The *Other* Munros

Anne Seth Mitchell-Munro

authorHOUSE®

AuthorHouse™ UK
1663 Liberty Drive
Bloomington, IN 47403 USA
www.authorhouse.co.uk
Phone: UK TFN: 0800 0148641 (Toll Free inside the UK)
*   UK Local: (02) 0369 56322 (+44 20 3695 6322 from outside the UK)*

Published by AuthorHouse 02/16/2023

ISBN: 979-8-8230-8059-0 (sc)
ISBN: 979-8-8230-8058-3 (e)

Contents

Dedication

In loving memory of my dear mother Joan Mitchell-Munro

Foreword

Around the time of the Scottish Highland Clearances, Murdoch and Janet Munro, along with their small children, were evicted from their croft in Sutherland, to be resettled on the bleak North East Coast of Scotland. Life was extremely difficult for the family.

When two of their sons – John and Murdoch junior – reached their middle teenage years, they decided to travel south to the richer farming areas of Lanarkshire, hoping to find work and make a future for themselves. Their lives followed parallel courses of love, sadness, joy, fortunes...good and bad... as well as the tragedies they suffered.

This is their story: as passed-on down the generations - from Munro to Munro.

Anseth Mitchell Munro is the pen name of Anne Seth Currie nee Mitchell. Her mother, Joan Mitchell nee Munro, was a direct descendant of the characters in this book.

The name "Anseth" comes from an incident in Primary One at Haghill Primary School in Glasgow, Scotland in 1937.

Anne' s older sister May (Mary) Wilkie Dunn nee Mitchell Munro was asked the name of her new-born little sister. To this, May answered "Anseth." So there you have it.

Chapter 1

It was a miserable, bitterly cold day at the beginning of February. John stepped out of the little fishing boat into the shallow icy water of the North Sea. He dragged the boat up the pebble shore and made it fast - barely able to tie the rope - his hands, red raw, painful and stiff with the cold. He was frozen to the inner core of his being - his feet like dead appendages at the end of his legs. It always seemed to be cold; even in summer, there was usually a thin keen wind blowing off the North Sea. Oh how he hated this barren, desolate God forsaken place!

He was a strong, well built handsome seventeen years old lad with a pleasant disposition. Every day either himself or his brother would take their little open fishing boat out to sea, to supplement the food supply for the entire family which, beside themselves, consisted of father, mother, two other younger brothers and a wee sister.

On this particular day, young John was very despondent– more so than usual. Looking at the meagre catch of fish lying on the bottom boards of the boat he thought: *this will not be much of a meal for them.* He vowed to talk to his brother again that very night about going south to find work. They had discussed it endlessly during the long winter nights, but had not come to any decision.

For generations his family, part of the great Munro Clan...had been crofters in Sutherland. When he was a very small boy they had lived inland on a croft with a milk cow, hens and good arable land for growing potatoes, vegetables and other crops...some of which were sold in the little market town nearby. This paid for the rent due to the landlord. Life was hard but pleasant and familiar.

All was well until the start of the despicable Highland Clearances when families were systematically thrown off their land to make way for sheep, which were much more profitable than people. No-one gave a damn what happened to these folk For all the landowners cared, they could sink, swim or starve to death...which some of them did. It wasn't the landlord's problem!

Lady Stafford, wife of Lord Stafford, landowner of Sutherlandshire, was quoted as saying *she would like to visit her estates but was uneasy about a sort of mutiny that had broken out in consequence of their new plans to transplant some inhabitants to the sea coast.*

Heavens! Did these people really think that human beings were like some unwanted plant to be plucked out of the ground and transplanted in some dark corner to struggle for survival, or wither and die?

John's father, Murdoch Munro, and his wife Janet, had been among these unfortunates.

Many Munro families went south: some to the Glasgow and Clyde area... others to Inveraray in Argyll. Those with a bit more courage, or no choice, went further afield to start a new life- to America, Canada, South Africa, Australia and New Zealand. However, Murdoch was reluctant to go south as he had two very small children and a six-month-old baby. Additionally; Janet was again pregnant with their fourth child, so the trip would be too long for her and the children. He therefore reluctantly accepted tenancy of a small cottage and a piece of ground near Dornoch on the East Coast of Scotland which was at least a place to lay their heads in the meantime.

Young John trudged home, wet from his hours out on the cold water. He was thankful to enter the cosy warm kitchen, where his mother was working. She looked up expectantly.

"So, how did it go today then, John?" she asked.

"As you can see, mother, not very well. The fish did not want to jump into the boat today," he answered, - trying to put a little humour into the situation.

"Och well, I am sure I can do something with this lot for the dinner." she said, trying to hide her disappointment. "You look frozen, son, away and get a heat at the fire."

It always amazed the family how their mother could produce a meal, which satisfied them all, from next to nothing. It was truly a miracle... like the feeding of the five thousand! After they had eaten, and everything was cleared up, they would sit round the fire and discuss the day's events. Everyone had a chance to tell their own stories. Then it was off to bed; there was no option but to do so. After all, when you were as poor as church mice; candles were used sparingly.

That night, as they lay in bed, John discussed the possibility of going south with his brother, who was a year younger than himself.

"Murdoch, are you still awake?" Asked John in a whisper; not wanting to waken his two other younger brothers who slept in the same room.

At his question, he could hear his brother suck in a gasp of exasperation. Undaunted, he continued.

"Do you remember we talked a while back about going south for work? Well......." - Not waiting for an answer -

"I think the time has come now to consider this seriously, what do you think?"

There was no reply. Then came a single question from his younger brother which gave answer to both his big brother's questions: "Who is going to tell Mother and Father then?"

John could feel the excitement of anticipated adventure rising in his breast... "We both will in the morning."

The following morning at breakfast Janet looked at the two of them and thought they were unusually quiet. "So, what is up with you two today, you look as if the world had fallen on top of you?"

"Nothing", they chorused.

"That is rubbish and you know it, so out with it."

Like most mothers, Janet instinctively sensed when something was amiss with her offspring.

John blurted out in one long sentence;

"Murdoch and I want to go south to find work. There is nothing here for us and what if we met a lass and wanted to wed; how could we?"

Janet had known for some time that one day this would happen. She knew perfectly well that what John said was true; there *was* no future for them here.

"Well, if that is what you want to do, I will not stop you, but you had better go and talk to your father first."

As soon as they had eaten, the brothers went outside to look for their father. They found him stacking fresh-cut peats for the fire. John was again the spokesman and told his father more or less what he had said to their mother.

Murdoch senior listened carefully to what his son had to say then was silent for almost a full minute before reacting to this momentous news. His reply was characteristic of the man – practical and to the point.

"What am I supposed to do without you two here to help with the work and do the fishing?" the head of their family grumbled; bushy black eyebrows raised in an arch to emphasise the question.

For the first time his son, Murdoch Junior, found his voice;

"Och father; our brother Angus is fourteen now, surely he will be able to do these things?"

The boys waited in fear and trepidation for the remarks that were bound to follow, however, they were astonished to hear their father's answer. It came with a mixture of reluctance, caution and advice.

"Well lads, if that is what you want, then go ahead, I will not stand in your way. You should be all right if you work hard and keep out of trouble." With that, he turned away from his two boys and got on with what he had been doing.

Murdoch Munro senior was a man of few words. That was the subject closed as far as he was concerned. Inwardly, he knew as well as did their mother that there *was* no life here for the boys...he had for many years, bitterly regretted his decision to bring his family to this place. The cottage was small, the ground was bad, and growing anything was difficult because of the salty sea air and the poor soil. They had survived, just, but life certainly was not a bed of roses.

At the beginning it was really tough - picking limpets off the beach along with other indescribable things that Janet tried to make soup and some sort of meals with - certainly *not* what they had been used to, and pretty awful at that.

And so, John and Murdoch decided to wait for spring to come before setting out on their journey. Meantime, they continued helping with all the odd jobs that needed attention. As luck would have it, the fishing improved, so they were able to store quite a lot of salted fish in the barrels for future use.

Janet was not looking forward to her boys going away. She loved them dearly and knew she would miss them terribly, but she had to think of their future and put her own feelings to the back of her mind. Being an ever practical woman, it occurred to her there would be two less mouths to feed, although she felt guilty even thinking that way, but things were difficult and these two big lads had big appetites.

The departure day finally dawned. After fond farewells, mother's tears and father's firm handshake, the two boys left the nest with warnings of... "Be careful you do not get robbed. Do not you go near these loose women hanging around looking for nice lads like you...".... "Beware of the demon drink." etc ringing in their ears, they were off to set the world on fire! The journey had begun.

Chapter 2

The obvious route from where they were to where they wanted to be would be a straight line, but it was all mountainous country with little or no habitation, therefore no chance of work, food, or a place to sleep so they had to stick to the coastline.

Spring was late in arriving and the cold easterly wind off the North Sea chilled the travellers to the bone. Then, to compound their misery, the rain arrived, slashing relentlessly across the countryside in a horizontal fashion, joining in the gleeful torture. Murdoch was utterly, utterly miserable and felt like turning back and going home, and said as much to his older brother. But determination and pride would not let John give in so early on. He convinced his sibling to keep going...that things could only get better. And so, they headed for Inverness.

On arrival at their first big town, they had a quick look around the place, and by sheer luck found a cosy little inn with a bright fire burning in the parlour, but as they had no money, they couldn't very well stay there. They approached the landlord and John, as ever the spokesman, asked:

"Would you happen to know of any farms near here that might be looking for extra hands just now?"

The man was not what one would call the friendliest of characters and gruffly told them;

"There is a farm about two or three miles to the west where you might get something." As far as he was concerned, if they didn't have any money to spend, he didn't want them sitting there.

As for the lads; they would dearly have loved to stay there by the fire, warm themselves and get something to eat, unfortunately they had to take their leave of the place. *Oh, to have just a little money!*

They trudged on in the direction indicated by the landlord of the inn and finally, after trudging for what seemed an eternity, they came to a small farm building that the individual in question had suggested. It was getting dark and they could see the glimmer of an oil lamp through the cracks in a shuttered window. John rapped the door loudly with a stout stick he had been carrying. They could hear the scrape of furniture from within and thereafter, the rattle of a bolt. The door swung inward revealing the farmer outlined by the light of a miserable oil lantern on the table behind him.

"Who the devil are you two then?" he asked gruffly. What do you want here?"

John explained that he and his brother were looking for work and a place to stay. The surly individual was about to slam the door in their faces but then...giving the two boys a closer look...he realised very quickly that he could get some good work out of the two of them.

"I can give you unpaid work, with two meals a day and the barn to sleep in, that is all – take it or leave it!"

The brothers conferred and decided it would do for the time being, albeit no money, but at least they would get food and a bed.

"Fine!" said John, "We will take it."

It was now getting dark. Although their new employer directed then to where they could sleep, he told them they were too late to get food. Besides, they hadn't worked for it yet. They would have to wait until morning. And so the boys bedded down in the hay of the barn with empty stomachs and only rainwater to drink. At least they were warm and out of the wind and rain.

Next morning, they were called at the crack of dawn and given the meanest breakfast they had ever seen. As soon as it was finished, they were put to work. Now that it was daylight, the two young men could see around the place and decided it was not a very well run farm. There were a few fields with crops growing in them, which looked quite good - not very far advanced as yet - but it was early days and the weather had not been good of late. There was also a field with cows grazing; they too looked quite good animals.

However, the few existing farm buildings – the barn and cow sheds were in a dreadful state of dereliction. Goodness knows when the cow sheds were previously mucked out... they stank!

The whole place stank and had an air of sad neglect!

Their first job was to muck out the over-full disgusting cow sheds, which took them the best part of the day. When eventually the job was done, they smelled as bad as what they had cleared out. But their contact with the evil smelling mass was by no means over. They were informed by their employer that their chore for the next day would be to transport it to the fields and spread it over them as a layer of fertiliser.

Finally, this first day came to an end...time to eat!

The evening meal proved to be a disaster - just as mean as the breakfast, but they said nothing; they were both starving and ate up every morsel.

The barn they were given to sleep in was infested with mice and who knows what else. It occurred to them that the farmer could be doing with having a few cats around the place to keep the vermin down. However, the boys were so tired they would have slept anywhere and fought off a hoard of cats, dogs and mice for the privilege of getting their heads down.

The next morning, they were rudely awakened before dawn broke. It was quite cold but there was to be no comfort or joy in visiting the farmhouse. Entering, they saw that the fire had not been lit. There was no decent food on or anywhere near the table and the farmer looked and smelled like he had been sleeping on the floor of the cow shed, before they had cleaned it out! He was a wee filthy, grossly overweight fat man who looked as if he had never done much work in his entire life. The condition of his farmhouse and surroundings bore witness to that. In addition; there did not seem to be any other workers, not that that came as any great surprise, considering that no-one in their right mind would want to stay or work in the place anyway.

The farmer never spoke to them except to tell them what to do and made no offers of giving them a bite to eat in the middle of the day. Talk about Shylock?...he had nothing on this fellow!

This situation continued for three days, by which time the boys realised they were being utterly exploited. After the evening meal on the third day, they agreed that enough was enough and decided to leave. They would tell their employer of their plans at breakfast time.

The following day, they were awakened before dawn as usual, and went to the farmhouse for breakfast. When they had finished, Murdoch disappeared to collect their belongings and stand outside ready to run while John faced up to the wee fat man:

"We are leaving now." he announced. "We do not want to work for you any more." He went on; his courage growing... "You think we are stupid *heilan* lads who will thank you for your awful food - which by the way, is not fit for a dog to eat - and work hard all day for you for nothing. It seems to us simple lads that you are the only one who benefits from this arrangement. It is no wonder you have no help here if you have treated past employees the way you have treated us. We might be young, - even simple, but we are not stupid!" With those few words, John turned on his heel and stomped out; slamming the door in the face of the wee fat man whose face had turned purple with anger.

Outside the door, John's spirits soared with relief. He gave a great shouting laugh and exclaimed to his wee brother...

"Come-on Murdoch! Let us run, brother, in case that wee greasy ball of lard in there comes at us with a pitchfork."

The two of them picked up there meagre belongings and too to their heels down the road, running for their lives and laughing all the way.

After that first encounter, the boys plodded on; working their way down the east coast of Scotland; getting work in the small fishing villages, helping with the fishing boats – mending lobster pots and creels. This was work they knew something about, and best of all...they got paid for it – hallelujah! Things were looking up. It meant they could buy decent food and get a comfortable, warm, dry place to sleep each night.

They stayed in the area for a little while, longer than they had planned. But they saved as much of their earnings as they could, before setting off on their southward journey yet again.

The road they were on led to Edinburgh, the Scottish capital but they decided to by-pass that great city and head westward across Scotland's fertile central belt to Glasgow by way of Stirling.

Eventually, after what seemed like a lifetime, they reached the *big city of* Glasgow, which had been their aim for so long, and which finally, they had safely reached after their adventurous journey.

Having come from a quiet, peaceful highland hamlet via an equally quiet shore-side settlement, the two boys were totally astounded by the sights sounds and smells of their first visit to a big city. The centre was a busy bustling place full of people and horse drawn vehicles, the former entering and exiting gigantic, ornate sandstone buildings like worker ants feeding their queen while the latter seemed to fill the streets from side to side with piles of steaming dung balls. They had entered the main city from the east and were skirting the centre, north of the cathedral.

As they continued to wander around bone weary and hungry, they found themselves in one of the poorest areas of the town. The streets were filthy, the people dirty, and the smells that assaulted their noses were indescribable. They were used to the smells of the countryside and sea and their mother was always scrubbing and washing, so this filth was alien to them. They were not enamoured by what they saw!

Eventually, they found a little eating place which looked reasonably clean compared with the rest of the places they had seen and quickly bi-passed.

Their money was almost gone, they had very little left so could afford little to eat. What they were able to buy would not have satisfied one of them, let alone two!

"This will not do Murdoch!" said John, "We will have to find work or we will starve in this dreadful place. The countryside cannot be too far away, we will surely find employment there?"

After their miserly repast, John approached a large man wearing a white apron whom he presumed to be the owner of the establishment.

"Would you happen to know of any farms in the area that might be looking for workers at the moment, sir? My brother and I are used to farm work."

The owner, who recognised the soft spoken highland lilt, and who had been similarly approached in the past, was civil to him and prepared to give out information.

"Aye lad! There are quite a lot of farms to the north and north east of here - in the Bishopbriggs, Kirkintilloch and Lenzie areas which take on hands at this time of the year. The bigger farms have large herds of cows; some of which will probably be calving about now so extra hands will be needed. There is sure to be a shortage of good hands." He went on;

"A lot of them have left the land and are now here in the city; attracted by plentiful work and the better pay. Are you sure you would not rather stay here for the better money?"

"No thanks!" the young Munros chorused." We have seen enough of the city for the time being."

"Right you are then lads! Good luck to you!" The Landlord finished by pointing out to them the right road to follow.

Thanking him for his kindness, they left, heading in the recommended direction; glad to be away from Glasgow and its smells with the bonus of not having been robbed or accosted by bad women which would surely have been their fate had they remained there.

And so they plodded north eastward. It now being summer, the rubbish and other horrors lying around stank abominably in the narrow streets.

They got lost getting out of Glasgow, having taken the wrong turning. As they were stopped at a corner, trying to decide which way to go, an old woman, filthy, ragged and toothless, watched them from across the road. She could see they were strangers, so approached them. As she got close, the lads automatically stepped back a pace; frightened she would touch them and give them some unwanted disease. She smelled horrible, and it reminded John of the smell when he mucked out the cow byre at the farm near Inverness!

"Now; wid youse two nice boys be lost, then?" she asked them in a cackling -type voice

"So it would seem," answered John. "We were given directions for Kirkintilloch, but we seem to have taken the wrong turning. We know we are in the North of Glasgow and that the places we want to go to are in this part but really, we have no idea where we are. Any help you can give mistress will be appreciated."

The horrid old woman's eyes brightened in their nest of wrinkles. Sensing a possible source of income, she pointed the boys in the right direction. Hoping to get something- money or a trinket for her trouble- she extended a filthy claw-like hand with nails that would have put a witch to shame. But the boys had spent their last penny on food and had nothing to give. They thanked the crone profusely for her help and left. As they turned away, they distinctly heard her spit on the road and curse them with the broad, lowland sounding exclamation of;

"Miserable wee bastards!"

Once out of the town and onto the country roads again, they thankfully breathed in the fresh air.

"I am glad to be away from there, it is far too big and has too many folk, all of them – seems to me - living on top of each other." commented Murdoch.

"Me too, I could not live there. I do not know what I was expecting, but I feel a bit disappointed. It is much, much bigger than I could ever have imagined. I have never seen so many folk in one place. I am afraid it is not for me."

In truth; they really were country lads - the only thing they *did* know about was working on the land. They didn't want any of the industrial type jobs they could probably have got, as they would have been obliged to live in the city. Glasgow had just gone through a severe cholera epidemic, so they wanted no part of it. They were just glad to be out on the country roads again away from the smoke and smells.

Chapter 3

They tramped onward.

The first two farms they came to didn't need any extra hands and they were sent off rather rudely.

"Heavens!" exclaimed Murdoch. "What was all that about? You would think we had two heads or something! We must have looked to them like a couple of villains - Highway Bandits!"

"No!" answered his brother with a straight face... "It was just yourself who gave them the scare. Have a look at yourself in the next rain puddle we come to. That is, of course, if you do not scare the water out of it..." this said while jumping out of the way of his young brother's boot.

And so the two of them continued on their way, exchanging friendly banter while continuously on the lookout for somewhere to spend the night. Time was getting on and they were hoping against hope to get somewhere soon... preferably not under a hedge.

They carried on as fast as their weary legs would allow. Soon, in the near distance they could see cultivated farmland – planted fields and next to them, cows grazing peacefully. Just then, as luck would have it, a man with a horse and cart came along and stopped beside them and spoke.

"Well now! Where are you two going out here in the middle of nowhere?" He had a friendly voice and open face which invited conversation.

John, looking up at him, replied; "We are heading for the next farm along the road looking for work, Sir."

"Right then!" exclaimed this Good Samaritan, "hop up on the cart and I will give you a little help in your quest."

"Thank you very much, sir", they chorused; in tones that conveyed relief as well as genuine gratitude.

And so, they continued onward... this time slowly but in comfort. The man was very curious about them and asked lots of questions *who were they?...where had they come from*? And so on.

They told him their family history...of being put off the land and ending up at the coast...of how hard life was up there and now they were down here looking for work and a future. Also that they could read and write.

The man was impressed; he liked these two. They seemed to him to be honest, well mannered, intelligent lads looking to improve themselves.

He was a Lowlander, born and bred. To him; the place these lads came from was as far removed from his way of life as the Moon from earth. He had always been under the impression that the folk from away up there were almost uncivilised savages and were *as thick as mince*! as the saying went. Yet here were these two boys one of seventeen the other eighteen years old... both of whom could read and write.

And so, the three of them continued along the road in this manner, chatting pleasantly and exchanging information. The boys were very curious!

Eventually, they came to a place where the little roads crossed. "Well lads, this is as far as I go. I can drop you off here if you wish to go onward in the same direction."

John and Murdoch thanked him profusely and were about to take their leave when their new acquaintance surprised them by remarking...

"If it is of interest, I could employ one of you but not both. I am sorry; I would if I could, but it is just not possible. He went on. "I can give one of you farm work with a reasonable wage, three meals a day and a place to sleep. What do you think?"

Initially, to the boys, this seemed too good to be true, but then doubts crept in. *Which of them was going to take up this offer of a job? If they split up; what would happen to the other one?*

John, being the older of the two quickly made a decision.

"You take it Murdoch and I will carry on looking for something for myself".

Murdoch would not hear of such a thing.

"Not at all John! It was your idea to come here in the first place; therefore you should get the first job offered." John protested at this suggestion.

While they argued, the man in the cart offered a solution. He told them about a farmer friend who had a farm about four or five miles further on. His friend's property was named *Eastfield*. It was a very large farm and its owner took on a lot of hands at this time of the year. It would soon be calving time and he would be needing extra hands. He finished with...

"Whichever of you decides to stay here with me, the other should go and tell the farmer at *Eastfield* - Mr. Mitchell is his name - that I sent you, and that your brother has a job with me. My name is Malcolm Lennox."

And so it was decided between them that young Murdoch would carry on toward *Eastfield* and seek work there. However, it was getting late... he would need to hurry.

Before Murdoch left, John had a quiet word with him.

"If you do not get work there, come back here and we will both leave together and find something else." Little did they both know at that time, Murdoch would land on his feet big style!

The brothers parted company, with John extracting a promise from Murdoch that if nothing was available at *Eastfield*, he would come back and find him. He felt very guilty about letting his little brother go off on his own. He felt that he should have insisted that *he* - Murdoch -took this job. He thought: *Here he was, the elder of the two and supposed to be looking out for his younger brother.* His mother would certainly not have approved of the arrangement! However there was no point worrying now - the deed was done. And so, John continued with Mr. Lennox toward his new employer's farm.

Soon the cart turned into the approach road to the farm. As it did so, John made out the name *"Kirkland"* painted on a board nailed to a fence post. They continued up the rough road towards the farm buildings; as they did so, John made a mental note of all he saw.

The first thing he noticed on the right hand side was a row of four farm cottages, then his eyes took in the wide vista of lots of fields with what seemed to be excellent growing crops. This was, indeed, a large farm.

As they continued along the road, the farmer pointed out to him the various barns and cow byres, of which there seemed to be an abundance. The road curved round to the left and as they turned the corner, an impressive, stone built, two storied building with a very elegant front door came into sight. He would learn that this was known as the *Big House*; in this case, even larger than the normally large farmhouse.

They alighted from the cart and as they did so, a man wearing what seemed to be a type of uniform came out the ornate front door and led the horse and cart away round the side of the house. Then, Malcolm Lennox told John to go round the opposite side of the house to the kitchen door and wait for him.

Arriving at the back of the house, John could only find one door, which he presumed was the kitchen. He waited for some time, wondering if he was supposed to knock on the door, but thought better of it and just waited.

During his wait, several people came and went; all of whom completely ignored him as if he was invisible. Eventually, after what seemed to be ages, the kitchen door opened and Mr. Lennox beckoned him inside. The aroma of cooking food and baking bread was almost more than John could bear: suddenly he realised just how hungry he was. His new employer told him that until something else could be arranged, he would have to sleep in the hay loft which was situated across from the kitchen. He would be fed in the kitchen with the other servants at breakfast and an evening meal and would be expected to be in the kitchen in the morning at dawn. After breakfast, the farm manager would give him work to do. In the middle of the day, there was a short rest period. Cook would supply him with something to eat for that time.

Having issued John with his instructions, Malcom Lennox turned on his heel and walked out of the kitchen. He had omitted to tell John that he was reluctant at this point to put him in the "Bothy" where all the other farm labourers lived...where they cooked their own meals and slept. He felt that John, being a Highlander, would be ostracised by them. He also knew that an intelligent young man with skills in reading and writing, which was more than most of these hands could do, would not be too well received in their company. Additionally, many of the farm labourers were transient...usually worked for maybe six months or so, before moving on.

Somehow, Lennox got the impression that this young man would stay at Kirkland longer than that. Thus he had made these temporary arrangements for his newest employee. He would sleep on it for the moment and give closer consideration to the matter the following morning.

After Mr. Lennox left, John looked around the room. There were three people in the kitchen, all females, who stood and looked at John as if he was some kind of sub-human. The atmosphere could have literally been cut with the proverbial knife. He surveyed the three, not quite sure what he was supposed to do now. The oldest, by the clothes she was wearing, appeared to be the Cook. She was a short plump woman with a face like a battleaxe. She stood there, hands on hips, looking him up and down and frowning. The remaining two were quite young, one of them about twenty years old and the other probably about fifteen. The younger one eyed John rather cheekily. Cook was the first to speak.

"We will just get the facts strait here and now. This one"; pointing to the older girl of the two - "is my daughter, Lizzie, and she is spoken for. She is wed to the Groom who looks after the horses. This one here is Sarah, and she has just turned fourteen, so keep your eyes off her."

Cook finished with: "If you are expecting to sit at *MY* table in *MY* kitchen, then you better get yourself a wash and a shave. You look and smell disgusting. There is a water pipe outside the kitchen door, so make use of it, and while on the subject, if you have any cleaner clothes with you, then change into them and leave those filthy things you are wearing here; they will be washed. Now be off with you!"

John felt as if a school marm had given him a dressing down. He thought this lecturing woman was roughly about the same age or slightly older than his mother, but nothing like the sweet tempered soul his mother was. He said

"Can I ask you a question?"

This was met with a stony silence, but John stood his ground and stared back with a question mark on his face.

"Well?" asked Cook.

John, very embarrassed and with a red face, asked; "Could you please tell me where folk relieve themselves" Cook almost had a smirk on her face, and enjoyed seeing this handsome strong young man taken down a peg with such a simple request! "There is a closet at the end of the building for that purpose", she replied.

Poor John, he hadn ' t said or done anything that would make this woman feel such animosity towards him. He vowed he would get round her in the long run...she was obviously the ruler of that domain. What she said was law in the catering department.

In fact, the average Lowlanders had no time for Highlanders; regarding them as inferior and uneducated. In John's case, they would be proved wrong. He could read and write, which most of *them* could not do. Like most of his kind, he was loyal and dedicated. He also had a way with words and enjoyed talking to people and had a sense of humour - all of which would prove invaluable to him, particularly in the kitchen. He would employ his talents and hopefully get Cook to like him. In the meantime, he contented himself by thanking the women and went about the task of making himself presentable, so as not to offend this gruff woman's sense of vision or smell. Consequently, he took his few belongings into the barn and up into the hay loft looking to see what would be more presentable than what he was wearing. Finding a clean shirt and a pair of trousers which weren't too bad, he then went down to the standpipe in the yard and washed himself down to the waist, then shaved; all the while hoping against hope that the door wouldn't open and the girls come out and see him in this state of undress.

He managed to get finished without incident and scurried back to the hay loft to get changed, feeling clean, fresh and much, much better.

After dressing, John waited what he thought would be a respectable time before venturing to the vicinity of the kitchen door. He hung about aimlessly, wondering what to do but principally wondering when this evening meal would be served...he was starving! Luckily, the girl Sarah came out of the kitchen and told him the evening meal would be served at sunset.

John's stomach complained at the enforced delay... it was summertime... he was going to have to wait for a few hours yet. What to do until then? He decided to wander round the farm and take stock of his surroundings.

Wandering along the back of the house, he saw a field occupied by a good number of nice healthy looking cows. He liked cows so stood, leaning over the fence, watching them for a bit. After a while, he got tired of staring at the animals and went round the other side of the house. To his delight, he came across a stable full of the most incredible looking horses he had ever seen in his young life. They were massive strong beasts with large hairy hooves, and beautiful long silken manes. He was admiring them when a young man came out of the stable. He was a bit older; slim and strong looking, and with a pleasant smiling face.

"Who are you?" asked this fellow.

"Mr. Lennox has just taken me on today as a labourer, my name' s John Munro."

"I am James Sinclair, the head Groom." the young man replied.

John's retentive memory reminded him that the young man in front of him must be the husband of the girl in the kitchen...Lizzie...Cook ' s precious daughter.

"Hello! I am very pleased to meet with you" said John, offering his hand.

"Likewise", replied the Groom, taking John' s hand in a strong but measured grip.

There was instant, mutual respect between them.

The two of them chatted for some time and seemed to get along pretty well. At the outset, John remarked that he had never seen such magnificent horses. In reply, James asked him where he came from.

The knowledge that John was a Highlander from the North seemed of little importance...the fact that he liked horses was enough for James. John was indeed very interested in these magnificent animals and asked if they were of a particular breed. James warmed to his subject.

"They are a very old breed indeed John. They were bred for their power and strength. The breed goes by the name of *Clydesdale,* taken from the place where they originated." He was steeped in facts about the horses, relating them to John as though reading from the breed manual. He continued: "They stand six feet high at the shoulder and weigh an enormous number of pounds. In the old days, in the seventeenth century, they were used as war horses. Nowadays, they are used on farms for ploughing, pulling carts, removing tree roots and all manner of farm work. In towns they pull carts and heavy loads. Not only that, they walk canal tow paths pulling heavily loaded barges." As he talked, one of the huge beasts rested its great head on the top of the stable door between the two of them and snorted. James absently stroked its ear and went on: "The hair round their ankles and on their manes is soft and silky - would you like to touch it?"

John was of course, all for this and tentatively put out his hand to the horse and stroked its mane.

"It is all right John! You do not have to be wary of these big beasts; they have a lovely calm and friendly nature, and are good to work with."

John felt the power and gentleness all in one sensation...he was looking forward to seeing these great beasts at work in the coming days.

"Do they need a lot of attention then?" he asked, very interested to know all about these animals. James was in his element and delighted to air his knowledge.

"As they work hard, they need to be well fed and groomed regularly, particularly the hair round their feet ...it can get muddy and tangled, but it is a pleasure to groom them when they" are finished working... make them look as they should be. Like all other horses, they need to have their hooves looked at often to make sure they do not have any problems and to make sure they are not in need of new shoes. We do not have a blacksmith here but if they do need shod, they are taken to the local Smiddy and he fits them."

It was obvious that James would have talked about his favourite subject all day and night but at this point, John thought he had better move on and not keep the man from his work. Being new to the place, he didn't want to be classed as a talking time-waster.

"Thanks for telling me about the horses James. I enjoyed hearing all about them. It is no wonder that you are so very proud of them."

Wandering on, John came across a building larger than a farm cottage, which was obviously some sort of accommodation or living place for people. There was no clue as to what it was or who might occupy it. He was extremely curious. Already he had many questions he would love to have answers to...there would be many more, but he would have to bide his time. Patience! And so he continued round the farm, meeting men here and there, all of whom ignored him, but he was happy just to look around and see how the land lay. After all, he was going to be working here, so he may as well familiarise himself with his surroundings.

The farm cottages he had seen on the way in came into view. On closer inspection, he saw there were indeed four of them... small, but with a good piece of land at the back of each. Some had hens and two of them had pigs. This surprised John, he wasn't expecting to see pigs! Additionally, they had areas with crops of potatoes and vegetables. Obviously the occupants were self sufficient in some things. However, he did not see any cows. Probably they got their milk from the farm. He had seen a dairy herd elsewhere on the farm...doubtless there would be a dairy and cow byre attached.

He knew there were families on the property because he had seen small children running around the farm earlier and had presumed they were the offspring of some of the farm workers. His presumptions were correct; his attention was drawn to a group of children happily playing nearby. It consisted of three little girls aged about three or four years old, a slightly older girl of about six or seven, and a little boy of around the same age as her. All five of them were absolutely filthy and looked as if they had been in the byre or somewhere equally as dirty. Hugely amused, he thought; *I wonder who their mothers are? No doubt someone will claim them at the end of the day.*

Coming back along the track towards the rest of the property and instinctively knowing that the left fork led to the main farmhouse - John took a right turn. Almost immediately, he came across the cow byre and a little distance from it, the Dairy. A man and two young boys were mucking- out the byre. The clanging sound of enamelled steel pails drew his attention to the dairy itself. Through its open door he could see a woman and girl were working with milk pails. He cheerfully shouted "Hello!" in the passing, and was rewarded with a simple nod, then was completely ignored, as the folk in question turned their heads away and got on with what they were doing. *Hmm!* He thought...*nice friendly people!* However, to be fair to them... they didn't know who he was. It would take time for him to become accepted by them...to be a part of the farm workers community.

He knew full well that he had another problem of acceptance. Strictly speaking, he was not one of them; he was not a Lowlander. He had been told about this strange form of southern ostracism before leaving home but could not understand it. After all, he too was Scottish, so what did it matter which part of Scotland he came from? None-the-less, it seemed to matter to these Lowlanders, and he would just have to get used to it. One would think he came from a different country altogether and did not speak English!

He had learned all things English the hard way but these were not English people! His native language was Gaelic, but when he attended school, he had not been permitted to speak it. All conversation and writing had to be in English and so he had been compelled to learn that language. It was totally ironic... here he was, still in his homeland and being subjected to a form of persecution by his own people. Had not he and his clans-people sacrificed enough? Still, there simmered in his heart, was a fierce resentment for what his people had endured. Not only had the Clan lands been taken away, but their very identity had been almost erased. Language, kilts and even bagpipes were also forbidden. Many highland people had fought against this enforced, alien way of life but had been severely chastised for ignoring the rules.

22

The Clan Munro was one of the oldest Clans in Scotland, going back before the time of the Romans. They had held the lands of Sutherland for centuries. However, lowlanders were not particularly interested in his history. To them, John Munro was simply a stranger from *away up there* and that was that. Most of them wouldn't even have a clue where Sutherland was!

And so, John decided to keep his mouth shut about his origins and, whatever tasks he was given, he would do to the best of his ability. Meantime, he was tired, so headed for the hay loft to lie down for a bit. Being absolutely sure that no-one would come looking for him if he was late - hee dare not fall asleep in case he missed his dinner. In his then state of mind, he figured that if he didn't turn up for his meal, the Lowlander attitude would simply *be "too bad!" It was his problem, and he would just have to wait till breakfast next morning before getting any food.* John didn't hink he could last that long!

Back at the hay loft, John lay down; trying desperately not to go to sleep. Eventually, as a precaution, he sat up and got himself into a comfortable position where he could see the kitchen door and hopefully, some of the other diners arriving.

Sunset seemed to be held up that night and on occasion, John had to stop himself dozing off.

Eventually, the sun finally went to bed. As its light began to fade, he saw a couple of men enter the kitchen, so he quickly arose then went across and knocked on the door. His knock was answered by another young girl - one he not seen before. He asked her if this was the right time to come in for his meal. The girl just stared at him without answering...obviously at a loss as to who he was and what to say.

They stood there in awkward silence until time was started again by the distinctive voice of the girl Sarah shouting...

"Let the big Highlander in."

John heaved a sigh of relief...*thank the good Lord for Sarah!* But for her, he may not have been allowed in and been doomed to go to bed on an empty stomach. This girl Sarah had a different accent from the others? - Not Lowlander and certainly not Highlander although there was a certain lilt to her tongue. It was a strange sound... he wondered where she came from.

Later, he would learn that she was from Ireland.

John entered the kitchen and sat down where indicated by cook's daughter. He looked round the table to see who was there and noted that James, the groom, was absent. Those who were seated included the man who had taken the horse and cart away from Mr. Lennox when they arrived, another older man, Cook, and the two young girls who were dishing out what appeared to be soup. There was lots of bread on the table, along with bannocks, and as soon as the soup was served, everyone delved in. Working all day from dawn to dusk on a farm makes a body very hungry!

Although John had been intent on looking at the food, he noticed Cook's daughter leaving...apparently she was not joining them. Another question unanswered!

Cook ladled out the next course, which was some kind of stew, with meat and lots of vegetables and included potatoes. This smelled very good, and tasted even better. If this was the kind of food he was to get here, he would be extremely happy! Some indeterminate pudding followed the second course, which was also very edible.

After cleaning this last plateful, for the first time in many months, John had a full stomach and felt totally satisfied.

As soon as everyone was finished, they rose from the table...Cook and the two girls remained behind to clear up after them. Hoping it would put him in her good books, John thanked Cook for the lovely meal, adding how much he enjoyed it. Apart from this nefarious reason for his profuse thanks...he had always been taught that it was polite to say thank you.

Cook's brief and to-the point-response was...

"You do not get fed rubbish or meagre rations in MY kitchen" and with that, got on with clearing up... totally ignoring him. However she had more to say!

As John was about to leave she added;

"Mind now, do not be late for the breakfast or you will not be served. As the Master said: be in here at dawn."

End of conversation. No *good nights* or otherwise!

Dog-tired and full of good food, John headed for the hay loft and snuggled down. He fell asleep almost immediately. His only concern, as he drifted off, was that he would not wake in time for the breakfast and get his instructions for work the next day. He just dare not blot his copybook at this early stage, or he would be out on his ear before he even got started. In seconds, he was dead to the world.

Having been used all his young life to getting up at the crack of dawn, John ' s biological clock wakened him just before dawn the next morning. When fully awake, he went down into the yard, quickly washed and then attended to his bodily needs. Thus, he was ready to enter the kitchen when the others appeared. He would be first in line.

As he waited, he wondered how many people would turn up for breakfast. He supposed it would be the same people who were at the meal table the previous night, although he did not know at this stage who they all were, he supposed someone would eventually enlighten him. If no one volunteered, he would get information from the girl Sarah. She seemed to be a bit of a chatterbox and willing to converse with anyone. This said; he had the feeling he better watch his step with that one and be careful not to bring the wrath of Cook down on his head - particularly when she took the trouble to warn him to keep his eyes off her. Sarah was only fourteen anyway and he was so much older than her, or so he thought - since he had then reached the ripe old age of eighteen!

Dawn broke and there were still no signs of anyone entering the kitchen. He thought he had better knock on the door and find out what was happening. His knock was rewarded by the sound of Cook's voice bidding him "come in."

On entering the kitchen, he found to his amazement that the only people in the kitchen were Cook, Sarah, the other serving girl who had opened the door to him the previous night, and the man with the kind of uniform. This uniform was in fact, a black jacket and trousers, white shirt and a black bow tie. *Who was he and what was his role in this household? Very curious...Yet another mystery to be solved.*

John was not the most patient of people when it came to wanting to know things. He had a very enquiring mind and liked to have answers almost at once, however, in this case, he was just going to have to curb his curiosity until he learned who was who and what their role was at this farm. He had worked the land for quite a few years, but had never seen anything as large and with as many people as there was at this establishment. Other things he wanted to know about concerned all the other hands: *where were they?* And *where did they eat? Could they be housed in that other building he saw yesterday and feed themselves?* Anyway, it was time to concentrate on what was going to be placed in front of him!

There were five plates on the table, one in front of each place, and Cook put a huge pot of porridge in the centre of the table. The man in the uniform was served by Sarah, who afterward sat down with the other two females. It then seemed to be a serve yourself situation.

John waited till the women took their share before helping himself.

It was good porridge, as good as his mother's, and that was saying something!

When everyone had finished eating, there was quite a bit left in the pot. John, who still had room in his stomach, boldly asked if he might have some more. At the same time being diplomatically careful to play down his hunger and to emphasise his reason; that it was the quality of the porridge. This of course pleased Cook. Beaming across at him, she told him to go ahead and help himself.

As well as the delicious porridge, the table was laden with plates containing bannocks, bread, a large pat of dairy butter and cheese, as well as a huge jug of milk. John was totally delighted with the breakfast situation and hoped it would be like this all the time he worked there. He would be in for a shock in the not too distant future!

On finishing his breakfast, John asked whom he should see about the work that he had to do. Cook - reverting to her former unpleasant tone - told him he would find the farm manager outside. With a little malicious smile on her face, she added...

"You will recognise him right away... he is the man who was sitting next to you last night."

John hoped he could remember what this man looked like...the previous night he had been more interested in what he was getting to eat than who was sitting next to him. He again thanked Cook for the good breakfast, and then just as he was leaving, she piped up

"When you have seen him and got your duties, come back here and get your mid-day food to take with you." *What a strange woman!*

Outside the kitchen door John looked for a man he hoped he would recognise - he spotted a vaguely familiar face. *Was this the farm manager?* Approaching this individual he asked him if he was the manager and received a curt, affirmative nod by way of an answer. He introduced himself.

"Good morning sir!" he began." My name is John Munro and I have been told to get my instructions from you for work today."

The older man looked him up and down before replying.

"Right then, lad, I want you to join the others in yonder field." he said - pointing to a large field where several men were working.

"If you will come with me now, I will give you a scythe, then take you over there and show you what is to be done. We are harvesting the hay and stacking it." With these words, he marched off with John hurrying after him.

Eventually they reached a shed in which all kinds of farm implements were stacked neatly in long rows. The manager, who by this time had introduced himself as Archibald Robertson, lifted down a huge scythe and handed it to John, adding with a chuckle,

"I reckon a big one like this is a fitting tool for a big highlander like yourself."

Thereafter the two of them headed for the field in which somewhere in the region of twenty men were working...some cutting hay and others making it into stacks to be dried... to John; this was familiar work.

He spotted James with his horses pulling a cart full of dried hay towards an area where hay stacks were being built. These would eventually form lines on top of the stubble in the areas where the hay had already been cut.

Mr. Robertson showed him how he wanted the hay cut, then left John to get on with it. There was another fellow working close by who shouted to him in a cheerful voice.

"You the new boy then?" He asked. Without waiting for an answer, he continued;

"The name's Liam, what would yours be then?"

"I am called John. Have you been here long then Liam?"

"That I have" replied the other, without actually saying how long he had been there.

Liam' s accent sounded familiar... the same as the girl Sarah I the kitchen; surely they came from the same place? Curious as ever he asked:

"So where do you come from then, Liam?"

"Ah now me boy-oh that would be the beautiful Emerald Isle, or Ireland to you, what about yourself?"

John was happy to exchange information with the Irishman.

"I come from a place called Sutherland, away up in the North of Scotland.

"Never heard of it", replied Liam; dismissing the information out of hand.

"Most folk down here have not heard of it either. It is a long way up from here, I can tell you that for sure. I can vouch for that, since my brother and I have walked almost every mile of it and it has taken months to get here", explained John.

Liam thought for a moment then exclaimed "I could not walk from Ireland, ye see there is water in between and I can not walk on that!" he said; finishing with a loud chuckle.

John thought; *Here was a likeable chap with a sense of humour... he would enjoy this one's company!*

And so, the two of them worked hard all morning scything the hay.

As the day wore on it got hotter and Liam remarked that the weather was perfect to help dry out the hay. "I hope it continues. Most of this stuff is used for fodder, so this is not a huge field. The other fields are much larger."

"What is growing in the other fields, Liam?" asked John.

"Now, that would be oats over there", pointing to the field in question, "and the other one beside it is barley. It is the next one to be harvested. After that, it will be the oats. By the time we" have finished with the oats, the turnips and potatoes will be ready for lifting; so there is plenty of work to break your back on, my friend. And that is not to mention the sore arms you will be having for the next few days." He finished, laughing at the growing worry on John's features.

Suddenly! it dawned on John that he had completely forgotten to go back to the kitchen and get his mid-day snack from Cook. *What an idiot he was! Now he would have nothing to eat till sunset!* He was tempted to sneak back to the kitchen but thought better of it. He couldn't very well leave the field and go back there, he would be seen and that would make him look a fool! Resigned to his fate, he thought maybe it would teach him a lesson not to forget in future.

As break time approached, he saw the kitchen girl Sarah coming towards him with something in her hand. She came up to him and held out a wrapped package. She had a wide smile on her face.

"You are a big oaf, John Munro. You did not come back for this and I persuaded Cook to let me bring it to you. I could not see you starving, now could I? She finished with a twinkle in her eye. She then turned on her heel and danced away laughing.

John was so embarrassed...all the other men were watching. Truth be known, they were more likely to be watching Sarah. After all, she was a very pretty girl with a laughing face and a huge personality. Liam, of course, had to make some remark.

"Well now, I would be thinking that this young girl has set her sights on you and will have you wed to her in no time at all. What did she bring you then?"

John, who had opened the package was delighted to find that it contained bread and cheese, However at Liam's remark, he immediately went on the defensive. Blushing, he protested "Absolutely not, I will *certainly not* be thinking of that. After all, she is just a child as far as I am concerned. She will not catch me!"

One day he just might eat those words!

When they stopped work, John asked "Where do you get something to drink? I am parched!"

Liam pointed - "There is a stream over there at the end of the field where we fill our bottles in the morning and again at mid day. It is good clear, clean water."

Going over to the stream, John had a long drink. It was indeed sweet and cool. *He must get himself a bottle of his own to fill.*

Thankfully it was mid day...time to have a rest and eat. John and Liam sat down together to eat their bread and cheese. John wanted to know more about the fields.

"As I told you", said Liam," the barley is next. It is scythed the same way as the hay. Then it is laid out nice and neat so that it will dry before threshing. Afterward, we move on to the oats and scythe them too. Oats are a very good crop to grow. They are fed to the cattle and horses, and the straw that is left after scything is excellent for winter bedding for them. It is dust free and keeps the place dry."

"Och yes. I know about that." said John." We grew plenty of them up north but we were more concerned with our own stomachs and used them mainly for porridge, oatcakes and bread."

"Right you are" agreed his companion. "Sure oats are great things indeed!" He went on, nodding his head. "Yes, very useful both for animals and humans alike."

John had another thought:

"I suppose the turnips and potatoes are next then. I have heard that turnips are fed to the horses, is that true? I suppose they are used in the kitchen as well?"

"Yes", answered Liam shortly.

By this short answer, John guessed that Liam was getting fed up with him asking so many questions about the fields, so decided to change tactics.

"You said you came from Ireland. What is it like there?"

"Not much different from here, in actual fact. Lots of rain! The scenery is very similar and there are lots of farms too, but things are not so good at the moment and work is scarce, that is why I came here. This is a good farm and Mr. Lennox is a fair man who pays reasonable wages. Mind you, you have to be working hard in the summer to earn them."

"So where do you live then?" continued John.

"In the Bothy; we cook, eat and sleep there as well. It is not all that wonderful, but it is sufferable. What about you?"

"I sleep in the hay loft opposite the kitchen and get my meals in there along with some of the other staff."

"Well, you are the lucky one" exclaimed Liam. "How did you manage that good arrangement? No-one else has had that privilege."

"I do not know, I just did what Mr. Lennox told me to do." replied John.

Liam thought for a moment - "There is a man in the Bothy moving on at the end of the week, so maybe you will be joining us there. You surely would find a big difference to your present situation."

John thought: *I would not know how to cook, that is women" s work, but I suppose if it comes to that I will just have to get on with it and do as the others do.*

"Time to get back to work now." said Liam abruptly. And so they started again and worked all afternoon.

It was hot work, so in the early evening they had another short break and a drink of water.

During this second break, Liam asked: "You said you and your brother came down here together, so where is he now?"

"I am really quite worried about him." answered John. "Mr. Lennox said he could only take one of us on so my brother Murdoch insisted that I took this job. The boss told him to go to a farm about four or five miles further on and to tell the farmer there that I was employed here. He said Murdoch would probably get work there. I insisted that if he did not get employed at that place, he was to come back here and we would leave together and get something else. I have not heard from Murdoch since that day."

"How old is your brother?"

"He is seventeen and I am supposed to look out for him. My mother would not be pleased with me right now for letting Murdoch go off on his own like that."

Liam thought for a moment then answered; "I am sure he will be all right! If he did not come back, he must have got work there, so I would not worry about him. No doubt he can look after himself at that age - he is not a baby!"

Eventually, Mr. Robertson came into the field and said it was time to finish for the day. They were all glad to straighten their backs and trudge back to the barn.

As each man reached the barn, the manager collected the man's scythe and replaced it in the neat row with its companions. Afterward, John went back to the farm and had a good wash at the pipe in the yard next to the kitchen but did not see or meet with anyone. He could smell the food cooking and it made his mouth water. Again he was starving!

After washing, he returned to the hay loft and lay down for a rest, but again was frightened in case he fell asleep and missed his dinner. He hoped things would not change as he thought the existing arrangement was perfect. Although Cook was a bit of a tyrant and apparently did not like him, he had to admit she was a good cook and gave him plenty to eat.

As he lay there his mind began to wander. His thoughts turned to Glasgow. *How could people live like that? All crowded into houses more or less living on top of each other? And the dirt and the smells – oh those smells - ugh! Better to have less wages and live in the clean fresh air of the countryside!* He supposed people had to work and live in places like that for better money if they had a family to support.

The people on the farm with their families seemed to do all right. He had discovered that even in the Bothy, the men were given peat or wood for their fires and potatoes and milk from the farm.

Thus, his mind was occupied. However, he kept one eye on the kitchen door.

As he thought and watched, he suddenly saw Mr. Robertson enter the kitchen. Quickly jumping down from his vantage point; he crossed the yard and knocked on the kitchen door. A loud *come in!* was the result.

Entering, he found all the same people there as the previous night. He took his place at the table.

This time, Cook ladled soup into plates...the three men present being served first. Afterward, the three women joined them at table.

A meat and potato dish followed the soup. John was in heaven! It was exceedingly good and tasty.

When the meat was consumed, platters of oatcakes, cheese, bread and butter were placed on the table, along with a huge jug of rich, creamy milk. John enjoyed every mouthful!

John's thoughts turned to his well dressed dinner companion.

He supposed that because Mr. Robertson was the farm manager, he was invited to eat in the kitchen, but wondered where he lived. What John did not know was that Mr. Robertson lived in one of the farm cottages and was actually *married* to Cook!

John hadn't set eyes on the other man since the previous night. He presumed therefore that the man in question only worked in the house and his job was to serve Mr. Lennox. Doubtless; one day he would find out about everybody.

Throughout the meal there were times when he could feel Sarah's eyes on him, but he chose to ignore her and got on with the task of eating. He felt it was safer to do so and not give her any encouragement at all. He had a feeling that if he showed any interest in her, she would hound him and bring down upon him the wrath of Cook who already didn't seem to care for him ... so why aggravate the situation?

There was no doubt about it that Sarah was indeed a lovely girl and when a bit older would be quite a beauty. *Turn you thoughts away from that, John Munro!* He finished his meal, thanked Cook and left.

The next day was spent the same as the one before; scything the hay. This time he remembered to get his mid-day food. No way was he going to have that girl coming out to the field to give it to him!

Just after the mid-day break, Mr. Robertson came into the field and told him to go over to the place where they were forking the hay up onto the cart... they needed an extra hand there. John was quite pleased to be doing something different, besides, Liam was a non-stop talker, which was getting a bit wearing at times. How on earth he could keep talking and working in the heat, John would never understand.

He went with Mr. Robertson as requested and was pleased to see that James was there with the incredible Clydesdale horses. These stood patiently waiting while the hay was forked up onto their carts. One had been filled and was about to pull away and be taken to another part of the field where men were building hay stacks to allow the cut hay to dry out. Once the carts were empty, the horses would then come back and wait for their next load. No wonder these animals had such patience; they needed it - just waiting to work.

John was given a pitchfork and shown how to lift the hay up on to the cart. Strong arms were needed for this purpose, but John was physically well endowed in that department. He quickly learned how to lift the hay up onto the cart and enjoyed the work. The other men did not talk much, but John didn't mind, it was a relief after Liam's constant chatter. *Are all Irish people like that* he wondered? Surely not? Because if so, who would listen to whoever was talking!

Having thought that...Liam was really a nice friendly man, who would tell him about the work but could not be serious for too long. He had an irrepressible sense of humour and was quite funny at times.

During a short evening break, John questioned James as to why he didn't eat in the kitchen.

"I see Mr Robertson, Cook, the two girls and your wife Lizzie there sometimes, but not you.

"No, Lizzie and I have one of the farm cottages and we eat there all the time." answered James. He continued;

"Lizzie's duties are to help her mother in the kitchen preparing the food, but her main work is looking after Mrs. Lennox."

"Who is the other man in the suit who is there at breakfast and evening meal?" asked John.

"That will be Forbes, well, his name is Alexander Forbes, but he is just called Forbes. He attends to the needs of Mr. Lennox - a sort of butler or valet, I suppose you would say. He is in charge of the household staff, but he is a nice man and not too bossy; unless of course, any of them step out of line. Cook is the boss in the kitchen and provisions area." John felt he was imposing.

"I hope you do not mind me asking all these questions, James...it is just to get to know who is who and what their duties are."

"Not at all." the other protested "I do not mind. I expect you will want to know who the other girl is in the kitchen. Her name is Jean and she is Cook's younger daughter and, of course, Lizzie's sister. She is seventeen and walking out with a lad from the nearest village. You know that Sarah is the other girl in the kitchen. She came here about a year ago. Her parents came here from Ireland for the father to find work, like a lot of the Irish have done."

"Thanks for the information, James; I have been wondering who all the people were and what their positions in the household were."

The break was soon over and the lads went back to work -carrying-on till nearly sunset. It had been another hot day, but clouds were amassing on the horizon, so maybe the hot weather was about to break.

John was curious. *How would they work if there was heavy rain? Would they still go on doing what they were doing?* He assumed they would *do so. Surely it could not possibly be? Down tools every time it rained? They would never get anything done!*

Time came to finishing work again for today, so things were gathered up and the horses led off to the stables for their evening feed and to be groomed. James still had all that to do before he was finished for the day, but to him, it was a labour of love and he didn't seem to mind. He adored these horses and John could see why.

Once more, John headed back to the farm where he had a wash then went up to the hay loft and changed his clothes. The clothes Cook had told him to leave for washing had been washed and left in the barn for him. After donning these, he felt cleaner but with all the heat in the previous two days he had been sweating a lot. *Tomorrow he would get up earlier and have a proper wash down to the waist at the stand pipe. Although he constantly dreaded that the young girls, particularly Sarah, would come out and see him.*

The evening meal that night was as good as ever. When he had finished eating, he retired to the hay loft and turned in for the night.

This state of affairs carried on until the end of the week, when John's euphoric bubble was burst. He was on his way to work when Mr. Lennox stopped him in the yard.

"One of the men in the Bothy is leaving today, so you will be transferring there where you will sleep and make your own meals. Like the men in the Bothy, you will be supplied with potatoes, turnips, milk, and oats. Chickens are also sent from time to time and some of the men trap rabbits. Anything else you will have to supply on your own. The Bothy is also provided with peat and wood for the fires for cooking purposes. I feel that you have got to know some of the men by now, so you should be able to mix in with the rest."

As he walked away, he turned round and said "By the way; I spoke to Mr. Mitchell yesterday. He informed me that he had employed your brother at his farm the same day as you came here and that he has settled in all right.

At this news, John felt a load lift from his shoulders. "Thank you for letting me know, Mr. Lennox, I was worrying about him."

The hay cutting and stacking was now finished and left to dry and the men moved on to the barley fields. The same procedure applied with the barley being cut by scythe then laid out to dry, when it would then be taken away and threshed later. The weather had changed somewhat, being cooler and cloudier which, in actual fact, was better for working. When they had the hot spell, it really was pretty gruelling work, so this suited the men much better. It was also getting dark a bit earlier now, which meant they could finish a little earlier.

Chapter 4

John did not take kindly to moving into the Bothy. He had always had someone to provide meals for him and he didn't have a clue what to do. It made him feel rather stupid when all the other men there were quite adept at making meals, if you could call them that! John had been used to Cook's super meals all week.... he just had to make the best of it and watch what the other men did.

There was a store in the Bothy containing all the basic ingredients to prepare a meal; potatoes and vegetables, flour, oats, and various other bits and pieces. There was also a stack of firewood. It seemed that the men got together in little groups round their own cooking fire at one end of the Bothy where they cooked communally.

In the morning big pots of porridge were put on the fires. While these were cooking, two or three of the men would go up to the farm kitchen and collect jugs of milk. If there was any bread available, they brought that back too. The same happened with the pots in the evening – this time they were filled with water, potatoes, vegetables, and whatever else was available.

All-in-all, they had enough to keep the wolf from the door, but, as John quickly learned, the food wasn't a patch on Cook's meals.

Meantime, Mr. Lennox had informed Cook that John would no longer be getting his meals in the kitchen. She had told him she had no objections at all about feeding this young man. He was polite, well mannered, and always thanked her for his meals and certainly seemed to enjoy them. Secretly, she would never ever have admitted to anyone that she actually liked this boy. He was a refreshing change from some of the uncouth ill-mannered farm workers, and he was also intelligent. Given a chance, she thought, that young man could go far, but he would no doubt be like all the rest, a farm labourer all his life till he had to retire.

She and her husband had three sons as well as the two girls.

The two oldest boys had left to go to Glasgow to get better paid work. One was twenty three years old and the other, twenty one. She worried about them being safe in the town, but they were sensible boys and had quite good jobs.

Her remaining son was only sixteen and was assistant groom to James, her son-in-law. She hoped that the fact he worked with James and loved the horses, would probably keep him on the farm.

She had compared her own situation to that of John's parents away up there in the North... being so far away - not knowing if their two boys were safe... had they obtained good work?

At least, in her case, Glasgow was not very far away, and her boys got home from time to time. At these happy reunion times, she fed them up and washed their clothes before sending them on their way again.

Communications with those in the north of the country were not easy, but things were beginning to improve. More coach routes were being established and of course, the railway was now beginning to be the preferred mode of travel. Perhaps, since John was able to read and write, he would one day be able to send his parents a note saying he and his brother were safe and had work on farms.

And so, as she worked, such thoughts passed through Cook's mind. She may have had the air of being a bit of a tyrant in the kitchen but at heart, she really was a softie where the young ones were concerned. That said, her own children had never been spoiled and a fair smack on the backside was not unknown when they stepped out of line. Cook was satisfied that she had done a good job with her own offspring; perhaps that was why she felt a "soft spot" for John Munro? He was simply a nice boy, well raised ... just a young lad away from home. *Perhaps,* she thought, *that it was just as well he was now in the Bothy and out of sight of that Irish colleen, Sarah Hendrie.* Cook had seen the wee vixen's eagle eye on him. Not that she blamed her... after all, he *was* a handsome young lad who no doubt would have an interest in the girls, but Sarah was too young and in her safe keeping.

The days moved on with much the same routine; scything the barley and laying it out, and afterward, moving into fields of oats.

There were two or three such fields so it took time to harvest them. All of the harvesting work had to be done before bad weather set in. Not only that, but the days were also beginning to shorten... time was precious

When most of the harvest was gathered, and the available hours of daylight for working got less, the men had more spare time on their hands. Some of them went into the nearby village inn at Kirkintilloch to relax, enjoy a change of scenery and have a few jars of ale. On occasion they would come back to the Bothy singing and almost unable to stand! The following morning, they would of course, have dreadful hangovers and have to be hauled awake to get to work.

This practice was not repeated too often during weekdays. However, on a Saturday night they would get absolutely helpless with drink. If the following day was the Sabbath - Sunday their only day off, they would have a full day to sleep it off.

John was a bit apprehensive about joining them; remembering his parent's warning of "the demon drink"! He wasn't too sure if he wanted to be coming back to the Bothy in the same state as he had seen some of his returning workmates! How they ever managed to get back at all, along the unlit country roads was a total mystery to him! He decided that in the meantime it would be best to decline any offer to join them. This was a bit difficult, since he didn't want them to think it was against his principles or he was frightened to take a drink, which, be it known, was much nearer the truth.

These men did not go to the inn and have just one drink. Obviously, to get into the state they came back in, they must have consumed umpteen ales.

Consequently, for the time being, John decided to stay at the farm on his day off and saved any money he earned.

On the other hand, John had been thinking; *it would be nice if he could meet up with his brother Murdoch and perhaps the two of them might try a couple of drinks on their own.*

Chapter 5

Finally the great day arrived! At last, it was John's Sunday off! Getting himself cleaned up he headed in the direction of the other farm to seek out his wee brother.

After travelling a couple of miles or so, he saw a figure in the distance heading in his direction. The person was too far away to recognise, but there was a certain familiarity about way the stranger walked or was this just wishful thinking?

As the men approached each other, it was with the greatest delight that John realised that it was indeed his brother. At the same moment, Murdoch recognised John and in turn experienced a great surge of delight and pleasure. The brothers quickened their pace; each reaching out for the other's hand and elbow. Shaking hands as if trying to break them off... laughing and beaming in sheer happiness. Arms round each other's shoulders, they walked on at a more leisurely pace. They had so much to catch up with, so much to talk about. The two of them wandered along the road with tongues going ten to the dozen.

"I heard from Mr. Lennox that you had got work at a farm further on the very same day as me" said John, "a farmer by the name of Mitchell?"

"That is right!" confirmed Murdoch.

"I was very relieved to hear that, as I was worried about you." said John with a sigh of relief. So what is the Mitchell farm like?"

"Very good!" replied Murdoch. He qualified that with..." We are quite well fed and looked after and there are lots of hands working there. It is a big farm with a good number of crop fields and fields for cattle.

41

My first job was helping to harvest the crops with an enormous scythe. Then I was moved on into the fields where the cows were calving ... some of the poor beasts were having problems giving birth, so we had to help with the animals. It was interesting work and the little calves are doing well now." He changed the subject.

"So how went things with you at the Lennox farm?" John laughed.

"I think they must start new people in the same way on every farm here. I too got to work with an enormous scythe. We have a fair number of cattle too, but so far, I have had nothing to do with them. The farm itself is really well managed. The food is alright, although it is nothing special, but adequate."

The brothers were heading in the direction of Kirkintilloch so decided to continue on into the village and have a look round. Being the Sabbath, they knew every shop would be closed so they had brought food with them.

Looking for somewhere to sit and eat; they finally found a nice spot on the banks of a canal that skirted the village.

As they sat there admiring the scenery, John remarked that the canal was a wonder indeed. It reminded him of one he had glimpsed near Inverness when they skirted that town.

"Right enough" agreed Murdoch continuing;

"This canal took twenty-two years to build and is thirty-five miles long with thirty-nine locks. Did you know that John?" "No, I did not - and just how is it that you know that, young brother?"'

It is a bit of a story," explained Murdoch.

"When Mr. Mitchell, my boss, found out I could read and write, he asked me if I would like to borrow a book from his library. All of course, on condition that I promised to take good care of it. His daughter, who looked after the library, would take me there and allow me to choose something I might be interested in."

"Well now, brother! exclaimed John. "You must have made an impression for him to allow you to do that, so what did you choose?"

"One evening, his daughter saw me coming back from work. She stopped me and told me that her father had told her of his offer to me and said that if I was still interested, I should come to the kitchen door and ask for her after I had washed and eaten. She would then take me into the house and show me the library so that I might choose something to read.

I followed her instructions and when I entered the Library, I was totally overcome. I have never seen so many books in my life! The walls were covered with them... so many that I had no idea what to choose. It must have shown on my face because the daughter - her name is Agnes - was most helpful. She asked me what I might be interested in. I told her I would like to know something about the history of this area, so she showed me what book I should read. So now you know where I got the information about this canal."

"What is she like - this Agnes lass of yours?" queried John.

"She is very plain looking, quite shy and quiet, but very pleasant. The lads in the Bothy tell me she is an only child and that her mother died when she was very young. Also that she was brought up by a governess and a nanny.

Apparently her father dotes on her, but I think myself that she is a bit lonely and missing company of people of her own age. But when we started to talk about the books in her father's library, she changed... brightened up a bit and seemed to enjoy our conversation."

"So, what age do you think she is? Is she an old maid?" asked John, laughing.

"Indeed not," answered Murdoch indignantly, "I think she is about the same age as me, or perhaps a little older. She told me to come back when I had finished with the two books she let me have, and I could get more if I wanted them, but warned me to take good care of them as the books in the library were the pride and joy of her father."

Chuckling at this John remarked; "Maybe she will take a shine to you and you could become rich, brother Murdoch? Funnier things have happened!"

"Do not be ridiculous!" protested his young brother. She is the daughter of a wealthy man, and clever as well. She keeps all her father's books, pays the wages, etc. What on earth makes you think she would even be allowed to walk out with a farm labourer, even if she did like me?" he scoffed.

"That is plain stupid! In fact, I have learned quite a bit about this locality. It has a lot of ancient history. Do you remember the school teacher up north telling us about the Romans?"

John nodded.

"Well, the Romans were here and built a Fort. It was on the wall of Antonine."

"Who was Antonine?" asked John.

"Oh never mind!" gasped his brother impatiently, and continued: "They built Antonine's Wall right across Scotland to keep us Northerners out! There is a railway here as well. It goes from here to a place called Monklands and it was built in 1826. Do you remember the big building we passed in the village?"

John nodded again.

"That is called the Barony Chambers and it was built in 1814/15. It is used as the Town Hall, Council Chambers, School, Court House and the Jail."

John was astounded at how much information Murdoch had absorbed. He knew he was a bright fellow, but to remember all this information was quite incredible.

The two brothers were different in many ways. While similar in stature – tall and strongly built – they were not facially alike.

John was without doubt the more handsome of the two and much more outgoing than his younger brother who tended to be quieter and shyer and prone to keeping his own council about things. He was very observant, missed nothing and had a mind like a sponge.

John was also clever. He too had a very inquiring mind, but did not have Murdoch's ability to retain vast amounts of information.

"With the amount of information you have stored in your head in such a short time, little brother, you continue to surprise me, No doubt you will be wanting more books from Mr. Mitchell's library in the near future. Where and when do you do all your reading? Do not the field hands make fun of you with your nose stuck in a book all the time?"

"Sometimes they make remarks, but none of them can read or write, so they do not say much. No doubt they have plenty to say behind my back about getting into the Big House library, but I do not care. I want to learn things and I have found the best way to do it, so they can think what they like."

"It would be good if we could both go to Glasgow some day, other than a Sunday," suggested John, completely changing the subject. "Perhaps next month before it gets dark early, we could ask if we could have a Saturday off instead of a Sunday, What do you think?"

Murdoch thought for a moment.

"It would be good, but I do not think we have been here long enough to start asking for favours, do you?" "I suppose not." his older brother agreed.

"How do you feel about the idea of us meeting next time at the Inn in Kirkintilloch on the Saturday night and having an ale or two? We would not have to get up for work the next day."

Murdoch thought again before answering.

"Some of the men in our Bothy do that and come back hardly able to stand. I would not want to get like that." came his cautious, ever practical answer. Although the younger of the two, Murdoch was blessed with more sense!

"Well!" protested John. "Nobody said we *have* to get like that, we can just to try it out like the other men." Inwardly, he wondered what it would feel like to be intoxicated.

He was willing to risk it, just to find out for himself.

Murdoch, on the other hand, decided he would humour his older brother and agreed to go with him the next time they had a day off.

They had now finished eating so decided to move on and explore the area a bit more. Nothing moved, of course, it being Sunday, but it was a pleasant day, and they enjoyed being with each other and away from the farms.

"It is quite an achievement - this canal, and nice to walk alongside." said John. *One day that same canal would bring him a great deal of sorrow!*

There was a large building on the opposite bank of the canal. Airing his encyclopedic knowledge, Murdoch told John that this was where the

Clydesdale horses were stabled and went on to tell him that the horses were used to pull the barges along the canal, all the way to Glasgow. There would be a man on the barge steering it and another walking on the towpath leading the horse.

Apparently it was a very busy waterway, taking all kinds of goods to Glasgow from the farms and other industries in the area.

Previously, it had taken much longer to get farm products to the market with horse and cart. The route followed by the canal took it to the north of the city of Glasgow...a much shorter distance than by the old roadways. This meant the people in the city could get fresher potatoes and vegetables, thereby improving their health.

Like all great cities...due to cramped living conditions, bad food and water supplies, health problems in Glasgow were rife. Things would improve but only when the filthy river Clyde was no longer used for drinking water.

While he was interested in all Murdoch had to tell about this place, much went over John's head, but the mention of Clydesdales caught his interest.

"I know about the Clydesdales pulling the barges. We have them on our farm. They are wonderful beasts, so big, strong and nice natured. Does Mr. Mitchell have such beasts?"

"Yes, we have them as well and as you say, they are magnificent animals."

And so the lads wandered on in pleasant conversation. Suddenly they were confronted with a pair of gleaming steel railway lines which disappeared in ever narrowing straight lines across the flat land until they joined together before disappearing round a bend in the distance.

Although never having seen these before, they instantly recognised them for what they were; each lad stood there, fervently wishing he could see a locomotive. This was a sight they could never have imagined in a million years. Progress had arrived in Scotland and these two would see many changes before they were much older.

In vain, they waited to see their first steam locomotive. Finally, they turned away in disappointment and headed back along the road...still talking endlessly about their work on the farms and comparing one farm to the other.

It was beginning to get dusky so the lads thought they had better head back in the direction they had come from; wanting to get back before it got completely dark. John had about four miles further to go than his brother, so they set off, endlessly talking all the way.

Both boys had thoroughly enjoyed their day out together and made arrangements to meet at the Kirkintilloch Inn on the Saturday, four week hence. Eventually, they came to the parting of their ways and wished each other well.

John continued smartly on his way wanting to get back as quickly as possible. He didn't want to lose his way in the dark or fall in the ditch.

As he travelled on his way he thought about Murdoch and had to admit to himself he was a bit jealous of the fact that his brother had access to all these books to read. How he would dearly have loved to be able to do the same. Knowledge from books was a great thing but there was no way he could see Mr. Lennox allowing him into *his* library! With the exception of the kitchen for Mr. Robertson and the household staff, the house area was taboo to the men.

John hadn't as yet, laid eyes on Mrs. Lennox or her two children. According to gossip; there was a governess who taught the children. She took her meals upstairs with the family. She also slept in the main house. As for gaining general knowledge; doubtless he would get a lot of information from Murdoch every time he met him. Equally doubtless, his brother would be only too glad to impart such knowledge... he would just have to make do with that!

He thought about the train and how he would love to take a ride on it to Monklands and back again, it would be quite exciting. *Ah well*! he thought, all *in good time*! There were lots of exciting things happening to look forward to. Progress was well and truly underway and he was thankful that he was young enough to be able to see it. One day, too, when roadways opened up a bit more to the North, he would write a letter to his family and tell them all the wonderful things that were going on down here. Although his parents could not read, his brothers and sister were able to do so. They would read the letter out for them.

John arrived back at the Bothy just before it was really dark. Some of the men were starting to cook their evening meal A few chickens had been donated so there would be a good meal that night. Liam was nowhere to be seen, but the others in his group had started a fire and were ready to begin cooking the chicken. He pitched in, peeling potatoes while another man prepared vegetables. It would be some time before the meal was ready, so what to do in the meantime? *If only I had some books to read* thought John, *it would pass the time and I could learn a lot of things.*

Liam returned while the men were waiting for the food to cook so they all decided to have a sing-song. The little Irishman started off the singing on his own by giving renderings of Irish folk songs in a surprisingly sweet melodious voice. Some of the songs were very humorous and had everyone laughing. The laughing encouraged him to get carried away and he began telling highly amusing Irish stories and jokes. His captive audience was so enraptured by his entertainment that the dinner was forgotten about and almost ruined.

The next night, was almost a repeat of the previous one except that this time, the others got a chance to air their singing talent. The lads had varying degrees of singing ability...some had very good voices... others were downright pathetic and totally tuneless. John ranked among the latter!

The days passed quickly, all the crops of hay, barley and oats were harvested from the fields. After threshing, the remainder of the straw from the grains was gathered and dried then stored in a barn along with the hay to provide winter bedding for the animals.

Potatoes and turnips had yet to be lifted and stored in their appropriate places. Afterward; during the winter months - the fields would be ploughed over and left to dry out, ready for the spring sowings of crops once again.

Ploughing was a laborious task, walking up and down behind a plough drawn by the horses with men following behind, taking out stones and helping break up the soil with forks and spades. Daylight was now in ever-shortening supply.

Once the vegetables had been lifted and the fields empty, more than seventy per cent of the field hands would leave and go into town for the winter. Some would go willingly, others would be paid off.

The men remaining on the farm would be assigned to mending barns and walls, and anything else that required repairing. New men would be taken on again in early spring.

As a result of this autumn exodus, there was more room in the Bothy for those remaining; a pleasant change from the crowded conditions during the hot summer nights. Doubtless there would be complaints about the winter cold, but fires could be kept smouldering all night to keep the place slightly warm and the worst of the cold out.

Chapter 6

Finally, the Saturday night arrived for John to go and meet Murdoch at the Inn in Kirkintilloch. He had been looking forward to this for weeks.

After he had eaten and got all spruced up, he headed, with the others, into the village. As they went along, he tried to fix his bearings so that he could find his way on the return journey. Doubtless he would be heading back to the farm a lot earlier than the rest of his companions since they would probably be coming back in the wee small hours. As for them: they all seemed to know the road by instinct... probably because they had travelled this way on so many previous occasions. It was certainly by instinct that they found their way back home...most of them being so drunk, they couldn't bite a finger!

Arriving at the Inn, John found his brother sitting on his own; patiently waiting for him.

The brothers were greatly pleased to see each other again. John joined Murdoch at a rough table in a corner while the rest of the hands gathered in another corner of the spacious sawdust floored public bar.

After ordering two ales at the bar, John brought them back to the table. Then the brothers took their first sip of the "demon drink." It tasted bitter to them but they persevered while catching up with each other's news.

John was particularly keen to hear what Murdoch had learned from all the books he was allowed to borrow from Mr. Mitchell's library as well as what he was now doing on the farm. They discovered that the work at their relative farms was almost at the same stage.

"I have been getting to know Agnes quite a bit better" remarked Murdoch, "she really is a very nice girl, but rather shy. It takes a bit of time to get into conversation with her.

I have found out she is really a very clever girl...well read on many subjects, probably from having read a good number of the books in her father's library."

His brother felt the pangs of envy.

"Oh, how I wish I could have the use of books too. The dark hours in the bothy seem so long without anything to do. If I even had some paper and something to write with, I would start writing down each day's events, which would keep me occupied at least" Then a thought struck him.

"Would there be any chance you could get something like that for me? Maybe your nice Agnes would get me some if you said it was for yourself."

"I could ask her and maybe say I wanted to take some notes from the books, or maybe I could just tell her the truth and say it was for you. I am sure she would appreciate the fact that you also have the desire to read...I know she thinks that people should be educated and that all children should be taught, whether they are rich or poor."

"Well," said John, sipping his drink, beginning to get used to it and thinking it was quite pleasant... "She certainly sounds like a nice person who thinks about people other than the rich ones she has been brought up with. Besides that," he said laughing, "methinks little brother, she has her eye on you."... again teasing his brother about Agnes Mitchell. Then he abruptly changed the subject. The alcohol was beginning to work and he was feeling faintly expansive.

"I am thinking of asking Mr. Lennox if I could have just one Saturday off instead of Sunday, so that I could go to Glasgow and buy some things. I was also thinking of writing a letter to mother and father. Is there any chance you could get pen and paper? If you cannot get me paper and something to write with, then I could buy them in Glasgow. Besides... I do not know about you, but I am sorely in need of some clothes. I have saved most of my wages for that very purpose. Would you be willing to ask Mr. Mitchell if you could also have the same Saturday off and come with me?"

"I suppose it would not do any harm to just ask" replied Murdoch.

"If he says no, well so be it. Now that it is getting darker and most of the fields will be finished soon, I do not see why not!"

Murdoch was also enjoying the taste of his ale! He finished with "We haven not, after all, spent any of our earnings till tonight, so I think we could treat ourselves to a day in town, do not you?"

John was pleased with this response, being sure the two of them would have a good day out in the "Big City." It was something to look forward to

They chatted on... deciding to order more ale... they were beginning to feel a little bit of a mellow "glow."

Murdoch related to his brother some of the things he had been learning from the books borrowed from his employer's library. Obviously he was getting very well educated from all this reading. He was using his twin assets of encyclopaedic memory and total recall to great advantage!

To John, who enjoyed knowledge, it was all very interesting stuff.

By the time they had finished the second pint of ale, they were both feeling decidedly tipsy and thinking it was a very pleasant feeling. Throwing caution to the wind, they ordered a third drink. At this point, most of the inhabitants in the Inn, who were in an advanced state of drunkenness, began singing. Everyone was in a merry mood... all were the best of pals, but as the night wore on and more alcohol was consumed, the fights would break out.

Murdoch, being the slightly more cautious brother of the two, decided after the third pint of ale, to call a halt, and advised John to do likewise. They had, by this time, joined the rest of the men and were also giving voice to song. The fact that they didn't know most of the songs being sung didn't deter them; they joined in anyway.

As the evening progressed, the singing got louder and louder, until it was merely a tuneless, incomprehensible shouting sound... an insult to the name of music and an assault on the poor landlord's ears. At this point the boys made the big mistake of ordering more ale...they were in full swing...enjoying themselves. Drink number four was quickly followed by yet another.

The ale in those days was pretty potent, rough stuff. This being the first time they had partaken of alcohol, the Munro brothers felt its effects rather badly. By now they were well and truly inebriated and the atmosphere in the pub had turned decidedly confrontational. They decided to leave just as the first fight broke out.

Once out in the fresh air, they felt like kings and set off... tramping their way along the road with arms about each other's shoulders... staggering from side to side, and singing at the top of their voices. They had no idea if they were going in the right direction, nor did they care.

The night was pitch-black. Despite this and by sheer luck rather than skilful navigation, they reached the junction in the road that led to Murdoch's destination...*Eastfield* farm. John would continue on the main road toward his destination.

After a great deal of back slapping and loud meaningless conversation, the brothers parted company, bidding each other goodnight... at least four times. Murdoch promised three times to ask about having a Saturday off. Finally, they arranged to meet on the Sunday, a month from then. It was extremely doubtful that these happy souls would even remember a single word of what passed between them that night! Oh how they would suffer! Little did they know how horrendously ill they would feel next morning. *So much for their father's warning*!

John managed to get himself back to the Bothy without getting lost or falling into the ditch.

Tumbling into bed; he became unconscious almost immediately. He didn't even hear Liam and the other men coming back, making the most awful noise and only vaguely stirred when he heard the others hauling themselves with difficulty out of bed to go to work next morning. Immediately they left, he went back to sleep.

Some time later he wakened and sat up, wishing immediately that he hadn't done so! He felt as if ten little men with hammers were inside his head hitting every part of it. He also felt extremely nauseous. He stood up and headed outside the Bothy, hoping the fresh air would make him feel better – it didn't! His father's words came back to him... no wonder he had called it the demon drink. Now he knew why! John was experiencing a massive hangover!

He walked around for a bit then headed for the water pipe outside the kitchen door and stuck his head under the cold water, the shock of which, felt invigorating and refreshing.

Just then, the kitchen door opened.... who should walk out? None other than Sarah Hendrie, the very last person on the face of God's earth he wanted to see right at that moment in time but there she stood; looking at him and laughing! *Why did this slip of a girl always make him feel at a disadvantage and a bit stupid?* She had a strange effect on him.

"Well now, John Munro, just look at you. I do not need to ask where you were last night. Feeling bad then are we?" This was said with a chuckle in her voice while her bright eyes danced.

John glowered at her, but had no answer. The way he felt was obvious to anyone who had their sight!

"Wait there, you big oaf!" his nemesis continued, "and I will get something to make you feel better. Now do not you go away."

In a few minutes she was back with a drink of he knew not what, but she made him drink every last drop of it anyway.

"Believe me, that will make you feel better in a wee while." she finished with smug satisfaction.

Thanking her he was about to go when Cook came out of the kitchen and added to his misery.

"You are a disgrace, young man; what would your mother think of you if she saw the state of you this morning? You keep away from that crowd and the drink, my boy, before it becomes a bad habit. It will get you nowhere." Having said that she went back into the kitchen and slammed the door behind her.

"I have an hour off just now" said Sarah, after Cook had disappeared.

"I can walk with you round the farm till you feel all right. You should get something to eat too. I will see if there is something in the kitchen." Again she disappeared, coming back a few moments later with some nice new bread and cheese.

John felt that if he ate anything, he would be sick, but just to please Sarah he ate the bread - actually quite enjoying it once he got started. He did not want Sarah's company but couldn't be bothered to argue with her, so went along with her suggestion. Inwardly, he thought about how he felt and said to himself *never again will I take strong drink!*

Now, how many times had that statement been heard then and since?

The two of them wandered round the farm, looking at the cows and horses and her, of course, doing all the talking. John questioned her about the people on the farm... who they were and the relationship between them all

"You have met James, Lizzie's husband, and the boy that workswith him; he is Cook's youngest boy.

The man who looks after the cows is Donald Kerr. Two of his boys help when they are not at school. He also has a girl at school, she is about six, then there is a little one running round the farm. His wife Jessie runs the dairy and their oldest daughter helps her." She paused at that point to take a breath

"What about another man I see with the plough, who is he?" A asked John.

"That would be Thomas McPherson, the ploughman. He works with James and the horses. Thomas has two sons at school, a daughter too young for school and a baby. When not at school, the older boy helps his father. Thomas ' s wife Agnes works in the laundry with the help of the daughter and keeps the baby in there with her. That's all the folk here on a permanent basis. They all live in the farm cottages" She stopped again for a quick breath.

Boy! John thought *could she talk!*

"Then there is Forbes" continued Sarah. "He is the boss' s servant and looks after all Mr. Lennox ' s personal things. He is single and has a room in the attic. So do I." She added.

"Jean, of course, stays in the farm cottage with her parents. Forbes is also in charge of the household staff, but he would not dare tell Cook what to do!"

John by this time was feeling better and there was no doubt that whatever the liquid Sarah gave him had definitely helped, plus the food. He was grateful for her thoughtfulness and not criticising him too much for being so stupid. *Well!* He thought...every young man is stupid at some time or another regarding alcohol. He had learned his lesson! *Or had he?*

Sarah was surely the greatest chatterbox he had ever met, with perhaps the exception of Liam, but he was actually beginning to enjoy her company and had learned quite a bit about all the people who worked on the farm. He asked her...

"Is Mr. Lennox quite a good boss then, or do you have any trouble with him?"

"No, we hardly ever see him. As long as we are doing our work and Cook and Forbes are satisfied with what Jean and I do, then all is well." Before Sarah could start talking again John quickly continued:

"I never see any of them around and I have never seen Mrs. Lennox at all. I saw the family all go out in a sort of coach thing one day, but that is all."

Sarah solved that mystery.

"Nobody sees them much except Lizzie and sometimes Cook. Lizzie tends to the personal needs of Mrs. Lennox, so she sees her quite a lot and says she is a very nice lady.

The children are in the nursery or schoolroom with the governess and take their meals there as well, so nobody hardly ever sees them either. I think they would love to run around the farm the way the other children do and have ones their own age to play with, but that would never be allowed That would be beneath their station in life!" she said pulling a face!

John sighed. "Thank you Sarah, for making me feel better... maybe I should take Cook's advice. My father warned me and my brother of the *demon drink;* now I know what he meant, that is for sure!

I wonder how Murdoch is feeling this morning? Probably as bad as I did, but he would not have had someone to give him something to make him feel better and he would have had to get his own food as well."

Sarah - suddenly remembering - said "I had better get back to the kitchen – I do not want to be late and get in Cook's bad books. You know: I think she really quite likes you and wants to look out for you. There is nothing that goes on at this farm that passes her nose... believe me!" adding, with a laugh: "She probably just wants to mother you. Her two older boys are in Glasgow, so You are their replacement!"

"I do not need mothered, I am old enough to look after myself", muttered John indignantly.

"Oh yes? I could see how well you were looking after yourself this morning, John Munro." retorted Sarah looking at him side-ways.

At this point, the two of them parted company but not before John, against his better judgment remarked casually;

"Maybe I will see you again sometime."

"Maybe you will at that." replied Sarah with eyes twinkling, thinking to herself *I will most certainly make sure of that.*

Thereafter, she flounced off to the kitchen, giving him a backward glance and a cheeky grin.

As John made his way back to the Bothy, he chided himself for getting involved with this little Irish she-devil! He should never have given the impression that he wanted to see her again. Cook would have his hide for even thinking about it. Sarah might be young, but she was older and wiser than her years. She was also a little flirt and could easily get him into trouble. *Better steer clear in the meantime,* he thought. But he had to admit he enjoyed her company. She was bright and laughed a lot, with a great sense of humour. *But again; she really was only a child, whatever way you looked at it.* He reluctantly stopped thinking about Sarah and concentrated on the present. Time to get ready and meet Murdoch. *Did they say last night that they would meet today?* He couldn't remember. No matter, he would just go and see if he was around. He made up something to eat and drink then set off.

That same morning, Murdoch thought he would never see the light of another day nor would ever feel well again. He stayed in bed for a while, and then made the effort to stir himself.

Once fully awake, he felt more or less the same way as had his brother John...- ghastly! To put it mildly. His immediate thought being... *If this was the way ale made you feel then they could keep it. It certainly wasn't worth feeling like this.* Like his brother, he couldn't remember what he said last night, in fact, he could hardly remember anything about the previous night at all.

He had no idea how he got back to the farm or got to bed. He had heard it said that drunken men get back by instinct, so it must have been that which guided him, or maybe someone made sure he got back to the farm. He didn't think it was John, for as far as he could remember anything; John was as drunk as he was.

It was stupid of him to go along with the idea of getting more ale when his instincts had told him to stop when they got to the tipsy stage. *So much for his common sense!* he thought ruefully.

He decided to wash and afterward go and see if John was coming along the road. Maybe the fresh air would make him feel like a human being again. His tongue felt thick as a strap of black tobacco. A drink and some food might help.

After consuming almost a pint of milk, he wrapped up some cheese and bread in a clean neckerchief, went outside and began walking along the road. Oh if only his head would stop throbbing and his stomach would settle down!

He trudged along for a bit, and then stopped for a rest... sitting on top of one of the stone dykes which lined each side of the road, separating it from the fields. He felt dreadful!

After a while, he made out a figure in the distance coming along the road in his direction. Presuming it must be his brother he wondered: *is he feeling as bad as I am?*

Sure enough as soon as the figure drew nearer, he saw that it was indeed John.

Sitting on the wall beside him John observed:

"I can see little brother that you are feeling not quite yourself this morning, would I be right in saying that?"

"You surely would be right about that brother." agreed Murdoch. "How do you feel yourself?"

"Not too bad now! When I got up, I went to the water pipe at the kitchen for a wash. Young Sarah Hendrie came out and saw me. She laughed at me, then went into the kitchen and returned with a liquid that she made me drink. Then insisted I ate some bread and cheese. After that I started to feel better and now I am not feeling too bad at all."

"Well, lucky you! The thought of eating makes me feel sick and my head is painful." moaned Murdoch.

"Do you have something with you to eat?" asked John. "Because if not, I have some bread and cheese here which I will happily share with you."

"No, thank you, I have food of my own here with me. I suppose I had better eat it now...anything to make me feel even a little better."

The two of them sat together for a while on the wall while Murdoch ate...every mouthful nearly choking him. But his brother John insisted he kept going till the food was finished; then gave him a drink of water to wash down the food.

After, they walked along the road towards Kirkintilloch, taking a detour before they reached the village and went to have a look at the railway.

As always, Murdoch was a fountain of information concerning this ever -growing means of travel and transport. He told John that the little nearby railway station had been named after the hamlet of Lenzie.

John remarked that this was strange since there wasn't much there at that time.

Murdoch told him that he had learned of great plans for the railway system. The train that passed through Lenzie went to Monklands and stopped there but eventually, it would go right into the centre of Glasgow. At Glasgow, another existing train could be boarded that would take passengers all the way to Edinburgh. However, he told him; that was not going to happen for some time yet.

Both brothers knew that businesses were beginning to start up in the Kirkintilloch area. Weaving, iron smelting and, because of the canal, even boat building. The area was becoming a little hive of industry.

More accommodation was being built to house the workers who came from other areas of Scotland.

They wandered about for some time, but it was cold and, it being Sunday, all public establishments were closed. Since they really had no specific destination, they decided to go back to *Eastfield* where Murdoch would show his brother the books he had borrowed from the library, courtesy of Agnes.

At *Eastfield*, John was really impressed when he saw the books Murdoch had, and dearly wished he could borrow a few of them. However, since he knew that was out of the question, he had to be content to sit with his brother in the Bothy, looking through them... reading bits and pieces here and there, until it was getting dark, and time for him to go.

As he was leaving, Murdoch promised he would ask Agnes... in the hope that she would be sympathetic to his request ...if she could provide some extra paper and writing materials which he would pass on to John. *Nothing ventured – nothing gained!* He also promised to ask her father if he could have a Saturday off instead of Sunday as he needed to go to Glasgow to get some personal things.

John thought this was a good idea and promised he would do likewise... they could perhaps have an answer when next they met in a month. Adding that he would dearly love to write a letter to their parents to let them know that they were doing all right and what was happening in Glasgow and surrounding area. Writing the letter would be no problem if Agnes provided the means to write it. He knew their parents and siblings would be delighted to get such a letter...to know they had good jobs and that they were well. Also to hear all their other news - minus of course, the bit about having too much of the demon drink and feeling ill with it. There was most definitely a *not a need for them to know*!

Once he had the means of writing, he would find some way to get a letter to them, even if it took a long time to get there.

John finally took his leave of Murdoch and set off once more for his own Bothy.

When he got back it was dark, but still fairly early, so what to do now? Most of the remaining men were just sitting around talking and telling tall stories. Liam, of course, was in good form as usual with his tales and songs, so time passed till it was time to cook the evening meal. If truth be known - John would much prefer to be working than sitting around with nothing to do, but he had to learn patience.

And so the weeks passed with all the usual work going on by day and the nights long and boring. It was little wonder that so many of the men went into the village to the Inn for a few drinks. At least it passed the time but it was an expensive way of doing so.

One morning, John saw Mr. Lennox in the yard. He decided to broach the question of swapping Sunday off for a Saturday. Doffing his cap he addressed his employer.

"Sir; as you know, all the shops are closed on the Sabbath. Would it be possible for me to have a Saturday off instead of the Sunday? I need to go to Glasgow to get some things."

"I suppose so John. I have no problem with that. An odd Saturday is fine but" he cautioned, "please do not make a habit of it" adding "Once you decide on a particular day - to keep things right and proper - you had better tell Mr. Robertson of your decision. Just to keep him informed you understand?"

John thanked him profusely, promised to keep Mr Robertson informed and said he would most definitely not make it a regular occurrence.

The next meeting of the brothers was quite exciting. Murdoch too had been successful with the Saturday, Sunday swop, so they planned a Glasgow trip on their next day off. Additionally, Murdoch brought some writing materials, courtesy of Agnes Mitchell.

John was delighted and asked that his thanks be conveyed to her. Now he would be able to write a letter to his parents and give them all the news. He had been thinking that if he didn't get any writing materials from Agnes, then there was no reason why his brother could not write a letter to their family up north. However, now he had the means, he could do it himself.

Just as well anyway, since Murdoch would have written in a short, matter of fact way and not given them the whole picture. Whereas, he knew he would be much more elaborate in his writings. He would start the letter soon and add to it after they had been on the train to Monklands. Going on the train would be exciting – what an experience! What a story to tell! More so, since the new Monklands to Glasgow line had recently opened for business so they would be able to travel the whole way to Glasgow and back by train.

And so the momentous Glasgow-trip Saturday duly arrived.

The two boys met at the bottom of the road to *Eastfield* and, in great expectancy, headed for the railway station at Lenzie They had already ascertained what time the train would arrive - there was no way they wanted to miss it! So many things to see! To these boys this was to be the most exciting thing that had ever happened to them; they would talk about it for years to come.

The arrival of the great hissing, clanking smoke blowing monster was their first thrill. Thereafter, all went well.

They boarded the train and sat on a bench at the side of one of the carriages. There was a moment of silence, broken only by the lowing of cattle in a field nearby and a blackbird emptying its heart to the world.

Suddenly there was a loud whistle followed by an ear-damaging shriek from the engine at the head of the train. Then came a loud rushing of steam from the locomotive, the vapour of which engulfed the station and all standing on its platform. At these alien sounds the brothers jumped up in alarm, the cattle in the field ran off with udders swinging and no one could tell if the blackbird sang or did not. It all happened in the wink of an eye and was followed immediately by a jerk on the carriages as the engine towed them - wheels squeaking - out of Lenzie station...which jerk, returned the brothers unceremoniously to their seats. They were off on their next great adventure!

Soon the train was chuffing along the tracks. They were fascinated! To be moving along iron tracks at a reasonable speed and no horses!

This was fantastic! The train picked up speed. They watched everything whizzing past them at what seemed to them to be an incredibly fast pace... faster than they had travelled in their entire short lives.

In what seemed no time at all, the train was pulling into Monklands station. When it finally stopped after much jerking and clanking, they alighted and were directed to another platform to board another train, which would take them directly into the heart of the City of Glasgow.

Shortly after that, they embarked on the second train journey of their lives...every bit as exciting as the first and every bit as interesting due to the changing scenery.

Soon, the train was passing through the outskirts of the city and finally pulled into the station. They had arrived at Glasgow for the second time since they left the north.

The city had not improved since their previous visit. It smelled as badly as before, and no one seemed to wash very much.

The children were filthy and some had no shoes on their feet. They were playing in gutters which were running with filthy water and in some places sewage. No wonder there was disease.

It was not a place to spend too much time in, so they quickly found out where they could make necessary purchases and headed there.

After they had visited all the stalls and small shops, they then wandered round for a while; had something to eat, then decided they had had enough and headed for the train to take them back from whence they came. They were now entirely devoid of cash, but did not regret one penny they had spent.

The nights were drawing in, but the farm work continued during the ever decreasing hours of daylight left of each day. Now the turnips and potatoes were all lifted and stored and the vacated fields ready for ploughing after the New Year.

Christmas was soon to be upon them and John had already written his long letter and found a means of posting it, albeit it would take a long time to get to his parents, if at all.

All work stopped on Christmas day and the only poor souls that had to keep slaving away were Cook and her helpers.

Mr & Mrs. Lennox were entertaining family members for the festivities, which of course gave the kitchen and household staff even more work to do, so no time off for them.

Those of the Bothy men remaining in the Bothy were given chickens to cook. With potatoes and vegetables these provided a fine dinner. Cook provided a huge plum pudding and an equally huge churn of fresh cream which when poured over the pudding finished the meal and made the day a little bit different for them.

New Year came and went. It was the depths of winter. But for the livestock, farm life all but came to a standstill.

The weather by now was bitterly cold, especially at night. Snow fell for a few days, making work of any kind impossible. This was quickly followed by a thaw which turned the snow to a watery slush, making the already heavy clay even heavier.

Soon though, the weather changed...less rain, a little more sunshine and with the east wind blowing more frequently... the earth began to dry out fulfilling the old prophesy that *A peck of March dust was worth its weight in gold!*

When the soil was dry enough, the ploughing began... making the fields ready for the sowing of the crops in the spring.

And so life trundled-on with nothing much changing from year to year. Both young men were quite happy to stay put at their respective farms; giving good and loyal service to their employers.

In the beginning, John and Sarah had become very good friends but this soon developed into a romance and they were then officially *walking out together.* John was twenty two years old and Sarah, at the tender age of eighteen, was four years his junior. This was quite acceptable!

Cook was pleased with their situation; she liked both of them and felt they were really suited to each other.

As for John; he thought the sun rose and set on his little Irish temptress. She in turn; adored her *Big Highlander* as she called him.

During the same time, fortune smiled upon Murdoch. Mr. Mitchell's manager had retired and Murdoch was asked if he felt capable of taking over and replacing the man as the new Farm Manager. Murdoch was delighted to accept. He now had a bit of status on the farm other than being just a labourer.

Agnes was, in turn, thrilled at this turn of events. *Perhaps she had wangled this?* She was very fond of Murdoch and felt comfortable in his company. Although her father had a lot of friends with young sons around her age, none of them were interested in her. She was not exactly the prettiest girl in the neighbourhood, and always very shy and awkward in their company. All these young men were so confident and voluble, and she seemed to shrink into her shell in their company. *Shrinking violet comes to mind!*

On the other hand, with Murdoch, she felt utterly at ease ...her father had not missed this. Quietly, he hoped she would not be disappointed if Murdoch went off and got married.

Although Murdoch was not really of their class, it had to be said that he had greatly improved himself over the years. He read many books and had learned many things. Since he had arrived, he had always maintained good manners and always been polite. *Time would tell.*

Chapter 7

*A*n announcement was made on the Lennox farm a wedding soon to take place! Cook's youngest daughter, Jean, was finally getting married to her young man, and so the preparations began, and Cook was making the wedding cake.

Between them; Jean and her sister Lizzie, were in the process of sewing the wedding dress.

The couple were to be married in the local church at Kirkintilloch and afterward, a feast would be held at the farm

The young man's family, consisting of his parents and a number of other relatives, would be there. Jean's two brothers in Glasgow were also coming to see their sister wed - it promised to be quite a gathering. Of course, the other farm employees would not be included in this celebration.

Sarah would have to work very hard that day as Cook would be wanting time off to enjoy the celebrations. She would still have to make the evening meal for the Lennox family and tend to her normal duties, but Sarah said she would help as much as possible to give Cook a break.

The great celebration eventually took place, and quite a *do* it was.

There were many people there and a very merry time was had by all.

John had glimpsed all this in the passing and thought *if it came to pass that Sarah and him were wed, nothing like this would happen. After all, her folk were many miles away in another part of Scotland, and so was his family. The only ones that would attend their wedding would be his brother and perhaps Jean, as witnesses, but that would be all. No great celebrations for them.*

However, at that moment in time, John was not planning on getting wed, although he knew Sarah would jump at the prospect, given half the chance!

For a start, they would have nowhere to live. Having said that, there might be hope on the horizon as they were building two new farm cottages. Perhaps some of the people already in the existing ones, like Cook, for example, would get the new ones. However - *back to earth*! Until something was established on that front, John was no way committing himself to marriage, and that was that, no matter what Sarah wanted.

The previous year, Cook's daughter Lizzie had given birth to a lovely little boy and Cook was now a very proud grandmother who fussed over this baby like there had never been one born on the farm before!

When Lizzie was doing her house duties for Mrs. Lennox, Cook would have the wee lad in the kitchen with her and would spend half her time fawning over him. This was easy since he was a very good contented baby with lots of smiles, who just stole his grandmother's heart.

The wee lad was also the apple of his father's eye!

John had told Murdoch how the situation was between him and Sarah, so Murdoch guessed there might well be wedding bells in that direction in the not too distant future.

Murdoch - Like John - thought about his parents. If this were to come to pass; it would be a pity that their parents could not be here to see their eldest son married. If it did come about, there would not be too many folk attending it since Sarah was herself in the same position with parents and siblings being away down in the Scottish Borders.

His brother's news caused Murdoch to think about his own situation. Agnes was a very nice girl and they got on so well together. Both were interested in the same subjects, and felt very comfortable in each other's company. He had a great deal of respect for her, and knew she was very fond of him.

But what would her Daddy say to that? - Even though he indulged Agnes in anything she wanted; would he like it?

In truth, Agnes had simple tastes and had no great wants at all. Nor was she a socialite. However, she had to behave accordingly when her father entertained guests. Since her mother was dead, she took the place as the lady of the house. Such social dinners and events bored her. She was not at ease among large gatherings of people.

Murdoch often thought that he would love to be a "fly on the wall" at the time...if it ever came to it...*when she told her father she wanted to marry and her choice was his employee Murdoch Munro!* It was just possible... he had a strong feeling that that was what was in her mind.

He would be quite happy to marry Agnes Mitchell, but thought it would be a marriage of companionship rather than mad passionate love! Then again, one could never tell what a person could be like underneath all that shyness! In the meantime, they would just act as friends until such times as some sign was given for their friendship to go any further.

As Manager, Murdoch was now eating his meals in the kitchen with the other household staff.

The Cook was a small friendly, kindly lady. The other staff consisted of two serving girls - who also cleaned the house - a kitchen girl, and a manservant who attended to Mr. Mitchell's needs.

Murdoch was lucky from the point of view that previously, he had had to live in the Bothy and do for himself for quite a long time, so it was absolute heaven to have someone else make his meals for him....excellent meals at that! He thought of his brother John over at *Kirkland.* John had enjoyed his meals in the big house at first, then had been relegated to the Bothy. What a let down it must have been for him. On the other hand, he, Murdoch; as Farm Manager had been given one of two vacant farm cottages. After all; the new Farm Manager living in the Bothy was not quite the thing!

The brothers continued to meet on their Sundays off and enjoyed being together, sharing all the latest news.

John was delighted that his sibling had been made farm manager but was not surprised. He knew Murdoch had the right temperament and was quite capable of doing the job.

Since a small boy, his young brother had been a stickler for detail... everything had to be done properly. This trait had never left him and now he would reap the benefits.

On one such Sunday, John broached the subject of his brother's relationship with Agnes Mitchell...was it turning more serious?

This was a touchy subject as by that time, Murdoch was beginning to consider Agnes as a bit more than just a good friend. Inwardly, he knew his feelings were stirring a little in that direction but no way was he going to tell John his thoughts, absolutely not! He would just be made fun of so he kept the conversation to what Agnes had done for the two of them.

She had been very kind and managed to get writing materials for John on several occasions, so that he had been able to write to his parents.

Murdoch had also written to his parents.

A letter from up north finally arrived at the Mitchell farm. It was from Catherine, telling John and Murdoch that their letters had been received. Their parents and the rest of the family were all well and everyone was so glad to hear that all was well with the brothers... that they were doing well for themselves.

They learned that their mother was particularly thankful to hear from them at last...to know they were safe and had jobs. Obviously, like all mothers, she worried a lot about her two first born children – *not that they were children any more, but, again. Like all mothers...she thought of them as such*!

One day, Murdoch was in the library with Agnes getting some more books. Casually, he remarked:

"It would be nice if perhaps sometime we could go for a walk along the canal bank together." continuing anxiously: "I value your friendship and hope you will not be offended by my suggestion. I thought it would make a pleasant change from us always just meeting here in the library and we could go walking in the fresh air on a nice day, instead of always being on the farm." Waiting equally anxiously with bated breath to see how she accepted his suggestion, he was rewarded when she blushed and said "That would be very nice, Murdoch, I would like that very much.".... adding cautiously... "But I would have to ask my father first."

It was left at that, but he hoped she would speak to her father soon about the matter.

Meantime, John was having his ear bent by Sarah, hinting on every available occasion on the subject of setting a wedding date. He didn't really want to make a positive commitment. Although he loved Sarah, he also loved his independence.

He felt that once a man got married, in no time the children would come along; one after the other...he was not ready for that yet! Bringing up, feeding and clothing children was such a responsibility. He had witnessed how marriage affected men on the farm...working all the time, just to make enough money to keep their families...no time of their own. Besides, he liked to meet his brother on a Sunday, and on a very odd occasion, go with the lads to the village inn for a few jars. Marriage would put a stop to that! Perhaps when he was a little older, he might feel more inclined to be a married man and take his responsibilities seriously, but not right at that moment.

Life on the farm went on as usual. Another baby was born to Lizzie and James - a girl this time.

As previously, Cook was thrilled with this new little girl child... she simply adored both her small grandchildren. Then her other daughter, Jean, announced that she too was going to have a baby. Soon there would be another little one for Cook to drool over.

All such goings-on made Sarah even more determined to talk her John into getting wed, but she was *barking up the wrong tree* as they say. John would not be shifted from his decision to remain single. His stubbornness caused many a row between them, but these were always patched up with a few kisses and vague promises.

With the passing weeks, months and years, things were progressing in the country. New railroads were being built all over many parts of Scotland and existing ones extended, making travel so much easier between cities, towns and villages.

Industry was flourishing in the Lenzie – Kirkintilloch area; many more people were coming to work and settling there. Consequently, the swelling population increased the requirement for accommodation. Building work went on apace. The local solitary Inn was doing great business on a Saturday night; the demand was so great that another one had to open to take the overspill!

Not everyone was happy with this though. The Church completely condemned it, saying it was putting temptation in the way of good Christian men. *Let Christian men rejoice!*

One afternoon, when the hands were all out working, a letter from Ireland arrived for Liam. So when they got back to the Bothy that night, Liam, - who could neither read nor write - asked John if he would read it to him. John was quite happy to do so, but suggested they went outside, in case the letter was of a deeply personal nature and not for all the other hands in the Bothy to hear.

Quickly scanning the letter first, John then told his friend:

"Liam, I am sorry, but the news is not too good. Your father has been taken ill. Seems it is quite serious and your family wants you to go home as soon as possible. The letter has been written by a friend of your family... I will read it to you now."

He read the letter from beginning to end. It was quite brief. After finishing, he asked Liam if he wanted a reply to be written... adding; "I can do that for you without a problem but it will take quite a time before it gets delivered. I think it would be better if you go home right now... You will get there quicker than any letter would."

Liam thanked him and said he would go and see Mr. Lennox immediately and tell him what had happened, and that he would have to leave right away. He told John that if he did go, he didn't know if he would come back. He was the oldest of his family. Perhaps his mother and the rest of the family might be dependent on him. He would have to wait and see what the situation was when he got home.

John looked at his friend's downcast face.

"I am truly sorry, Liam, about the news of your father and that you have to go home. I, for one, will miss you, all your chatter and bad jokes, and particularly your terrible singing very much." He was trying to keep the situation from being too sombre.

Perhaps when Liam got home he would find the situation not to be as bad as the letter suggested and he would be able to return to be back again among his friends.

"Maybe the friend who wrote this letter could write a short note for you to send here to me and let me know how things are with you. I would be anxious to know."

"Thanks John, for reading the letter to me and for your concern. I, too, will miss you and all the lads here. They are a great bunch, particularly at the inn on a Saturday night. I must go now and try to see Mr. Lennox if he is available at the moment Once I get back home, I will indeed get my friend to write and let you know how things are with me."

Next morning Liam was gone, and John would never see him again. A short note arrived many weeks later informing John that Liam's father had died and he had to stay to look after his mother and the rest of his family.

As before, John and Murdoch had agreed to meet at the Inn on a particular Saturday night and have a couple of drinks. The Sunday following would be John's day off.

When they were seated in a cosy little corner, a sad, lonely looking older man came over to their table and asked if he might sit with them. He told them he was there on his own and was curious about them...two young strangers sitting together. The brothers were relaxed and saw no reason to ignore this stranger so they invited him to join them.

When seated, the man began by asking them their names, where they had come from and where did they work? The lads found him to be an interesting person, with quite a few local tales to tell.

Suddenly, he asked them "Did you arrive here after 1832? ... Did you know what happened here in that year?"

His questions immediately caught their interest. They told him they had arrived after that date and finished by asking "so what is the big mystery about 1832?"

"Well!" began the man, "no doubt you will know that cholera struck Glasgow with a vengeance, but did you know that it started right here in Kirkintilloch? This was the very first place on the West of Scotland to get it."

"No." They chorused. "We did not know that at all and nobody has ever said anything about it to us in the few years we have been here. Did people here die of it then?"

"As a matter of fact, yes, they did, thirty six of them in total; three of them being my wife and two of my children. It was a terrible thing! It was in the water you know. After that happened they cleaned up the water system so that it would not happen again. It must have got into the canal and headed for Glasgow - poor souls."

"Having been to Glasgow and seen conditions there" said John "and them using the dirty water of the River Clyde, I suppose it would go rapidly round like wild fire. It must have been a terrible time for you. We are so sorry to hear about your wife and children."

"Did you have other children and did they survive it?" asked Murdoch, feeling real sympathy for this pleasant man. He thought; how would he feel if it had been his brothers and sisters or worse still... *his children?*

"Yes." replied their companion. "I have three more children, but they are all older. One of them...my wee girl...caught the disease, but she fortunately recovered. The other two boys and I were lucky, I suppose."

"Yours is a sad, sad story friend." added John. "No doubt lots of families lost someone. The whole village would have been in mourning for a while."

"Och well now, time is a great healer! Let us change to a more pleasant subject", said the man, who had introduced himself as Hamish McFarlane. "I am hearing rumours that soon they are going to introduce gas lighting into the village. Now, will not that be something! Just think; with reasonably good lighting, and not be straining their eyes; if people had gas lighting in their houses, they would be able to do so many things during the dark hours. Now that so many children are getting schooling and have learned to read and write, it will be good for the scholars to be able to read when they want to...even at night during the long, dark winter months."

"That would be a great asset to all properties and perhaps the streets as well." said John. "Street lights would be quite something, do not you think?" He was really interested in this rumour. *How exciting* he thought, *to have the streets lit up!*

Thus, the conversation flowed back and forth for quite some time, until after just one drink, the man eventually said, that he had better head for home.

As he said his goodbyes, he told the boys he had thoroughly enjoyed their company. They, in turn, noticed that the man's expression had less sadness.

After their new friend had left, Murdoch turned the conversation to his brother's love life. John was adamant about how he felt regarding the whole thing; he just didn't want to commit himself to marrying Sarah as yet. "John," pleaded Murdoch, "you can not go on in this way forever... It is not fair to Sarah! One day she will tell you to forget it all and will go and marry someone else. You keep telling me how attractive she is, so no doubt there are lots of young lads waiting in the wings. How do you feel about her, really? Do you love her?"

"Yes, I do," anguished John. "It is just that I can not see myself married with a bunch of little ones. Oh I know; it is not that a man has to do much with them, that is the work of a wife, but they have to be fed and clothed and have a house to live in. The wages I have as a farm labourer would not go very far. Even coming to meet you here at the Inn on an odd occasion would not be affordable. It seems like a pretty boring existence, if you ask me." He finished with a gasp of dismay.

"Well I think it would be rather nice" said Murdoch, "to have a good wife and some little ones running around. They could give a person a lot of joy once they are past being a baby."

John was astonished at his brother's opinion of marriage and children.

"It is alright for you." he protested, "If you married Agnes you would no doubt just move into the big house and have a fine place for your children, plus enough money to keep them. Agnes's father would make sure of that, so you would have nothing to worry about."

"I suppose so," agreed Murdoch reluctantly, "I am maybe in a different position from you. Living in a small farm cottage with a lot of children would not be much fun. We had enough of that ourselves when we were small after we had to move to the coast. That cottage was tiny. Our parents also had the terrible problem of having no money and bad growing land. It must have been a nightmare for them to feed us all. I suppose you just do not think about it when you are young and it is not your responsibility."

"Well!" exclaimed John, "Neither of us is in that position as yet and I for one do not intend to be for some time. Nobody is pushing us into anything, although, as I said, Sarah is certainly trying her best!"

They both had a good laugh about that. John continue:

"Sarah is always hinting about folk being wed and how she does not want to be left an old maid. Not much chance of that for Sarah Hendrie, I can tell you - even if she has to drag someone to the altar." he finished ruefully! "I do not see much of her anyway as she is working in the big house most of the time and at night helping with the dinners. She gets time off in the afternoons, but I am working then.

Her Sunday off is different from mine so she thinks I should stay at the farm on *my* Sunday off and see her when *she is* off work for a couple of hours in the afternoon. I told her it was the only time I could meet her, but she was not too pleased with that and said *Hmmmm - some romance this is!*"

They continued to talk for a while on other matters until it was time for them to go home. On parting, they agreed to meet the next day which would be Sunday.

When next he met John, Murdoch was very well pleased with himself. He told his brother that Agnes's father had agreed to her occasionally walking out with him.

"She was all blushing when she told me but declared she was looking forward to it."

For Murdoch; things were moving along in the right direction!

The boys walked along the banks of the canal for a while, before sitting down to eat their food. As they sat, they watched some young children playing a little further along the canal bank. Suddenly- as they watched- a little boy stepped backwards too near the edge of the bank – lost his footing - and fell into the canal.

The lad splashed about, but it became obvious to the watching brothers that the boy couldn't swim. So John tugged off his heavy boots, dived into the water and swam strongly towards the child who was going under the water for the second time. He managed to grab a hold of the wee boy's clothing and haul him back to the surface. Then - towing the terrified child behind him - he headed into the bank where the hands of spectators were waiting to grab him.

Because the bank was almost vertical below the surface; there was no footing, so John had to dive under the water, and then push the boy upwards so that the folk on the bank could get a hold of him and pull him to dry land. Thus, the boy was returned to safety but there was no sign of his rescuer. John did not re-surface!

A minute passed and still there was no sign of John. Murdoch could wait no longer...barely taking time to think... he tugged off his own boots and jumped into the canal at the spot where he had last seen his brother. Beneath the surface and searching round desperately in the muddy brown water, he made out John. He had caught his foot in some kind of metal rope and couldn't get it free. His eyes bulged in his head and his cheeks looked to burst as he tried to retain the last vestiges of air in his lungs. After a struggle, Murdoch managed to free John's foot and the two of them came to the surface spluttering, coughing and gulping in massive quantities of sweet, fresh air. Waiting men then hauled the two of them clear of the water where they lay on the bank gasping like two giant fish.

Eventually, they got their breath back. They were soaking wet but seemingly no worse for wear. As for the rescued boy - he was fine and was already back to normal.

The boy's parents eventually arrived on the scene. When they heard the story of their son's rescue, they thanked John profusely for saving the life of their child. John in turn thanked his wee brother Murdoch for saving his life.

The unusual activity had brought people from their houses. John was now a local hero!

Time passed with the usual work going on...Sarah moaning that she didn't see John very much while Murdoch's romance blossomed beautifully.

If things kept going as they did, it looked very much like Murdoch would be wed before his brother.

Sarah was getting rather frustrated and annoyed at not being able to see John very much. It always seemed that when she had any time off, he was working, so it was not a very happy situation. She had asked him on several occasions to stay at the farm on his Sunday off...when she could get a few hours off in the afternoon and they could go out for a walk. He always answered briefly, that it was the only time he saw his brother and that was that!

Well, Sarah was not about to put up with that much longer, after all, she had known him now for five years, so she reckoned it was time to do something about it herself if he wasn't going to!

To this end, she asked Cook what she thought about her idea to change her Sunday off, to coincide with John's Sunday off; did Cook think Forbes would allow it?

"I have no problem with it" answered Cook," but remember; all of the staff except Jean have firm commitments so they will not be able to change. You will just have to get Jean to agree to changing days off with you."

Fortunately, Jean readily agreed to the change. Her husband didn't work on a Sunday, so it was fine with her. Sarah's next task was to clear the arrangement with Forbes.

He too was amenable to the new arrangement saying that as long as the house was run in the proper manner and there was always enough staff, it didn't much matter to him who had which Sunday off.

Having crossed all these hurdles with comparative ease, all Sarah had to do then was to tell John the good news. *How would he take it?*

In fact, John was not particularly pleased when she told him; protesting that she might have asked him first.

John's response to her news riled Sarah who retorted... spitting like a cat... her temper showing...

"I am not about to ask you for permission to do anything, you are not my boss. I thought you would be pleased that we could be together for a day. I do not think you love me at all. As far as you are concerned, I am just *PART OF THE SCENERY*" she shouted.

John was a little taken aback at her ferocity and realised she was really quite upset about his lack of enthusiasm to spend some time with her. But Sarah was not finished with him:

"Just go and stick with your precious brother on your Sunday off, but do not expect me to be waiting here to suit you."

With that last remark, she furiously stamped off without a backward glance, headed for her room. With door closed, she lay on her bed and wept. Poor Sarah, he really was not treating her very nicely.

Sarah's outburst gave John food for thought ... he decided he *did* really love her very much and didn't want to lose her so he decided do something about it.

When his next Sunday off came round, John contacted Sarah and suggested to her that she got dressed up and they would go for a walk first then later in the afternoon, they would meet with his brother Murdoch.

His suggestions pleased Sarah immensely. She hurried off to get ready... putting on her *Sunday best* so that she would look nice when at last she would meet John's brother.

And so it transpired; they had a pleasant walk as planned, then met Murdoch that afternoon.

Sarah discovered the brothers were not in the least alike...except in stature. Murdoch had plainer features; was much less flamboyant than her John and didn't talk as much. However, he was very pleasant and polite to her, and she liked him instantly.

Sarah was nervous at that first meeting and chattered incessantly but Murdoch's reaction had the effect of calming her down and much to John's relief, slowed her verbosity to a pleasant pace.

So now she had finally met this elusive brother. Unbeknown to her: John had decided the future arrangements for the Sunday off would be that he would see her in the morning, Murdoch in the afternoon and her again in the evening.

Chapter 8

When the Munro/Mitchell wedding was announced, it caused a lot of gossip in the village and surrounding area. The daughter of the master, marrying the farm manager? *She must be stuck for choice,* they said.

Not that they thought badly of Murdoch, because everyone who knew him liked him very much and considered him to be reasonably well educated and mannerly; but as far as they were concerned, he really wasn't of the same class as the Mitchells! In act, they were completely surprised that Mr. Mitchell had actually allowed his one and only daughter to marry the big Highlander. Then again, they all agreed that her chances of getting another husband of her own class were virtually nil. They also speculated that Murdoch would do very nicely out of it all, and would eventually inherit the farm when the old boy was in his box. However, they never for a second considered that this thought had ever entered Murdoch's head...that in fact, he simply was marrying Agnes because he liked her very much and was happy in her company.

Preparations got under way for the wedding to take place the following Spring. Murdoch, of course, asked John to be his *Best Man.* The latter had been expecting such a request anyway... *who else could have been given such an honour?*

John reckoned it was going to be a very posh affair and the two of them would have to get all dressed up. No doubt they would find out in good time what they were expected to wear but in the meantime, he thought, he had better start saving his money to buy a proper suit.

Sarah was all excited about the coming nuptials and chattered to John incessantly about the wedding. While doing so, a possibility occurred to her.

"As you and I are walking out, do you think I might get invited to the wedding too? What do you think?"

John replied that he didn't know. Inwardly he didn't think that she *would* be invited. He was Murdoch's brother and *Best Man* at the wedding but after all, he was only a farm labourer. It was highly unlikely that the Best Man's lady-friend, who was only a house servant, would even be considered.

John's other most pressing problem concerned his wedding present to the bride and Groom. He didn't have very much money, so it would have to be something small. He wished he could give them something substantial and in keeping with the other presents they would no doubt receive from the rich friends of the Mitchell family but that was impossible. The knowledge that Murdoch and Agnes would understand did not make him feel any better!

Murdoch received a letter from the family advising him that their sister Catherine had married a nice young man and that the two of them had moved south to Inverness. Only Angus and Dugald were now left at home. As he read, it occurred to him that his parents had one less mouth to feed!

Angus had been able to find work fairly close to home so was still around some of the time to assist his father. Young Dugald remained at home.

Murdoch passed-on the letter to John, who after reading it, penned a reply.

While expressing his delight at the news of his sister's wedding and the success of Angus in getting work, John didn't say anything about Murdoch's impending marriage as he felt it would be proper for Murdoch to tell them himself.

As he wrote, it occurred to him that they would be so pleased to hear the news, and about how well Murdoch was doing. It also struck him that it was such a pity they could not be here to see him married.

He had often wondered what would have happened if Murdoch had taken the Lennox farm job and he had got the one on the Mitchell farm. By the sound of Agnes, albeit her being a nice girl and that; she would not have been his *cup of tea*. He needed someone with a bit of spark and Sarah certainly had that, to be sure.

There *were* times when Sarah was a little fiend and argued with him - spitting like a cat - but making up afterward was worth it!

He had heard it said that the Irish had very short tempers... if she was anything to go by, that was certainly true. Having said that; Liam was never like that. He was such an easy going fellow and got on with everyone. He thought; *Must just be Sarah herself!* Anyway, she made life interesting, and it brought a bit of spice to their relationship. He would not have liked a woman who was docile and obeyed his every word. That would be so mundane and make a very uninteresting marriage.

Despite her faults, (which she denied the existence of) Sarah was really a lovely, lively, happy girl, with an occasional outburst when she was upset about something. She certainly came straight out with whatever was not pleasing her at any particular time. One of these days he *would* wed her, there was no doubt about that, but *when* was another question!

Murdoch had asked him: *would she wait forever or until it suited him?* He thought she might. *Perhaps he was being big headed and presumptuous? Maybe she would get fed up and find someone else.* He wouldn't like that at all... he really *did* want to marry her. In any case, he supposed he had better not keep her waiting too long.

When some of the local Gentry - friends of John Mitchell - heard of the forthcoming wedding and who the bridegroom was, oh boy, did the tongues wag! *What was John Mitchell thinking about?* They asked each another... *letting his only daughter, and only child, marry his manager, and the fellow only recently having been promoted from farm labourer. A man who doesn't even come from this area.... even worse... probably an uneducated and uncouth savage from the north.*

Despite these snobbish observations, all of them, particularly the women-folk, would not have missed this wedding for anything, if for nothing else, but to prove their suspicions concerning the bridegroom. *Heavens! His equally underclass brother was to be the best man,* - for these people, this would be quite some wedding; the likes of which *they* had never witnessed in their lives. Little did they guess that they would have the tables turned on them when they finally came face to face with the brothers Munro. They were to be utterly flabbergasted when they met these two charming, intelligent, smiling, perfectly mannered young men.

Finally the wedding day of Murdoch to Agnes dawned! Both Munro brothers were turned out impeccably in their smart new attire. Predictably, both behaved as to the Manor-born... each extremely careful not to put a foot wrong. The polite and mannerly teachings of their mother were paying off handsomely. All those ladies who had previously criticised them so severely were now as putty in the hands of the brothers Munro. *How charming they both are, and so well mannered and polite!* they would tell each other.

Oh how proud their mother would have been of her two big boys on that day!

From beginning to end, the day went perfectly. The bride was radiant and shone with sheer happiness. Noting this, her father was so glad he had allowed this marriage to take place.

He just hoped and prayed it would work out all right for them both.

And so little brother Murdoch was wed. He would now move out of the farm cottage and into the big house where the bedroom and sitting room formally occupied by Agnes, had been tastefully redecorated to suit a married couple. Murdoch had never lived in such a huge place. Well, to him it seemed huge. He really enjoyed the idea of being fairly rich instead of poor. It was a nice feeling, albeit it was Mr. Mitchell's home and not his own.

As time passed, Murdoch settled in nicely at *Eastfield* House. He never took for granted what he had...always remembering his humble beginnings and always being careful not to give Mr. Mitchell, any reason to think that just because he, Murdoch, had married his daughter that he could act like the lord of the manor. He got on very well with Agnes's father, and he wanted to keep things that way. He hoped, too, that perhaps one day they would give his father-in-law some grandchildren to be proud of.

Chapter 9

Over that winter, the *Kirkland* men were set to finishing the two new farm cottages. Mr. Lennox had decided Cook and her husband should get one of them and Lizzie and James the other. However, Cook suggested to Mr. Lennox that she would stay where she was and the ploughman Thomas McPherson and his wife should get one of the new cottages. There were only herself and her husband living at home now and their youngest son slept in the accommodation above the stables... only eating his meals at home. The McPhersons had seven children and were more in need of the space.

Mr. Lennox commended Cook on her generous offer; adding that he was sure the McPhersons would be extremely grateful to have a bit more space. This arrangement would mean there would be two vacant cottages. Which change of affairs caused John's thoughts to turn to Sarah and marriage. The obstacle of where to live would be removed... they would now have a place to stay!

Consequently; one Sunday morning, as the two of them were out walking... without preamble, he turned to her and said:

"I was just thinking, Sarah, would you be interested in marrying me soon?"

For the first time in her life, Sarah was robbed of speech, but not for long. Jumping up and down, eyes bright with sheer joy, she threw her arms around his neck and said

"Oh yes, Oh yes please John Munro, I will marry you tomorrow if today is too soon! Oh I am so happy!"

When she got back to the farm, Sarah couldn't wait to tell the rest of the kitchen staff. At her news, they were very happy for her. They all knew she had waited a long time for this to happen and were full of questions as to where and when the event would take place.

"It will not be much of a wedding." she advised them ruefully. "We have very little money, but I suppose we will go on the train to Monklands...to the place where they marry folks, then just come back here. John said we might get one of the farm cottages when they are empty.

If so, we would just go there and have something to eat."

Thus she continued, in full chatter... talking of the forthcoming wedding.... what she would wear... that maybe she could even afford a new dress.

Unknown to Sarah, Cook, Lizzie and Jean immediately started planning things. Lizzie was very good with the needle and, with the help of her mother and Jean herself, had made Jean's wedding dress. The three of them decided they would surprise Sarah and offer to make her a nice dress for *her* wedding day. Sarah could decide on how she wanted it to look and they would make it for her.

Cook also planned to bake a wedding cake and, after the wedding; to arrange some kind of little celebration, as an extra surprise. She liked both of these young people and wanted to help them have a day to remember. None of *their* close relatives would be able to attend and help them celebrate. Just to go to Monklands, get married, then come back and sit on their own in their little cottage seemed to her pathetic. *No* she thought *that would not do!* And so, preparations for the nuptials continued apace.

Meantime, the Munro brothers received a letter from home giving them the news that their sister, Catherine had produced a lovely healthy baby boy and had named him Murdoch and that their parents were well and sent their love.

Murdoch answered the letter; sending congratulations to his sister and her husband and letting his parents know that they would be having another addition to their grandchildren...that his wife Agnes was pregnant and hoped to give birth in about five months time.

Brother John also wrote to congratulate his sister and gave her the news of his forthcoming marriage to Sarah.

Such letters often disturbed John - awakening a longing to once again see his family but it was out of the question...they were so far away. Although the railway links were much better than before, and the coach roads had been much improved, it would be too expensive for him to travel so far... he just couldn't afford it. Maybe one day he would go back up North.

When Cook and her two daughters told Sarah they would be happy to make her a dress for her wedding, she was overcome by their thoughtfulness, and her eyes filled with tears.

"You are so kind to have thought of me and I would be very happy for you to make me a nice dress. Maybe you can tell me where I would be able to get the material?"

Lizzie replied.

"We know of a place. It is where we got the material for Jean's dress. We will come with you and help you choose", adding: "We can take a couple of hours off one afternoon when things are quiet."

She did not disclose the fact that Cook had got the cake underway while Sarah was away on her Sunday off. Nor that Cook was working on it at night after Sarah had gone to bed.

Cook was really a kind soul, although one would not think so by her expression at times! Sarah was delighted to tell John the plans for her wedding dress.

John's choice of wedding attire was simple...he would be wearing the suit he bought for his brother's wedding. It was still new, since he had not had an occasion to wear it since that time.

He had already made the necessary arrangements about going toMonklands and of course had asked Murdoch to be *his* Best Man, Murdoch was, in turn, delighted to comply, thinking to himself, *thank goodness at last he has decided to marry the girl The lass has waited so very patiently for so long for him to make up his mind!*

He knew instinctively that even although the two of them would argue and have many differences of opinion, they would be happy. This was the kind of girl his brother needed. A quiet girl like his Agnes would have bored John to bits.

In the meantime, Sarah had asked Jean if she would be *her* witness and come with them to *Monklands*.

And so, the arrangements for the wedding of John to Sarah were thus complete!

The wedding day duly arrived... Sarah was beside herself with excitement. In her pretty new dress, she felt like a queen. She and John together with Murdoch and Jean boarded the train at Lenzie station and set off for *Monklands*.

John had mixed feelings that day - *was he doing the right thing? Well, this was it, no going back now, freedom ended! Next thing the babies would be coming along. Was he ready for this? Too bad – too late to be thinking this way.*

They arrived at the Registry Office early and had to wait some time; there being a few couples who had arrived earlier and who were to be married before them. Another Highlander named Currie from the Hebridean island of Islay was in the queue ahead of them

Eventually, their turn arrived. The whole thing was over and done with in the shortest space of time. Sarah was astounded how quick it was, but she was now Mrs. John Munro. She now had that elusive gold ring firmly round the wedding finger of her left hand!

And so the new Mr. and Mrs. John Munro headed back for *Kirkland*. accompanied by Murdoch and Jean, As they entered the yard, they were surprised to see Cook, Mr. Robertson, Lizzie and James, and some of the other farm staff all gathered together... even Forbes was there. Everyone came forward to wish the couple well and invited them, along with Murdoch, into the kitchen. There, at the centre of the scrubbed kitchen table, in all its glory, stood a lovely wedding cake surrounded by a delicious looking spread of various kinds of good things to eat. John and Sarah were speechless... totally astounded!

Sarah was first into action; rushing over to Cook, she gave her a big hug and thanked her so much for all of it. Cook was very pleased with herself for doing this for the young ones - more so since they obviously appreciated it.

John also thanked Cook and Lizzie for all their hard work, but he drew the line at giving Cook a hug! That was going too far! This little celebration just made their day a perfect one.

Eventually, Murdoch left to go home. Everyone went back to their chores and the newly-weds; Sarah and John went to their new home... the little cottage, which previously had been home to Lizzie and James. The furnishings were sparse. All they had was a small table, two chairs and a bed... eventually they would gather bits and pieces to make it nice.

And so married life had well and truly begun for both the Munro brothers. Never did they think that day, when they left the North, that within a few years, they would both be married men. Now... one of them, Murdoch... was about to become a father!

Maybe it wouldn't be too long before John himself would become a father. That would be fine but he hoped he and Sarah would have a little time before it happened... time to collect some household goods and make this cottage a fit place to bring up a baby.

Sarah would, of course, go back to work right away, as would John... no time for a *honeymoon; that was only for the very rich!*

Soon thereafter, with the little gifts they had received from the farm people, and the very generous gift of lots of crockery from Murdoch and Agnes, together with the things they themselves purchased with their wages, their little cottage was beginning to become quite comfortable. Of course, there were still many things they would like to have, but wait they must, till cash became available.

Chapter 10

*I*n a short space of time, Sarah announced that a baby was on the way. She was overjoyed. John was a bit uncertain how he felt about it. On the other hand, his brother had been delighted when *his* wife, Agnes, had made her announcement.

John decided that if Sarah gave birth to a boy, he too would name the child Murdoch and follow normal tradition that the first born son was called after its paternal grandfather, and the first girl was called after her maternal grandmother. Anyway, Sarah may have a daughter. In that case, he would break with tradition and name the child Sarah after her mother. His mother-in-law was named Susan, and he wasn't having that - simply because he did not like the name. He would wait and see. As long as Sarah was all right and the baby was a fine healthy one, then what was in a name?

In the meantime, Cook's daughter Jean had given birth to a girl... Cook was delighted...she now had three little ones in the kitchen to keep her eye on!

Mother and the baby were well and in no time at all, Jean was back at work.

As time passed, Sarah's tummy grew ever larger until she began to find it difficult to do some of her chores. But work she must! They needed every penny they could get.

The Lennox's seemed to be entertaining more than usual and there were many nights when Sarah was very late in finishing her work.

Cook wanted to make sure that in Sarah's condition, she would be well fed so that when she did get home at night, she could go straight to bed. To this end, she arranged for Sarah to have her meals in the kitchen with the rest of staff. Normally, Sarah would have gone back to the cottage and prepared a meal for herself and John, but he didn't mind this situation. He knew it was for her benefit, so he would set-to and make something for himself.

John didn't see as much of his brother as before. They each now had wives. Murdoch had already started his family and soon both brothers would have families, so more time would be spent at their respective homes and work. Additionally; Murdoch was having to socialise more.

As Agnes's husband, he would join his wife at dinner parties where she normally took her dead mother's place beside her father. Stepping up the social ladder made little or no difference to him; he remained the same nice pleasant young man he had always been.

One day, in the middle of the morning, as Sarah worked in the kitchen, she suddenly bent over, gasping in agony. A searing pain took her breath away, so much so that she could hardly stand up. At this, Cook had a quick look at her and with a knowing nod said

"Looks like baby has decided to arrive. We had better get you down to the cottage lass and wait and see what happens." Adding; "No harm in being prepared."

She and Lizzie helped Sarah back to her cottage, settled her in her bed then put water on the fire to boil. Then at Sarah's direction, they looked out towels and cloths. All the time, Sarah lay on the bed moaning.

Cook comforted her and said cheerfully "You will be fine, my lass, both Lizzie and Jean have recently gone through this with no problems and so will you. It will be over in no time at all, you just wait and see, and you will have a bouncing baby to nurse."

Sarah felt calmer at this... Cook was such a reassuring and matter of fact person! Little did she know what was in front of her...it would certainly not be over *in no time at all.*

Cook had to go back to the kitchen for a while, but Lizzie stayed with Sarah. Time passed, yet there were no signs of the baby arriving, but Sarah was in agony, screaming and moaning continuously.

Eventually, Cook returned to see how things were going. When she saw and heard Sarah, she was most definitely unhappy with the situation. A flicker of worry crossed her brow.

"I think we better get the midwife to come; I will go and see if I can find someone to go for her." Inwardly, she was becoming increasingly concerned... *this birth was not going to plan; things were not looking too healthy.*

Cook came back a little later and told them she had sent her son to the village to fetch the midwife adding; "I hope he finds her quickly, it will be a time before she gets here."

Eventually, the midwife arrived. After a brief look at Sarah, she declared that Sarah needed a doctor. Just then, John arrived home. He had left his work as soon as he had been told about his wife. Before he even entered the cottage he heard her screaming in agony, the sound shook him to the core.

"Is this normal?" he asked anxiously.

Cook explained that it was not. There was something wrong and that the midwife was doing the best she could.

John was beside himself with worry. The situation brought home just how much Sarah meant to him. He was not a religious man, nevertheless, he paced up and down outside and prayed that both his wife and baby would get through their ordeal and things would turn out all right.

Mr. Lennox had gone to the kitchen to speak to Cook and was told by Jean what was happening. He went down to the cottages to see if there was anything he could do to help having had experienced of this kind of situation himself. His wife had gone through a terrible time giving birth to their second child and afterward, had been told she would never have any more children.

As he approached the cottage, he could see John pacing up and down and heard Sarah screaming.

"John" he began sympathetically, "I am told things are not going too well with Sarah, is there anything I can do to help?"

Before John could answer, the midwife came out and declared that she couldn't do anything more for the girl and therefore she would need to send for the doctor.

Mr Lennox reacted immediately.

"I will get Forbes to take the pony and trap and go to the village for the doctor." Turning on his heel, he set off for the big house. "It will be quicker that way."

Arriving at the house, he called for Forbes. "Get the pony and trap ready and go to the village. Find the doctor, as quick as you can, and bring him back to John Munro's cottage. Tell the doctor it is urgent. The girl Sarah is very much in need of him."

In no time at all, James had the pony hitched to the trap and Forbes set off down the road at a fair speed.

Meanwhile, back at the Munro cottage, the midwife came out to find John still pacing back and forth.

"Your wife is asking for you, would you go in and see her."

John was extremely apprehensive as he entered the room; he didn't like to think of Sarah in all this pain and he wasn't sure what to expect. He was shocked when he saw her. Her face was pale as death and she was soaked in perspiration. Big tough man that he thought he was...at the sight of his wee wife, a lump rose in his throat, threatening to choke him.

Sarah looked up at him as he towered over the bed. Her eyes round with fear and brow lined with anxiety she spoke in a small pathetic voice: "Am I going to die, John?"

"No of course not" replied John gently, wiping a sweat soaked wisp of hair from her forehead, "it is just that the baby is having a wee problem being born. You will be fine! Forbes has taken the pony and trap and gone for the doctor. As soon as he arrives, all will be well and he will fix you up just fine.

"If me and the baby are going to die, will you stay with me and hold my hand?" she asked.

John could hardly answer her, feeling the tears welling up in his eyes. *Men do not cry, it is not manly*! Besides that, he didn't want anyone to see him do so...especially not Sarah. He pulled himself together and mustered a firm positive tone.

"You and the baby are NOT going to die, Sarah, so get that idea out of your head. Once the doctor arrives, this will be over quickly and you will both be fine." Inwardly he hoped and prayed that this would be the case.

Thereafter, John stayed with his wife, mopping her brow with cold cloths, comforting her and holding her hand. She really was suffering - poor girl.

Fortunately the doctor was at home when Forbes called, so the two of them were back at the farm cottage pretty soon; although to John it seemed an eternity.

Entering the cottage with the midwife, the doctor sent John and Lizzie outside to wait while he examined Sarah.

After a few minutes, the doctor emerged and gave John his report.

"The baby is laying the wrong way round, so we will have to do something about that. We need plenty of towels and lots of hot water, can you arrange that quickly?"... The last said with a sense of urgency.

Lizzie told him there were pots of heated water all ready on the fire... she would boil them up again. Turning to John, she told him to go up to the house and get her mother.

John was grateful to have something to do and set off in the direction of the kitchen.

Finding Cook, he brought her back to the cottage. Afterward, he hung about outside... absolutely distraught, not knowing what to do.

A short time later, James came along. He said he had heard Sarah was having problems and that he had come along for a short time to see how John was doing and if he could be of any help. John was glad of the company.

"I cannot understand why Sarah is having so many problems. As far as I know Lizzie and Jean, and even my brother's wife, had no problems; so why my Sarah?"

"I think it is one of those things, John, answered James -nodding sagely. "It sometimes happens, but I am sure that now the doctor is here, all will be well. He will know what to do. Take heart, my friend, all will be well, believe me."

John very much appreciated James coming to see him and give him some comfort. Everyone else around him except the doctor was a woman... it was nice to have another man to talk to.

James stayed for a little time, but then had to get back to work. As he left he told John that he hoped all would be well for Sarah and the bairn and that no doubt he would hear how things went.

After a great deal of time and a lot of screaming from Sarah, all was quiet. Poor John thought the worst had happened. A moment later, the doctor came out of the cottage and told him that Sarah was very weak and ill, but with good care, attention and rest, she should be all right. She is a strong healthy girl.

"However she will have to take it easy for some time to recover her strength." Adding, almost as an afterthought "By the way young man, you have a fine healthy big boy, congratulations."

At this news, John could have wept with relief. He rushed into the cottage. He found Sarah looking like death; but smiling weakly as soon as she saw him she said proudly "I did it John, we have a son, and neither of us died."

The effort of these few words left her exhausted.

John kissed her gently on the forehead, telling her in a soft voice; "I am so very proud of you my sweetheart. Thank you for our wonderful son. You must rest now close your eyes; sleep and get back your strength."

By the time he had finished what he was saying; she was asleep.

He now had time to see his new-born son for the first time...his chest filled with pride. He was as proud as any father could be.

Into himself he said a little prayer of thanks for the lives of both his wife and son. Going outside, he questioned the doctor.

"Will Sarah really be alright, doctor, and will she be able to have any more children after this?"

The doctor thought for a moment then replied.

"I do not see why not, but ", he cautioned, "It might be better if she did not get pregnant too soon after this. Not until she gets her strength up again and the new Munro baby is a little older" He finished with "I will send my bill to you."

John thanked him profusely for what he had done for Sarah and promised he would make sure she did not get into that condition again for some time to come. He knew it would be difficult, because he loved

Sarah deeply but first and foremost, he had to think of her health. This incident had given him quite a shock. He had always thought that women just had babies without any problem. Much like the cows and the sheep on the farm!

Now he thought differently!

It seemed that Sarah and his son were out of danger and would make a full recovery; the next worrying thing for him concerned his medical debt. How on earth was he going to pay for the doctor? He really couldn't afford a doctor, but he would never see Sarah in any danger and not do the best he could for her. He would find the money somehow.

It took Sarah quite a time to recover from the birth of her son. During that time, Cook made sure the girl got all the right food to build up her strength. To this end; each day, she sent bowls of good nourishing soup down to the cottage, as well as meat and vegetable dishes and lots of fresh milk.

John had to go back to work right away, but between Cook, Lizzie, Jean and some of the other women on the farm, Sarah was never without help during the day when John was away at work. They really were all so kind. Both Sarah and John appreciated their kindness and help very much.

One evening, when John was at home, Mr. Lennox came to the cottage to see how Sarah and the baby were progressing. He stayed just long enough to satisfy himself that all was well then left. Just as he was leaving, he turned to John.

"By the way lad, do not worry yourself about that doctor's bill; I have taken care of it"!

John's heart leapt in his breast.

"Thank you sir, thank you. How on earth can we ever thank you enough for your kindness?"

Mr. Lennox replied with a twinkle in his eye.

"You lad, by working hard." And, turning toward Sarah;

"And you lass by getting well and letting us see your happy smile up at the big house." With that he turned and left.

John had been worrying about his debt to the doctor and wondered what he was going to do. He had even thought of asking Murdoch to give him a loan of some money, but that would have been a last resort. However, no need to worry now, the weight had been lifted from his shoulders!

Jean and Lizzie had been at work with little scraps of material, making clothes for the baby. Sarah couldn't believe how kind everyone was. Wee baby Murdoch as the child was called, was getting a fine start! They had named the child after John's father. Meantime, John's brother Murdoch eventually got news of the baby and came along to see his new infant nephew.

He was sorry to hear the story of Sarah's bad time giving birth, however, like everyone else; glad to hear all was now well.

Although he thought Sarah was looking very poorly; he did not voice his thoughts. He had brought gifts for the baby as well as some flowers for Sarah... just to cheer her up. These brought out a glimpse of the old Sarah he knew.

Before Murdoch left for home, he and John arranged to meet at the Inn, in a month's time to catch up with all the news. It had been some time since they had done just that. John thought that now he did not have to worry about the doctor's bill, he could afford at least one drink!

As Murdoch was leaving, John told him of Mr. Lennox's kindness in paying the doctor's bill.

Murdoch was surprised and commented "Did you not know that the master of the house is obliged by law to take care of a sick servant anyway?"

"Yes, I did know that" John confirmed "But you must remember, Sarah was not sick, merely having a baby. That is not considered as being sick, even if something does go wrong. I still think Mr. Lennox was extremely kind to settle the doctor's bill, as he really was not obliged to do so. John felt he had to defend his boss, as the man had always been fair and considerate.

Since it appeared that Sarah was going to be away from work for some time, Cook spoke to Forbes, saying that another pair of hands was needed to do all the extra work. The latter promised to speak to the master about it. But before doing so, he considered the options open to him...*one of the farm girls* or someone from outside? He preferred the former. *Perhaps the oldest daughter of Donald Kerr, the herdsman, might be suitable?* She was now seventeen years old and, since she was not working at a specific task, she might like to have the job until Sarah had fully recovered? He put this to Mr.Lennox who agreed it was better to share the work within the existing farm families and gave Forbes permission to make the necessary arrangements.

Meantime, John and Sarah were certainly missing Sarah's wages... not that they were very much in the first place, but they didn't have very much to begin with so every little extra counted. Sarah continuously wished she could go back to work, but there was no way she was anywhere near fit for that. The birth had taken its toll on her health; it now took all her efforts just to look after the baby and cook a few meals. She felt so weak and washed out and she didn't like how she felt. Feeling like this was alien to her...previously she had always been so fit and healthy.

John had written to her parents, telling of their new grandson. He didn't tell Sarah that he also told them how ill their daughter had been. This he had done in the hope that maybe her mother, at least, would be able to come and see her. He knew that Sarah would be so pleased to see her mother. However, they were a long way off. Her parents were not wealthy and probably wouldn't have the money to undertake the journey.

Meanwhile, Forbes spoke to the Kerrs about their daughter temporarily replacing Sarah. The girl, whose name was Catherine, accepted the post with delight. She hated working in the dairy all the time with her mother and was on the lookout for something a bit better. *Pity* she thought *that it was only a temporary position!*

So Cook got her extra help!

Young Catherine fitted in nicely and worked eagerly. As for her mother in the dairy? Catherine's sister was eleven and perfectly capable, so when she came home from school, she could help her mother.

When Sarah heard of the arrangement, her main hope was that this girl Catherine would not permanently take over - leaving Sarah without a job - particularly since they badly needed the money.

The brothers met at the inn on the Saturday night as prearranged.

Murdoch seemed to be doing well. Agnes was well, and their baby was thriving. While he went off to get two ales, John reflected on his brother's life.

Agnes was lucky to have Murdoch. He was a good caring husband and father.

There was no doubt that she had blossomed since the wedding. She was far more confident, friendly and talkative. Probably she was happy to have a husband and a baby. It had no doubt crossed her mind in the past that she may have remained a spinster, living with her father.

When Murdoch came back with the ale John remarked -

"I was thinking how Agnes has changed. She seems to be very happy and contented, and is much more outgoing than she used to be. Marriage agrees with her, it would seem."

"Yes, I have noticed the changes in her myself. Her father said to me that he too saw such a difference in her." adding that even his friends had noticed that she seemed to be very happy and much more at ease with everyone.

"That is your good influence, little brother, you are good for her!"

John changed the subject and spoke about *his* life.

As usual, things were tough and would be until Sarah got on her feet and back to work again. It was taking some time for her to recover from the birth.

Murdoch would have offered to help his brother financially a little bit, but he knew him only too well... no way would John have accepted any help.

They talked of other things... particularly about the new gas system just installed in the village and some of the bigger houses and farms nearby. The brothers agreed it was amazing to see the streets lit up on a dark night. To the older generation and some of he younger ones, it seemed a miracle! Everyone wanted to know how it worked!

Murdoch, as usual was a fountain of information. He told John that they had just had the new gas lighting installed at *Eastfield*.

"It is fantastic!" he enthused. "They mount light fittings up on the walls. These have pipes running up to them behind the wall. The fittings have little glass domes which cover little gauze things over a tiny hole where the gas comes out... they are called *mantles*. You turn a little knob, the gas hisses out, then you light a taper at the fire and hold it to the mantle which glows through the glass cover and gives off quite a lot of light. It is brilliant! You have to be careful though, when putting them out before going to bed at night... to make sure the knob is fully turned off. Apparently, you can die from breathing in the gas in a closed room. So you have to be careful, but it is worth the small risk to have such good light."

"But how does the gas get to your house, Murdoch?" asked John. "It comes from a huge iron tank just outside the village and is piped into each property through underground pipes."

"Well, what will they think of next? That is modernisation for you. Talking of which, we got a new plough the other day... It is an incredible machine that turns up the earth much better than the old one we had. Thomas McPherson is delighted with it. The men do not have to follow up behind the plough with shovels and spades chopping up the big clods of earth and taking the stones out. This machine does it all. Only when there are a lot of stones in the ground in places, do the men follow up, but it is a huge improvement to the soil and makes it much better for sowing in the spring. It also improves the drainage dramatically."

"I have also heard a rumour" said Murdoch, not to be beaten "that the young Queen Victoria is to be wed next year to a German called Albert."

"I do not think that will affect us much, do you?" chortled John.

"I suppose not." replied Murdoch. "She is very young to be a Queen with all the responsibilities that go with it. No doubt she will want to have children to carry on the line."

"I think that would be taken for granted. All right for her, though, no problem with money or accommodation. Also, a Nanny would be looking after them, and the Queen would probably hardly ever see them. Is that not the way it goes with royalty?"

"It certainly seems that way," ventured Murdoch, who got the distinct impression that his brother was feeling a bit low, which was not surprising. He was short of money, worried about Sarah, and just feeling a little depressed. No doubt due to all this talk of how much money and nice things the royalty had, while people like him, who worked hard all their lives, had next to nothing.

Murdoch's next piece of news was about Agnes. She was pregnant once again.

She cannot be all that shy then, thought John. Still, it was very nice news and good that Murdoch was so pleased. *No money or health problems for Agnes! Little brother was doing very nicely, thank you.*

A new baby on the way was the last thing John wanted to hear from Sarah. He had curbed his feelings for her to allow her to get better. Now, she was sleeping like the baby at night, which helped her on the way to full recovery.

For a while longer, the brothers talked of many other things...village gossip and just general chit-chat then decided it was time for each of them to go home. On parting company, they agreed to meet again in the near future.

Sarah received a letter from her mother, obviously written by someone else since, like Sarah, her mother could not read and write. John read it out to her.

Her mother was delighted to hear her daughter was on the mend... that Sarah had a lovely baby boy and that she had a new grandson. She could not get time off from her job on the farm where she and Sarah's father worked and because of this, could not come and visit her daughter and new grandson. Maybe one day soon they would all meet.

The letter continued with news of the rest of Sarah's family. They were all well and sent their best wishes to her and her husband. It finished by wishing lots of luck adding that her mother was pleased her daughter had a good husband.

Sarah was so delighted to get news from her family that she asked John to read it to her again. One day when she was feeling better, John would teach her to read and write. The subject had been broached many times...she would just laugh and ask; "Why do I need to bother when I have you to do it for me!"

John had tried to teach her before but she could not concentrate for two minutes. Eventually, he had given up in frustration, vowing that one of these days he *would* make her do it. He knew she would get so much pleasure out of being able to read and write. It was so beneficial to a person, but Sarah's philosophy was *why would a serving girl need to do this? What difference was it going to make to her work?* Perhaps this letter would be the key to changing her mind? He would suggest to her that if she could read and write, she could write as often as she liked to her mother and father and tell them all her news, and when she got a reply, she could read it herself as often as she wished. *Would that work?*

Sarah was strong enough to go back to work. Her stand-in Catherine thought that she would now be dismissed from the house and sent back to the dairy. However, as things on the farm were going very well and profits were being made, Mr. Lennox decided to give some thought to the situation. He was entertaining much more these days, which meant the house staff were finding it difficult to cope with all the late dinners, etc. More to the point, Cook, the last person he wanted to upset, was beginning to complain a little. That lady was a huge asset... a truly great cook who ran the kitchen like clockwork. She had been there for many years and he valued her greatly, so he decided he could afford to keep this girl Catherine where she was.

When Forbes told Cook that Catherine was to stay on, Cook gruffly stated "I should think so too, I am getting a bit tired with all the late nights and the work of clearing up with only Jean and one other to help wash all the dishes."

She wasn't going to admit to Forbes that she was actually delighted to have the extra help. Catherine was a good girl and did what she was told with good grace. She had made a few mistakes at the beginning but she was learning fast.

When Catherine and Sarah were told the news, they were ecstatic. Catherine; because she was being kept on, and Sarah; at having extra help for herself and Jean. Besides, it would make life a bit easier for Sarah - particularly since she was not yet quite her energetic self. Even better still, Cook told her to bring baby Murdoch with her and she would keep her eye on him as well as the other three of her own grandchildren already in her care. All the babies in the kitchen! It was becoming like a nursery. One of these days someone was going to complain but until someone did, there they would stay.

Lizzie's first born, Thomas, was now walking and becoming a menace. He was too young to let outside in the yard on his own. He strongly objected to being kept in a sitting position for too long and howled when he wanted to get down on the floor. Something was going to have to be done with all these children soon, but what? Nobody could afford to pay a woman to keep them while their mothers worked. The girls started very early in the morning... had perhaps an hour or two off in the afternoon, and then were there till late at night. Who would be able to look after them for all that time? *Good question!*

John was glad Sarah was now able to go back to work. The extra money she earned was sorely needed. Nevertheless, he hoped she wouldn't overdo it and wear herself out. It was also good news that this other girl was being kept on.

As for Sarah, she was glad to be back among her friends in the kitchen...to hear all the latest gossip! It livened her up and gave her something else to think about other than the worry of having less money to live on, her own health and the health of her baby.

And so, things were improving. Little did they think that in the not too distant future life for John and Sarah Munro was going to change dramatically forever!

Agnes's second pregnancy was not going quite as well as her first. She was not very well and took to her bed on several occasions. Eventually, a few weeks early, baby decided to make an entry into the world.

Agnes had a pretty bad time...not nearly as bad as her sister-in-law Sarah, but strangely enough, not as good as her first birthing.

Finally, a quite perfect little girl was born... and Agnes was content. She now had a daughter and it was all over.

She and Murdoch decided to name the child Agnes after her mother and maternal grandmother.

Murdoch was delighted with his beautiful little new daughter and made a great fuss of her. John Mitchell was also thrilled, as he now had two lovely, fine, fit and healthy grandchildren

John's dreaded day of apprehension finally arrived. Sarah announced she was pregnant again. She too shared her husband's apprehension; she didn't want to go through the same painful difficult birth she had experienced the previous time, but she was fit and healthy again, and little Murdoch was now over a year old. During that year, she had had plenty of time to build up her strength again. And so her second term of pregnancy began.

She remained very well during the pregnancy and when her time came, this second child wasted no time in arriving. In the middle of the night, Sarah wakened John and told him things were on the move. John's immediate thought was; *if this is going to be difficult, how will I get a doctor here in the middle of the night?* He had no idea what to do.

Sarah told him to go and get Lizzie who duly arrived in minutes; still dressed in her nightclothes, and got to work looking out all the necessary towels and cloths. She told John to build up the fire, put big pans of water on to heat and then to go along and fetch her mother. Secretly, Lizzie also hoped this would not be a repetition of the last time. Shortly after that, John arrived back with Cook. They waited... everything was ready!

They were all taken by surprise when suddenly, and without Sarah getting the usual prior warning; the baby's head appeared. In another 10 minutes, it fully entered the world without too much effort on Sarah's part.

No one could believe how quick this birth had been but everyone was relieved that it had gone so well.

John had gone outside and was pacing up and down waiting and listening for the worst.

When Cook emerged and told him he had another lovely son, he couldn't believe his ears and asked her if she was sure.

"Of course I am sure, you silly man! Your wife has just given birth to a baby in the shortest time I have ever seen and she is fine. Do not just stand there with your mouth open like a barn door... get yourself in there and welcome your new wee son to this wicked world!" adding "and while You are at it, tell that wife of yours she is a miracle-worker!"

John entered the house and was surprised to see Sarah sitting up in bed with the baby in her arms.

"Come and meet your new son." she greeted him with a wide grin on her face. "That was wonderful! It was so quick and much less painful than the last time. What are we going to call him? And before he could answer: "I suggest we call this one John after you, what do you think?"

John was so relieved to see Sarah so well and the baby fine, he would have agreed to anything at that moment.

"John's fine by me" he said - kissed his wife, then profusely congratulated her on her achievement.

In no time at all, Sarah was on her feet and back to work. Now the problem was with all these babies in the kitchen.

Jean had solved her problem...her mother-in-law offered to keep her little girl, who was now over a year old and eating solid food. That was one less in the kitchen.

Lizzie still had her two, but after James was finished work, he would take them back to their cottage till Lizzie was finished at night.

Sarah still had Murdoch with her and now new baby John would be joining them. Surely the complaints would come soon?

Chapter 11

Murdoch Senior and his wife Janet were still living on the North East Coast of Scotland with their son Dugald.

One morning, a letter arrived at the Munro croft. Being unable to read, Murdoch sought out Dugald and asked him to read it for him. Examining the envelope, Dugald confirmed that it was properly addressed and was indeed for his father.

It transpired that the letter was from a lawyer in Glasgow requesting one *Murdoch Munro Esq.* to visit his law office in the great city whereby he might hear something to his advantage.

On hearing this, Murdoch senior didn't know what to make of it. Except for his two sons living on the outskirts... he didn't know anyone in Glasgow at all. Since his sons were not mentioned in the letter, it could have nothing to do with them. This was a mystery indeed! *What could possibly be to his advantage in Glasgow?* Janet was equally mystified but as always practical.

"Maybe you should go and find out what this is all about, "she advised.

"Now how will I be able to do that?" her husband asked. "I do not have any money to go to Glasgow. Maybe we should just forget about it. We will just wait and see what Angus thinks of it when comes over to visit."

Curiosity is a great thing! While waiting impatiently for Angus to show up, Murdoch senior got Dugald to read every word of the letter again and again...in particular, the name and address of the lawyer.

After two days, Angus showed up and the letter was given to him to read and comment on.

"Well, well!" he exclaimed. "This is all a big mystery indeed. What could a lawyer possibly want with you father? What could he possibly tell you that would be to your advantage?"

"Maybe you have come into a fortune, father!" chipped in Dugald. They all laughed at this suggestion, particularly since Murdoch senior didn't know anyone who had a fortune, let alone one to leave it to him.

After the laughter subsided, Murdoch senior sought the advice of the older of his two boys.

"What do you think I should do, Angus? I do not have any money to go to Glasgow anyway."

"I think I can solve that problem" answered Angus. "I have a little money saved from my work. I would be happy to give it to you for your fare to Glasgow. I just hope it will be enough."

"Anyway," he went on: "It says here you will be reimbursed for any expenses."

Nobody knew what this big English word *reimbursed* meant, but Angus guessed it might mean his father would get his money back from the lawyer when he went there.

They discussed the subject inside out, upside down, round and round; wondering what it could all be about.

Finally, it was decided; that to put everyone's mind at rest; Murdoch senior would *go* to Glasgow as requested.

And so the day arrived when Murdoch senior would go south. He had one *good* suit, which he wore to church on Sunday, Thus attired; he said his farewells to Janet and the boys and set off on his journey to see the Glasgow lawyer.

As day broke, he boarded the coach for Inverness, and soon found the journey interesting, more so, since he had fellow passengers to talk with during the journey, which made it seem shorter and helped to pass the time.

On arriving at Inverness, he bade farewell to his fellow travellers and set off to find out when the coach for Edinburgh would leave. He was a bit upset to learn that it was an overnight journey and that he would have to sleep on the coach. The departure time was four o'clock that afternoon and the coach would not arrive in Edinburgh before Noon following day.

He had time to wait before the coach departed, so he wandered around the area for a bit before seeking out a place to get something cheap to eat. He was wishing he had sent word of his time of arrival to his married daughter, then living in Inverness. Perhaps they could have met up and spent a few hours together? Ah well - too late now.

Eventually the time came for him to board the Edinburgh coach. On doing so, he discovered there was only one other passenger on this trip... a quiet lady who spoke little. And so, Murdoch kept his council, deciding instead, to try and get some sleep.

He dozed off and on till they had a short stop for refreshments and to relieve themselves if necessary. Thereafter, the journey continued... Murdoch sleeping - waking - dozing off - and waking again by turns, for the rest of the journey.

The coach finally reached Edinburgh.

On alighting from the coach Murdoch was awestruck by his first sight of Scotland's capital with its regal buildings and great castle standing so proudly on the high hill overlooking the city. It was indeed a magnificent sight.

He had to ask how to get to the train for Glasgow several times before finally finding the new railway station situated at the bottom of the slope leading up to the castle. He discovered it would be another hour before the Glasgow train was due to leave, so he was able to have a look around the city.

The number of people and the buildings totally amazed him. Not only was this his first time in Edinburgh, it was, in fact, the first time he had ever been in *any* city...he had never seen anything like this before. It all made him rather nervous... he felt very small and vulnerable in this great, noise-filled place all on his own and with so little money. He was also very tired and hungry and beginning to wish he had never undertaken this journey. However, once he boarded the steam train for Glasgow, he lost such thoughts. He was completely fascinated with this,

his first train journey. Such noise! Such speed! And the countryside as they travelled through... very flat, with miles and miles of green fields. *This was really something! If only Janet could have come with him, she would have loved to see all the things he was seeing.* He continued avidly looking out of the train for the entire journey until they reached Glasgow.

Arrival in that city was a bit of a let down. It was, as his sons had discovered years earlier, not exactly the cleanest place in Scotland. Lots of people and bustle, with so much industry and noise. Murdoch felt as if his eardrums were being assaulted by the racket.

Leaving the train station, he asked the way to the address of the lawyer and eventually found the place. He felt rather dirty and crumpled after his long journey, but it couldn't be helped.

Entering the front door of the red sandstone building, he looked at the brass plates advertising the occupiers. Finally with great difficulty, - since he could not read - he was able to make out one that matched the writing on the letter he had with him.

His destination proved to be on the second floor. Climbing two flights of stairs, he found the lawyer's office and knocked on the door. A voice from inside bade him - *Enter!* He did so and found himself in a dark, dingy, stuffy little outer office occupied by a sour faced looking woman behind a desk, who looked at Murdoch as if he had crawled from under a stone.

Murdoch senior told her who he was and she told him to wait, then disappeared into another room. She returned and, holding the door open, bid him enter.

This inner room proved to be about as dark and musty as the outer office. It had a large desk piled with books and papers behind which sat a little bespectacled man. Murdoch was only able to make out the top half of the man's face behind all the paperwork. In a dry voice, he told Murdoch to sit down in an empty chair in front of the desk, then completely ignored him for the next five or ten minutes.

During this time, Murdoch had a good look round the room. He had never seen so much literature in his lifetime, all, it seemed, piled in a most untidy, haphazard manner and distributed all over the room. *How could this man ever find anything?* He wondered.

The little man finally spoke. He greeted his visitor formally then introduced himself as Mr. Beaton.

"Mr Munro" he began. Do you have knowledge of a relation named Edward Munro who had left the Highlands and came south with his family many years ago?"

Murdoch thought for a moment then replied.

"I remember having a cousin I used to play with when we were boys in Sutherland, and I also remember he and his family left suddenly around the time of the Clearances. I missed Edward for some time after that. As boys, we were great friends. The last I heard of him was many years ago.

A friend from the south told me he had met Edward. He told me that my cousin had never married but had done quite well for himself. In turn; I told my friend that I had eventually married Janet Bennie and that we had two small sons, John and Murdoch."

The little man hurumphed! to clear his throat, then in a thin voice announced: "Well, Mr. Munro, I have here the last will and testament of this same Edward Munro, who died recently, and it appears he has left his entire estate to you and your two sons."

Murdoch senior couldn't believe his ears... he just could not take this in! He hadn't seen Edward for all those years...since they were boys...why on earth would he leave anything to him and his sons?

Mr Beaton continued.

"His estate consists of large farmlands including a quarry adjacent to the property. According to the terms of the will, the farmland is divided into three portions, one for you, one for your son John Munro and one for your other son Murdoch Munro. In addition to the farmland, each portion contains a house and associated farm buildings. I do not know what they grow on these farmlands or if they contain cattle or any other livestock since there is no particular listing in the will; all I *do* know is that it all belongs to you and your sons now." He went on. "There is also an amount of money involved, not a vast sum, I hasten to add, but sufficient to run the estate and pay the wages of the workers there."

Not given to verbosity at the best of times, Murdoch senior was well and truly dumb-struck! He was still struggling with the word *adjacent*. Finally he found his voice. "Where is this farm?" he asked, barely able to hide his rising excitement.

"It is in a place called Boghead, which is near Kirkintilloch. Perhaps you have heard of it?"

Murdoch senior was amazed at the coincidence of this information..." Why, both my sons live and work on farms in that very area already!"

Lawyer Beaton hardly reacted; he simply suggested: "Then perhaps you would wish to visit them then and all three of you could go and look at the property in question?" Continuing;

"I have taken the liberty to inform the staff there that you will no doubt be coming to view your inheritance, so they know to expect you sometime."

Murdoch senior was almost beside himself with excitement, but managed to hide it from the other man. Inwardly he thought *Thank you Lord - soon I will see my boys once again* but he contained himself and answered simply.

"Yes, I think, now that I have come all this long way, I would like to do that."

"Well that is that!" exclaimed the lawyer. "Now, the matter of your reimbursement of travelling expenses; how much did it cost you to come here today Mr. Munro?"

Murdoch senior noted the other man's new tone of respect. *Amazing how a little land and property concentrates minds* he thought. He told him exactly how much he had spent on coaches and trains. At this, Mr Beaton asked:

"Surely sir, you also spent some money on food on the journey?"

Murdoch senior almost felt ashamed to tell this man how little he had eaten throughout the journey, and that he had eaten so little simply because he couldn't afford any more. However, like most Highlanders, Murdoch Munro was one of the most honest people on the face of the earth. He was not going to say it was more than it was...that was dishonest! The man wanted to know, so he told him.

The lawyer raised an eyebrow at the mention of such a meagre amount, but made no comment. He withdrew a black enamelled cash box from a drawer and counted out a sum of money equal to Murdoch senior's declared expenses and handed it to him across the desk.

"That will no doubt come in handy Mr. Munro. I have taken the liberty of adding a sum to cover your return fare back to your home in the north as well as money for food and, if necessary, lodgings for one night here in the south."

Murdoch was about to say that he didn't need lodgings for the night, hoping that he might get a bed in one of his son's houses, but thought better of it. He just might not be able to find them and end up needing to find somewhere to stay before starting on the long journey back home. He therefore thanked Mr. Beaton for his kindness and prepared to leave. As he turned to leave, the lawyer said

"Mr. Munro, would it not be a good idea if I gave you instructions as to how to get to your new property?"

Murdoch gave a short, embarrassed laugh "Oh, yes, how stupid of me, I wasn't thinking."

"That is understandable," replied Beaton. "Considering the news you have just received. I am sure it has come as quite a surprise to you."

A surprise, thought Murdoch, *more like a great shock!*

On a scrap of paper, Beaton drew out directions for Murdoch to get to the farm, saying that he could get a train from Glasgow to Lenzie… the train station for Kirkintilloch. He then asked Murdoch if he could read and write, but Murdoch had to admit that he could not.

"When you have viewed your inheritance and your sons have done likewise, it will be necessary for the three of you to come back to this office to sign papers of ownership. Can your sons read and write?"

"Oh, yes," said Murdoch proudly, "they read and write extremely well""

"That is good, they will be able to sign the appropriate papers and I will get my secretary to witness your mark. When do you expect you may be able to come back here?"

"If I go straight to Kirkintilloch and see the farms, then I will find my sons, take them there and hopefully, the next day come back here. I think that would be possible. I also have to get back home soon"

"Good! exclaimed Beaton. "I will look forward to seeing you all in a short time. I will inform my secretary to expect the three of you sometime soon"

At this point, Beaton stood up. Murdoch senior, who was taller than the average person, towered over him. *What a tiny little person the other man was!* They shook hands and Murdoch left.

On his way down the stairs to the street, he felt like dancing. *What an upturn to his luck! Wouldn't Janet be delighted when he got home and told her all about it? THEM... farm owners of a large farm and a quarry too! Well now, wasn't that something!*

Although he was saddened to hear of his Cousin Edward's death, he just could not believe his luck. Inwardly he exclaimed; *thank you, Edward!*

It had been many years since he had last seen his cousin. Then, they had been great friends and had enjoyed each other's company, as young lads getting up to all kinds of tricks. *Thank you again Edward!*

When Murdoch senior got down to street level, he asked for directions to the railway station where he might board the train for Lenzie. After a few attempts he finally arrived at the station in question, there, to learn that his new found luck was holding up... a train for Lenzie was due to leave in about twenty minutes.

The time passed quickly and he boarded the train and settled down for the journey. Again, he was fascinated; looking at everything as the train left Glasgow and headed out into the countryside.

He noted the large and lush farmlands on the way and hoped the ones he and his boys had inherited would be as good as some of the ones he was seeing. *Wouldn't it be so nice to live and work in a place like this,* he thought?

During the short journey, he took out the drawing given to him by the lawyer. He didn't know anything about large farms. His little piece of land at home as well as the small croft he had previously been forced to vacate in Sutherland were nothing like the size of this inheritance. He reflected on how poor his circumstances were. Because of these, he had taken on part time work at a local quarry... an extra job to make ends meet. Life was really pretty tough...things were not growing well on the poor land he had. The extra income from the quarry work helped to supplement his meagre family income. *Well!* he thought; *maybe those days would soon be over and perhaps the quarry experience will come in handy.*

Soon the train *chuffed* its way into Lenzie station and Murdoch senior got off.

A local man gave him directions for Kirkintilloch. He also asked the man if he knew the whereabouts of the Lennox farm.

"It is the second farm you come to, about five or six miles from here" was the answer.

Although Murdoch was well used to walking long distances, it was normally after a good night's sleep. Now he was *really* tired, however; needs must, so he trudged on along the seemingly endless road.

Murdoch senior thought he was never going to get there when at last, the first farm came into sight. *Not far to go now* he thought Not so!

His pace had slowed down considerably and he was getting more tired by the minute. He sat on a stone dyke for a wee while to regain his strength. *After all,* he thought to himself, *I am getting on a bit now. Not as young as I used to be.* He was fifty-nine years old!

At long last, he reached the second farm - *Kirkland.* Leaving the main road, he walked wearily up the winding track towards the farm, hoping that John would be around. No doubt his son would look quite different; he would be twenty eight years old. Not only that - now a married man with a wife and two children. It was to be expected he would have matured somewhat. At least he hoped so!

As Murdoch senior approached some farm cottages, a young girl came out of one of them. There was a small boy by her side and she carried a baby. With a pleasant smile she came towards Murdoch and asked... "Can I help you sir...are you looking for someone in particular?"

"Yes please." replied Murdoch. "I am looking for John Munro, do you know him?"

The young girl's smile broadened to a wide grin. Replying with a laugh she said

"I most certainly do, I am his wife Sarah, and who might you be then?

Murdoch senior - tiredness completely forgotten...replied with an equally wide grin.

"My name is Murdoch Munro and I am John's father."

"Oh Mr. Munro, I am so pleased to meet you!" exclaimed Sarah. "John will be delighted to see you. Please come into the cottage and have a seat and I will make you a cup of tea, then go and find John. I am afraid our cottage is not very big, but it is home to us at the moment." gesturing to the children she told him:

"These two are your grandsons, Murdoch and John. The big one is named Murdoch after you, and the wee baby is named after his father. Turning to the wee boy - who was shy with strangers and had been sheltering by his mothers side - she said "Murdoch; this is your grandfather, your father's father, say hello."

"Hello, grandfather," said little Murdoch dutifully. He was quite in awe of this strange tall old gentleman in front of him.

Sarah was full of curiosity and her tongue went into top gear. "You must have had a long journey to come here, Mr. Munro, and I think you must be very tired. Where did you come from today then? Is everything all right with your wife and family at home? I hope you haven not come with bad news." She finished this plethora of questions with an anxious look.

"No lass!" exclaimed Murdoch senior. - laughing loudly. "Not at all, just the opposite, I have come with very good news, but I will tell you all about it when John arrives.

As to your first question: In fact, I came from Glasgow on the train to Lenzie, then walked here. Before that I took a coach from home to Inverness, another one to Edinburgh, and a train from there to Glasgow. I had to sleep on the coach from Inverness to Edinburgh as it was an overnight journey. I did not get much real sleep so I am very tired"

"Well I hope you will not be rushing off again to go all the way back without at least one night's good sleep." said Sarah, anxiously.

"Och no, Lass. I could not face doing all that again so soon after the first time... I was hoping that perhaps I could get a bed either with you and John or with my other son Murdoch?"

"Of course!" exclaimed Sarah. "We would be pleased to have you here. Are you going over to see Murdoch next or have you been to see him already?" she asked; while she busied herself making tea and sandwiches.

"No, not yet, I want to get both the boys together, but I wanted to talk to John first, him being the older of the two."

"This sounds all very mysterious and interesting." smiled Sarah -adding- "There now! Your tea is ready and there is something for you to eat. I will go and look for John and tell him you are here. He is probably out in one of the fields. I will not be long."

With that, Sarah hurried off, taking her children with her. The boy would not have stayed with this stranger in any case - grandfather or not - and the baby might cry. *Besides,* she thought *Mr. Munro wouldn't know what to do with a crying baby.*

After Sarah had gone, Grandpa Murdoch...for now that is what he must be called...was glad to get a seat, something to eat and a cup of tea. Sarah seemed to him like a very nice girl and she certainly had made him welcome. She appeared to be a good wife and mother. Looking round him, he noticed that the cottage was tidy and clean - just like his grandchildren. *Oh these children were so beautiful!* He almost fell asleep as he waited for Sarah to return with John. Just before he drifted off, the two of them appeared.

John was surprised, thrilled and delighted to see his father after all those long years. He hadn't changed all that much...more gray hairs and worry lines but still strong and tall So many questions to ask him and things to tell *him.* He thought that it was a great pity that his mother could not have been here too, but it would have been too expensive for both of them to come. He also wondered how his father had got the money together just to come here on his own and say hello. There had to be more to things than just that, surely?

Sarah had told him on the way back to the cottage that there was no bad news, and that his mother and the rest of his family were all well. *So what could it be? Something was afoot!*

He strode forward and clasped his father's great work-worn hand, casting his arm over his sire's shoulder.

"Father, father! I am so glad to set eyes upon you again! What a wonderful surprise!"

Standing back after the initial meeting, Grandpa Murdoch studied the man standing before him. The tall gangly youth who had set off from the north all these years previously had been transformed into a fine, tall, handsome mature man. His heart filled with pride at the sight of his eldest son.

The next hour was filled with an exchange of news between father and son. When this had been exhausted, Grandpa Murdoch got down to the real reason for his visit... the inheritance!

After he had finished his report as to what had transpired at the lawyers office, John and Sarah sat in dumfounded silence...never were two people more dumfounded at that time than were these two!

What was this going to mean for them? Land owners! ...house and farm owners! Even a share in a quarry as well? They just could not believe it! Sarah's thoughts had already soared upward and away ahead: *Maybe a nice house with separate rooms in it and a proper kitchen, which would be wonderful. Then again, it might just be a small house. Whatever! Anything would be better than this.* She was getting carried away already!

John and his father continued discussing all the pros and cons of their new situation. John's brother Murdoch would need to be informed and brought into discussions about the future. The latter was in a better position to know about large farms. Although John had a lot of knowledge about working on a large farm, he did not have the experience of actually running one... his brother did.

John left the cottage and went up to the house to find Forbes or Mr. Lennox. He would explain that his father had arrived unexpectedly and ask permission to take the rest of the afternoon off and go with his father to visit his brother at *Eastfield*. He very rarely asked for any extra time off so he did not expect objections.

After he had gone, Sarah explained to Grandpa Murdoch that she had to get back to work soon ... that she had but two hours off in the afternoon. However, she would make a proper meal for the two men before she left so that they would have something decent to eat before they left for *Eastfield*.

Grandpa Murdoch was curious. As she prepared the meal, he questioned his daughter in law.

"When do *you* get the chance to eat Sarah, if you have to work?"

"Sure I get my meal in the kitchen with the rest of the staff; Cook prepares a really good three course meal for us each night. We all have to help her of course, but I do pretty well."

"What then does John do for his meal at night?"

"I leave a decent dinner for him and all he has to do is heat it up when he finishes work. I *had* said I would wait and get mine along with him when I finished work, but he insist I keep eating up at the big house." She went on to explain: "It all started because I was so poorly after wee Murdoch was born. I had a very bad time giving birth and it left me exhausted. Cook and John insisted I got a good meal every day to build up my strength and Cook made sure of it...she is so kind."

"Sounds like a good place to work. Do you like it here?"

"Well...I like all the company and the gossip in the kitchen, but I would much rather be at home with my little ones but we need the money. Life is hard if you do not have enough money. When I was off work for ages after wee Murdoch was born, it was really hard making ends meet. However, we managed."

"Yes," agreed Grandpa Murdoch... "my wife and I know what it is like to have nothing and no prospects either. Hopefully this piece of news I received will change all that for us. I am anxious to see the place for myself... I hope it meets our expectations."

"It certainly *sounds* good anyway!" said Sarah excitedly. Adding "So here is hoping"

John reappeared just as Sarah finished preparing the meal and the two men sat at the table.

As she served them she asked "How did you get on up at the big house?

"Fine!" said John; telling them both that he had permission to have the rest of the day off.

Sarah left for work shortly after, taking the two children with her.

Grandpa Murdoch was still curious.

"John; where does Sarah take the children when she goes to work?"
"They go with her to the kitchen. There are other little ones there as well... Cook loves having them all around her; three of them are her own grandchildren.

Sarah thinks that very soon some other arrangement will have to be made as there are now too many children in there. She reckons if Mr. Lennox sees them all in the kitchen, he will definitely not approve. So far, Forbes - who oversees things - has given hints in that direction, but has not said outright that the girls cannot bring their children to work. But if you think about it - at the end of the day - he is the one who will get the blame for allowing it. Cook has pointed this out; saying something will have to be worked out pretty soon."

As they ate the food, Grandpa Murdoch observed: "If we all decide to live on this farm or farms, then that will be two less children to go to the kitchen! Would you have any problem about leaving this place?"

John thought about that for a moment before replying.

"I have been happy here and had no problems with Mr. Lennox. He has been a good, fair minded employer and I will be sorry to leave all the friends I have here but it would be nice to be working for myself for a change. I have an annual contract for work and would probably have to work out my agreement however; by shear luck it is due for renewal next month. I suppose, if I wanted to, I could leave then?" He went on;

"I suppose you and me will have a lot to learn about running a farm, but this is where Murdoch comes in he knows what he is doing and would keep us right."

His father continued the conversation, warming to it.

"I have been doing a little bit of quarrying at home myself. To make ends meet, I put in a few hours at the local quarry, so I know a little bit about that kind of work. Perhaps they will have a manager there already running it."

With that, father and son finished their meal, left the cottage, and started back along the road the way grandpa Murdoch had come earlier.

Chapter 12

As they approached *Eastfield* Farm where Murdoch lived, John told his father; "Murdoch is quite the gentleman! Now that he is married to Agnes, he lives with her in the big house. He has done all right for himself; a good job, plenty of money and a nice house for him, his wife and children. The children want for nothing. They are Mr. Mitchell's grandchildren so he makes sure they get everything they need."

"What about Murdoch's wife Agnes?" inquired his father.

"Agnes is Mr. Mitchell's only child; his wife died many years ago. She is a really nice girl and Murdoch is very happy with her"

They finally arrived at the farm house and walked round the yard, hoping to see Murdoch, but he was nowhere in sight, so they went around to the back and knocked on the door. They would never have thought of going to the front door - that was only for the gentry and special guests.business.

The door was answered by a kitchen maid who inquired of their

"Is Mr. Munro at home?" asked John.

A voice from within the kitchen called out... "And who wants to know"?

The question came from a kindly looking little lady who turned out to be the Cook.

"I am John Munro, his brother, and this is our father Murdoch Munro'

"Och yes!" She exclaimed. "I recognise you from the wedding day.

Just wait a minute" she beamed, "I will see if he is around" After a short time, Agnes appeared at the door.

"John! How nice to see you." Then, turning to the older man "So this is your father!" I am so very pleased to meet you too Mr. Munro. My Murdoch often speaks of you and your wife; are you all well at home? I hope you do not come with disturbing news?"

Before Grandpa Murdoch could answer, she went on: "Now, John Munro; how many times have I told you that you do not need to come to the kitchen door like a servant or delivery person? After all, you are family! Come away into the house."

Turning back to Grandpa Munro she apologised for talking so much. "I am sorry Mr Munro; I interrupted you."

"No, not at all." protested Grandpa Murdoch. "And I am very pleased to meet you too Mrs. Munro, I have heard a lot about you from letters Murdoch has sent to us." adding; "Everyone at home is just fine thank you."

"Please call me Agnes - Mrs. Munro is far too formal for members of the family. Could I offer you some tea, perhaps?"

John replied for both of them;

"No thank you Agnes, we have just eaten at home. Is Murdoch around?"

"Yes, he was here a short while ago. I will send one of the staff to find him." She rang a bell and a maid appeared.

"Would you please go and find Mr. Munro and tell him we have guests?" She then sat down beside her visitors.

"Did you have a long journey getting here, Mr. Munro? It is rather a long way I fancy."

"It was indeed a very long and tiring journey." replied the older man. "But it was also very interesting. I was sorry I could not bring my wife with me, as I know she would have enjoyed the trip - there are so many things to see."

Grandpa Murdoch felt a little uncomfortable sitting in this rather elegant room, he didn't know people like this and it seemed inconceivable that his second son actually lived in such elegant surroundings. He thought; *Young Murdoch has certainly come up in the world.*

Young Murdoch eventually appeared and rushed over to his father to shake his hand vigorously, at the same time exclaiming his joy at seeing him after so many years.

"How are mother and the rest of the family?" he queried, "So many times I have thought about you all and hoped you were well. It was good to get letters from Angus, telling us how things were at home. So, are you here just for a visit? What is your news?... not bad, I hope."

Grandpa Murdoch was quick to reassure his youngest son.

"No, not at all! In fact I have very interesting and happy news for you. Can you spare some time while we discuss it?"

"Of course father," replied Murdoch, "as much time as is needed!"

At this point, Agnes said she would leave the gentlemen to discuss business and go and see what the children were up to. When they had finished their discussions, she would bring them in to meet their grandfather. Grandpa Murdoch then proceeded to tell his son of their inheritance.

When the full story had been related once again - like everyone else, Murdoch was astounded.

"But this is wonderful news father! It means we can all be together again...living in the same area as before. I would of course stay where I am and not move from here, but we can sort out these details later. The main thing for us to do is to go and see the extent of this place we have inherited."

"We will be relying on you to guide us in this matter Murdoch" said his father. "I know nothing about big farms, and while John works on a big farm, it is a far cry from running one.

"Of course father! I will be only too pleased to help where it is needed. I presume the farm, which your cousin lived on, will be the largest of the three on the estate and he probably had a manager to run it. If not, who is running it at the moment? We will have to go there and find out about this and other such things.

When will it suit you to have a look at the property?"

"Anytime will suit me" replied his father. "But John will probably have to make arrangements to have a day off to join us. I imagine it will take some time to see over the whole place and the quarry as well."

He continued...

"We will also have to talk to the folk involved who are living there at the moment. I think Edward must have rented out the other two farms, so we will not know if they are occupied until we get there. If there *are* people there, we cannot exactly throw them off the land. Heaven knows; I saw enough of that horror during The Clearances! I would not have that on my conscience!

Anyway; I do not want to stay down here too long. Your mother and the rest of the family will be anxious to know what my visit to the lawyer was all about. So; if it can be arranged, I would like to start on my way back north the day after tomorrow. This being so, perhaps we can arrange between us to go and see the place tomorrow morning. Would that suit you Murdoch?"

"Of course!" exclaimed Murdoch. Then turning to his brother: "You, John, can just take tomorrow off. Do not you worry... even if you do have to go without a day's pay, I will see to it that you do not have to be out of pocket over this, brother. Now please do not argue about it, I can see you are about to protest. You can pay me back when you are a rich farmer!" he finished.

All three Munros laughed excitedly at his final comments.

They continued discussing the thing over and over for a while, then Murdoch asked:

"Where are you staying tonight father? Adding: "You know you are more than welcome to stay here, we have plenty of space, and you can have a room of your own."

His father apologised. "Sorry my boy. It is kind of you and Agnes to offer to have me but Sarah has already offered to give me a bed for tonight and I do not want to disappoint her, so I will just go back home with John. We will come back here first thing in the morning."

"Fine", replied Murdoch shortly... a little put out at his father's refusal. Inwardly he thought that his father would have preferred to stay in comfort at *Eastfield*... a good bed and good food rather than John's tiny miserable cottage. Little did he know that the older man would not have wanted to stay with him, and that he felt out of his depth there. Also - that he would rather crowd into John's humble little home.

The business was now finished and the arrangements for the morrow made. Murdoch left his father and brother and went to find Agnes and the children; eventually bringing them in to see their uncle but specially their Munro grandpa.

Little John was three years old and infant Agnes eighteen months. They were very pretty children.

While the boy had a decided Munro look, the little girl looked like her mother.

Both children, although a little shy at this first meeting, were very polite. On cue from his parents little John stepped forward with his small podgy hand outstretched...

"Hello, I am pleased to meet you grandfather"

"Hello to you little man" replied Grandpa Murdoch solemnly, observing that his cute little grandson had a spark in his eyes that suggested he was not exactly a little angel! "I am very pleased to meet you as well," he chuckled.

Little Agnes smiled at her grandpa from behind her mother's skirts... a wee charmer in every way!

After a short while, John announced it was time that he and his father left to go back to *Kirkland*. Grandpa Murdoch secretly did not relish the thought of the walk all that way. He was so weary. However, Murdoch noticed how tired his father looked and offered to take them back in his trap. The old man was thankful and accepted the offer.

Arriving back at the *Kirkland* cottage, John made something to eat. Not long after, Sarah came home with the children. She had told Cook that John's father had arrived. Cook had responded by telling her to go home early, adding that they would manage fine without her.

After the children had been tucked up in bed, the three adults discussed the day's meeting with Murdoch over at *Eastfield*.

During the conversation, John asked his father why he had decided not to stay there and enjoy the extra comfort; observing that the older man would not have had to walk all the way back there in the morning.

"It is too fancy for me, son - and I felt a little out of place there.

Do not get me wrong; Murdoch and Agnes were very kind. It is just that I am a simple country man and not of their class."

Point taken, thought John, he would have felt the same himself.

When they had finished their discussions, a bed was made for the older man. He was very glad to lay his weary head down and soon he was asleep.

After his father was settled, John went up to the farm to request the next day off work.

Forbes, who was still around, said he would have to ask Mr. Lennox.

Fortunately, Mr. Lennox and his wife had finished dinner and were in the drawing room having a nightcap.

His employer considered the request then told Forbes;

"I suppose if his father has arrived, he will want to spend some time with him. It will be all right for him to have tomorrow off. He can either make up for it by working on his first Sunday off or by relinquishing a day's pay. It is up to him."

Forbes relayed this message to John who thanked him, saying that he would forfeit his pay instead of working on his Sunday off. He had plans for that day! He would surprise Sarah and take her to see the property: knowing she was desperate to do so.

He would pretend to go out for their usual Sunday walk, but take her there. It wasn't really all that far...both of them were used to walking for miles anyway. Besides, he knew that to see this place, she would walk from here to England if necessary!

Next morning John and his father left for *Eastfield* farm. Sarah having gone to work earlier, wished she too had the day off and be able to go with them.

The two men hadn't travelled very far along the road when Murdoch appeared coming towards them with the pony and trap. *Oh good*, thought Grandpa Murdoch, *we will not have to walk for miles today.*

Although he had slept reasonably well the previous night, he was still tired from all his walking and journeying.

Murdoch greeted the two of them.

"Good morning to you both! I thought you two might like a ride today in case this place is quite a bit away, I am not really sure where it is. Do you know father?"

"I have a drawing from the lawyer as to how to get there.." answered his father handing over the drawing in question.

After studying I oment Murdoch exclaimed...

"Of course, I know where this is! Actually it is not very far from here at all!"

They were all quite excited about seeing the place... each filled with curiosity... each with secret dreams about how it might affect their lives. John was particularly excited...this could fundamentally change the life of his family. As things stood, he could not visualise much change in their future lives.

Such thoughts depressed him... Now, here was the opportunity of a lifetime! He *would* make it work, even if he had to work every available daylight hour. His wife would no longer have to slave long unsociable hours for someone else for a pittance of a wage. She would be able to have the children with her all the time. Perhaps even, there might be a nice house!

If they had originally been dumbfounded by the news of their inherited property, they were doubly dumbfounded when they finally beheld it. It was enormous... a veritable Estate which encompassed three separate farms, each having its own "Big House."

A dirt road led from the main entrance to the first farm and continued onward, leading in turn to each of the other two farms.

Shortly after leaving the main road, a fairly large, sandstone house came into view. Two farm cottages were situated by the side of the road, just beyond the main house. Since the big house was rather grand, the Munros presumed it was the house that Cousin Edward had lived in.

As the trap got nearer, an elderly, neatly dressed servant came out of the house and greeted them. He advised them they were expected. At the same time, a young boy appeared from nowhere and took the trap away.

They were then ushered into the house by the serving man.

Once inside, the man lifted a small brass bell in the shape of a crinoline lady from a hall side table and gave it one loud ring... Almost immediately, a girl, dressed in maid's uniform appeared. The serving man inquired if they wished to *take tea*. They hesitated long enough to seem polite then declined the offer. Tea was the last thing on their minds! However, they politely accepted an offer from the serving man to show them round the house itself.

Thankfully this was brief and soon over. Then they were free to go outside to see the real focus of their interest...the farm itself.

As they emerged into the farm yard, they were confronted by a man who politely doffed his cap.

"Good day, gentlemen, I am Douglas Mackintosh, the farm manager." adding; "I have been here for quite a number of years. Since Mr. Edward's death, I have carried on running things here ... seeing that the farm is still run properly. I hope you approve!"

He went on. "I did not have anyone to give me instructions. Mr. Edward's lawyer told me just to continue as usual until the new owners came. As a matter of fact, he was here last week and paid out the wages to the staff and field hands here and to the hands on the other farms, so everything in that direction has been taken care of." He stopped there and waited for one of them to make a comment.

Murdoch, barely able to conceal a smile, spoke first.

"Thank you Mr. Mackintosh for your report. Things certainly seem to be well under your control and yes, we are glad to hear you have been taking care of things on our behalf. Forgive me for not making the proper introductions earlier; my name is Murdoch Munro. The gentleman on my right is my father; Murdoch Munro Senior and this other gentleman is my brother John Munro. Mr. Edward Munro was my father's cousin.

Grandpa Murdoch, who had been in a semi daze during the conversation, abruptly came down to earth. He shook hands with Mackintosh and expressed his thanks... John followed suit.

"And now Mr. Mackintosh!" exclaimed Grandpa Murdoch "to the thing that interests all of us here... the farm itself. If you would be so good as to show us round - perhaps as you do so you will explain to us how it is organised."

"I confess, it will be a pleasure for me to do so sir."

And so, the four men set off on a grand tour... during which the manager kept up a running commentary.

"There are the usual casual hands taken on, as and when necessary. We have around fifteen of these at the moment, and they all live in the Bothy. We grow barley, oats, hay, potatoes and turnips."

"What about livestock?"

"We have two Clydesdale horses, and a pony... the pony to pull our little carriage."

"Do you have a Groomsman and a Ploughman?" asked John. "Yes, we have one man and a boy who look after the horses and also to do the ploughing. The Ploughman, John Currie and his wife...who also acts as Cook...live in one of the two farm cottages you saw as you arrived. I live in the other one"

As they walked round the barns, the Munros noticed that the machinery and tools were good quality and in excellent condition. They also noted that the farm was equipped with one of the latest ploughs.

"Do you sell all of your crops at harvest time?" inquired Murdoch...

"Yes, we do, but keep part of each crop for our own use. We have no cattle here so, except for the horses, we do not need much hay. We also sell to other farms that have a lot of cattle."

"What about the other two farms?" asked Grandpa Murdoch. "I believe they are both rented out."

"Yes they both were", answered Mackintosh "but the nearest one was occupied by an elderly couple. When Mr. Edward passed away, they decided to retire, so that farm is now empty. However, I took the decision to keep on the hands of that farm to work its fields. There seemed little point in letting the crops go to ruin."

"That was a good decision." agreed Murdoch. "Better to keep things running for the time being. It will be a week or two yet before any of us can get settled in. What about the other farm? Is it still rented?"

"Yes; by a young couple with a family - will you be wanting them to leave?"

"No, not at all!" protested Grandpa Murdoch. We would not dream of throwing them out. My family and I had enough of that despicable nonsense during the Highland Clearances. I was a young man then, with little ones. We were evicted out of our croft without warning, and transported like cattle the East Coast. I have first hand knowledge of what eviction does to a family and would not think of inflicting the same on any other family. No, Mr. Mackintosh, you may tell the young family on our other farm they are safe from such treatment. I will never ask them to leave unless it is absolutely necessary!"

"I am sure they will be glad to hear your decision sir. Since Mr Edward's death and the impending sale of the property, they have been a bit worried as to what might become of them.

"Right!" announced John." Is there any more to see here? If not we will move on and take a look at the other farm and its fields. We believe it too includes a house."

"You have seen all there is to see here gentlemen." confirmed Mackintosh. "There is indeed another house on the next farm but it is a bit smaller than the main house here. Having said that; it is quite adequate. Do you want to see it?"

"I think we would like to have a quick look." agreed the three Munros, so they moved on to the second farm as planned.

It too was well equipped with machinery and, like the first one... well maintained.

The house itself was as Mackintosh had said, smaller than the previous farmhouse but, as far as John could see, had more than enough accommodation.

The kitchen, which was what Sarah would want to know about, would, he was certain, more than delight her. This said; he wasn't sure what the final arrangements would be. He had not discussed the details with his father. *Would he and Sarah be in this house on this farm and his parents in the bigger one, or would it be the other way round?* Secretly he would like the larger house and farm, but it would be up to his father and mother to make the decision.

And so, the inspection of two of the three properties was completed. "Will you be wanting to see the last of the three properties?" asked Mackintosh.

"We will not bother with the other place at the moment" answered Grandpa Murdoch "Next time we come we will speak to the people there and assure them we will not be asking them to leave. In the meantime you can tell them from us not worry about it.

Now I would like to know about the quarry. What can you tell us about that, Mr. Mackintosh?"

"Not very much! You had best go there and see the Quarry Manager yourself, Sir."

"Fine, we'll do that, which way is it?"

Having pointed out the way to the quarry, the farm manager excused himself, saying he would see them again before they left.

They followed the manager's directions for the quarry and found it to be quite a distance from the farms. There seemed to be no one around so they walked about for a bit, taking-in the area.

Eventually they spied a little building, which appeared to be an office of some sort. At that moment, a big, burly, unpleasant looking fellow exited from this place. Spying the three of them he came to meet them.

Having rudely looked them up and down he asked

"Who the devil are you lot then? And what do you want?

If ever there was a person who was disliked on sight by these three people, it was that man!

Young Murdoch answered in a very cool, level voice

"We just happen to be the new owners." adding... "Perhaps you might want to change your tone of voice."

John was quite amazed at his brother: the one who never had too much to say and didn't like unpleasantness.

The ugly brutal looking man didn't change his expression one bit. Obviously he did not care one hoot that they were the new owners. John thought to himself; *with the agreement of the others, You are fired! No way will father put up with this kind of attitude!*

"Perhaps, if we are not disturbing you too much, you would show us round the quarry and tell us something about the place... who you sell to" added young Murdoch - sarcasm dripping off his voice like poison.

Even after this obvious dressing down, the moron in front of them simply grumbled:

"I just see that the stone is cut properly and that those lazy good for nothings do their work. Who the stone is sold to? I do not know and I do not care either, as long as they get on with quarrying it. The decision as to who buys it and what they pay is nothing to do with me. The last boss handled all that"

"Thank you for your time" said John exceedingly politely. And with that, turned away in dismissal.

After having seen all there was to see, the three of them left the area and headed back the way they had come. As soon as they were out of earshot, they unanimously agreed the manager would have to go.

"I am not putting up with the likes of him!" commented Grandpa Murdoch. "Insolent, lazy looking man! I somehow think he gives the men a hard time and is exceedingly nasty to work for. I also suspect he does little for the wages paid to him. Well, I will soon put a stop to that! I will run the place myself!"

"You will need to watch that one!" cautioned Murdoch. "I think he would bear a grudge and take to being violent. So father... do not you approach him on your own when firing him. Besides; it will be better if you have a legitimate reason for doing so. I am sure firing him without an obvious cause will invoke violence." adding; "He might just decide to knock you about a bit."

"I would have the law on him if he did, to be sure."

"Fine!" retorted John. "But it would not be before he hit you, now, would it? He might just even put you in the Infirmary!"

Although it might not have been a laughing matter, they all laughed at the thought.

Back at the first farm house, Mackintosh asked them if they would like some refreshment. He told them that Cook had made some tea and cakes for them. They thanked him and asked him to join them.

When they were settled, John asked: "Who is that most unpleasant person running the quarry? He was very surly and rude and not the least bit likeable."

"I did not think you would like him." answered the manager." rnobody does. "I never understood why Mr. Edward kept him on. The men hate him. Besides which, he is very nasty and lazy. Apparently, though, he *does* have a good knowledge of the different types of stone and how they are cut, so I suppose that is why he is still here."

The Munros decided to say nothing to Mackintosh about firing the man, thinking it was to best keep the matter under wraps for the time being. Time enough to cross that bridge when they came to it!

While in the house, John paid a little more attention to his surroundings than previously. Sarah would want to know everything when he got back.

Personally, he wasn't interested in the house. Except that it was bigger and better than what they had. However it had to have a kitchen! That was the priority for Sarah.

The young girl they had seen on arrival, brought in tea and cakes, and John used this domestic scene to ask Mackintosh more about the house.

The latter informed him that there were three large bedrooms upstairs above which, were two small attic rooms where the manservant and the girl slept.

On the ground floor; besides the sitting room where they were having afternoon tea; there was a large dining room.

The back of the ground floor was taken up by a very large kitchen which had a pantry leading off it. This was beside the back door.

"How many staff are here? Asked John.

"Let me see: there is Cook and the girl. As well as these two, there is my wife... she comes in three days a week to do some cleaning and the laundry. The girl does what she has time for. Then there is James, who you have already met. He was Mr. Edward's manservant and has been here a very long time. I do not know if you will have much use for him yourselves. He is getting on now and has really nowhere else to go."

Grandpa Murdoch immediately exclaimed:

"Of course we will keep him on! We will find something for him to do, we would not dream of putting him out after all those years."

"That would be very kind of you sir; I am sure he will appreciate it. He has not said anything to me, but I know he has been worried about what will happen to him."

"You can put his mind at rest then." assured Grandpa Murdoch.

They chatted on a bit about the farms. Then, having finished afternoon tea, the Munros decided it was time for them to leave and head for home. Thanking Mackintosh for his kindness and information; they promised to be in touch with him again just as soon as they got things sorted out.

On the way home, Murdoch asked his father and John if they would like to come in and see Agnes and the children for a short time. In politeness they agreed, although John was desperate to get home and tell Sarah all the news before she had to go to work.

As it transpired, they only stayed for a short time and Murdoch offered to take them back in the trap which arrangement they were happy to accept.

On parting company, the three of them agreed they would visit the lawyer in Glasgow the next day and to this end, arranged to meet at Lenzie railway station first thing the following morning. There was an early train, which would give them plenty of time to go and see the lawyer, and get things signed and settled.

Their plan was that after seeing the lawyer, they would find somewhere to eat, and then see Grandpa Murdoch safely onto the train for Edinburgh. The latter knew that their mother, Janet would be anxious to hear what had transpired at the lawyer's office.

As soon as John and his father entered the cottage, Sarah started the questions: What was it like?...Was it a big house?...Did it have a kitchen?... Did they have staff?.. Were there lots of fields?...Did they have cows?... on and on and on she went.

"For goodness sake, woman, give your tongue a rest for a minute will you, and let me answer some of your questions" retorted John in exasperation. "Yes, it was quite a good sized house; not as big as the one here...Yes it does have a kitchen." adding: "and it also had three bedrooms upstairs and that is just the first house, which Edward lived in."

Sarah's eyes were wide with astonishment...her mouth forming a silent *ah*! John continued.

"The second farm has a smaller house, but you will be glad to know that it too has a kitchen! And no!... they do not have any cows, just the usual fields, not as many as here, but quite a few.

This second farm is empty so that will suit our purpose very well. My parents and brother can live in one and we can have the other. Now then woman," he asked with a huge laugh... "does that answer most of your questions for the moment?"

"Oh, John!" Sarah's voice danced with excitement... "I am so looking forward to seeing this place...wish I could have gone with you today!"

"We will get things moving along as soon as possible, but in the meantime you will just have to be patient. Is it not time for you to go work?"

"Unfortunately it is." she replied. "I wish I could stay here with you and talk and talk and talk!"

Secretly John was glad she could not stay!

"Just leave the wee ones here with us, no need to take them up to the house tonight. Oh! And by the way...please do NOT say anything about all this to the other staff at the moment. Wait till we come up with some kind of a plan as to what we are going to do." Then a thought struck him...

"Or have you been so excited about all this that you have already told some of them?"

"No, honestly, John." Sarah protested... "I have not said a word. Sure now, I would love to have told them in the kitchen. Do not worry... I promise I will keep quiet about it in the meantime."

Having said this, she then left for work...

After his wife had gone, John gave the children something to eat, and then made a meal for himself and his father. When the meal was over, he put the children to bed, and afterward sat down to have a serious quiet talk with his father about the day's events.

"I presume you will be living in Edward's house and working that farm father, and that Sarah and myself will run the other smaller one?"

"I was thinking about that" said his father. "There will only be the four of us: your mother, Dugald Angus and myself. But Angus is walking out with a nice girl from the next village and hopes to wed her soon, so he may not want to come down here. That will just leave the three of us at home. Besides, he has a good job where he is and may choose to stay.

On the other hand, you and Sarah have only two children at the moment and no doubt more will be added in the future. Seems to me that you would be better with the bigger house. You are young and able to handle a bigger farm than me; I am getting on in years. Besides which; I want to take an interest in that quarry, so all-in-all, the smaller farm would suit me, your mother and Dugald much better."

"As long as you are sure about this." cautioned John. "I would be happy to have the bigger house and run *that* farm. But what about Mackintosh the farm manager? Maybe we could get him to divide his time between the two farms and that would leave you free you see to the quarry."

"Yes, that might be an idea. He seemed to be a reasonable man, and as long as he is still getting his wages, I suppose he will not mind. We can ask him anyway."

"The big problem I will have is all the paperwork...keeping accounts and paying wages." complained John. "Who is going to do all that work? I can only presume that your cousin Edward did it before. My worry is that I know nothing abut that side of the business. At least I can read and write!"

His father laughed. "Here is another worry for you! You know I cannot read and write. So you would have to do it for *me* as well! Adding: "It will be like the blind leading the blind!"

John thought about that for a moment then suggested: "Perhaps Murdoch can help us out and show me what to do, although I do not know if he has much to do with that side of things either. Apparently it is Agnes who has always done it for *her* father, and probably still does."

This would be the last opportunity they would have time for a quie discussion so the two men spent the remainder of the evening attempting to cover all the possibilities. After tomorrow, when Grandpa Murdoch boarded that train for Edinburgh, communications would be difficult. The next time they would all meet would be when Grandpa Murdoch, his wife Janet and son Dugald arrived to stay permanently in the south. Goodness knows when that would be!

Meantime, John needed to speak to Mr. Lennox and find out how much time of his agreement remained and when Sarah would be free to leave. So many things to think about and do. While it was all very exciting, it was also a little daunting. He was stepping into the realms of the unknown...for the first time in his life he wondered if he could manage it all. Being a Farm Manager was one thing, but to be owner as well and have to successfully do what was expected of him made him a little nervous... although he would never have admitted it!

The following morning father and son ventured forth to the railway station where Murdoch was already waiting for them. Soon after, they boarded the train for Glasgow via Monklands.

Arriving at Glasgow, they made their way to the lawyer ' s office. Fortunately for them, Grandpa Murdoch remembered the way.

Entering the drab, stuffy little outer office, they were met with the sour faced glare of Mr. Beaton's secretary. At the sight of her it occurred to John; *there are really some terribly sour faced unpleasant folk in this world. What is so wrong about having a smile on your face?*

They gave this creature their names and were told to wait...same procedure as before. This time, they were kept waiting for quite a long time. Young Murdoch was getting rather impatient when finally, they were told to go in.

On entering Beaton's inner sanctum, Grandpa Murdoch introduced his two sons. Lawyer Beaton bid them be seated.

For the benefit of John and Murdoch, the lawyer went over the details of the will... answering any questions asked by them... particularly with reference to staffing and allocation of assets and portions of property. Everything was perfectly above board. In particular, there were no catches, such as keeping on certain people, etc. which was as well since there was no way the Munros wanted to retain their horrible quarry manager.

Entry to the property was formally granted. Occupancy would take place on the basis of when the three Munro families could get their existing affairs settled.

It was noted that Murdoch would not be occupying the third farm; it was to be left rented to the existing tenants for the time being.

The rent was to be paid to Murdoch in lieu of occupancy.

With all the legalities covered and discussed, the two Munro brothers signed all the relevant papers and Grandpa Murdoch made his marks... these being witnessed by the sour faced secretary who had been called in for that purpose. Seeing that Grandpa Murdoch was unable to write, this witch gave him such a look of disdain which clearly said; *how ignorant can one be? Imagine not being able to sign your own name!*

Thankfully, and with business finally completed, the three men left the lawyer ' s office clutching copies of all the necessary legal documentation. Murdoch warned his father of the need to be very careful with these ...to make sure he kept them safe during his long journey back north. *At all costs, he must not lose them!*

The Munros, father and sons, eventually found a place to eat and rejoice in the fact that they were now the proud, legal owners of rather a large estate. What a wonderful feeling it was... particularly in the case of Grandpa Murdoch and John... both of whom had never previously owned anything at all. It meant even more to them than Murdoch. He already had a nice place to live and he and Agnes would inherit the house and farm they lived in when Agnes's father passed away.

Having eaten, the brothers accompanied their father to the railway station where they discovered he had about two hours to wait until the next train to Edinburgh was due to leave. Normally this would have been a boring wait but they had much to talk about and the time soon passed.

Saying their goodbyes; the boys reminded their father once again about keeping his ownership documents safe. They parted company on a very happy note. The brothers would be seeing their father, mother and at least one brother very soon... not long to wait. Their father told them that the family would give up their cottage, pack up their belongings and come down as quickly as possible... there was nothing up there to keep them from doing so

"When John finally got back to the farm, Mr. Robertson, the farm manager, came looking for him.

John could see that Mr. Robertson was very angry with him.

"Where have you been all day? You never showed up for work this morning. What is going on? I am afraid I will have to report this to Mr. Lennox. Obviously you are not ill. Sarah was asked where you were but she said she did not know...that you left early and that she did not know when you would be back."

"I am very sorry Mr. Robertson, I will go and speak to Mr. Lennox myself, I need to speak to him anyway.

"Make sure you do' said Mr. Robertson, who was only annoyed with John because he hadn't told him beforehand that he would be off work for another day.

John had completely forgotten to tell his employers that he would be away that day to see his father off on the train to Edinburgh. At least that was the story he had decided to tell them until everything had been settled. Now he *could* tell them the truth.

Since Sarah was at work; John collected the two children from the kitchen; telling her all was well and that his father had safely boarded the Edinburgh train. He didn't want to say any more in front of the others... his news would have to keep until Sarah came home later.

Sarah, on the other hand, was desperate to hear how everything had worked out, and hopefully, confirmation that all was in order with their inheritance.

Finally her day's work ended and she was able to go home. When she arrived at the cottage, John told her all that had happened. It was now a matter of seeing Mr. Lennox and finding out how long they would be required to work for him.

John told her he thought his work agreement was due for renewal in about a month's time. If so, he would have to wait at least that length of time or perhaps a little longer.

They both knew that Sarah's work agreement was also due to be renewed soon, so they could be away from there and into their new house in a matter of weeks.

Sarah was thrilled to bits when John told her his father had suggested that they should have the bigger house and farm, and he and his family would have the smaller farm and house. It suited her just fine...now she would become the lady of the manor instead of the servant! What a nice prospect to dream about and look forward to!

The following morning they both asked to see Mr Lenox. They were worried about what his reaction would be to their news, but to their relief, Mr.Lennox told them he was pleased for them both but would be sorry to lose them. He said he would check when their agreements were due for renewal and let them know as soon as possible.

A little time would be needed to replace them, particularly Sarah. However, as far as a replacement for John was concerned; he did not expect this would take much time since extra hands for the farm work were always available at fairly short notice. Meantime, he would tell Forbes to get on with making some arrangements to replace Sarah.

And so, it all went fairly smoothly.

That same night, John visited Murdoch and while there, asked him about keeping accounts, paying wages and all the other paper work involved in running a farm.

"You are asking the wrong person, John, I really do not know too much about that side of things. Agnes has always dealt with them... you really need talk to her about this... Agnes!" he called... "Have you a moment to come through and have a word with John?

They heard her laughing reply.

"Of course! I always have a moment to talk with your big brother!"

After she joined the brothers and found out what it was all about, she turned to her brother-in law:

"John! I can teach you about all the things you will require to know, but I must caution you; it will take a little time for you to learn all that you need to know. It is not just about paying wages and grocery bills - far from it! It also concerns keeping records of all the income and outgoings. Not only those I have spoken of...but accounts for the Quarry will have to be kept separately. It is all quite complicated enough but you must also remember that Murdoch's share of the Quarry profit will need to be recorded separately and copy provided for *our* accounts.

And that is not all of it; you will have an additional burden! Did not Murdoch tell me, that since your father and mother cannot read and write, you will also have to do their accounts as well?"

John merely nodded glumly in the affirmative. Agnes continued...

"If I may make a suggestion... if I can teach you how to do all this, you could then instruct your younger brother Dugald in turn and he could eventually take over the accounts for your parent's farm and share of the quarry. What do you think?"

This was the longest speech John had ever heard Agnes make but he felt his heart lighten somewhat!

"Agnes, that would so kind of you. You are indeed my saviour. I would much appreciate your help... I have absolutely no idea what to do or where to start."

"Fine, that is settled then!" exclaimed Agnes. "We will make arrangements to start once you have moved into the property and we are able to see what accounts they have and the record keeping system they employed. I believe Mr Edward Munro did all the book keeping work himself?"

"So we understand" said Murdoch. "At least that is what the lawyer told us."

Agnes had another idea.

"You could of course get yourself a book-keeper and he or she would do it all for you, but it would cost you quite a bit of money. Having said that; it is not really so very difficult when you get to know how to do it. The secret is in keeping it all up to date and keeping receipts for everything.

Once you move into the house, I will be quite happy to come along an occasional morning and instruct you in the art of book keeping. At the end of each morning's instruction, I will write down all we have discussed, so that when I leave, you will have notes to refer to. Would that be suitable to you?"

John beamed his appreciation.

"Indeed it would, Agnes, and I thank you again for offering to help. I will try and learn everything as quickly as possible so as not to impose on your good self for too long."

My goodness! Thought Murdoch. *Agnes certainly is very voluble today, but then she is talking about a subject close to her heart!*

The following day, John and Sarah received a summons from Mr. Lennox. He informed them that their work agreements would expire in six weeks. Consequently, he would have enough time to replace them both. Therefore, they could make arrangements to vacate the cottage at that time.

After thanking him profusely, the two of them left... Sarah dashing off to the kitchen to spill the beans at last... to tell all the other staff of her and John's good fortune. She had been absolutely dying to tell them since she first found out and had found it very difficult to keep her mouth closed tight shut. Her moment had arrived!

Cook, Lizzie, Jean and Catherine were all together in the kitchen when Sarah burst in on them.

"You are NEVER going to believe this, BUT" After that, he never stopped to even take a breath; not until she had told them the whole story every single detail of it.

During the entire time, the other four stood open mouthed. They just couldn't believe their ears! Cook was the first one to recover from the shock! Rushing over to Sarah, she gathered the excited girl into her ample bosom and gave her a big hug. In quick succession, the remaining three females followed her example.

"I am so thrilled for you and John! exclaimed Cook. "If any folk deserved a bit of good luck like that, it is you two."

"Oh I am going to miss you all so very much." responded Sarah, bursting into tears. She had spent many years with these people and they were like family to her.

"Come, come now." said Cook, hugging her again and patting her like a baby, "You are not going very far away, now, are you? You can come and visit us in your pony and trap... and you a lady at that! Think of it!"

"Oh I know" sobbed and laughed Sarah... "I know, but it is just that you have always been my family and have all been so good to me and John, both when we got wed, and when I was so ill at the time of Murdoch's birth. I have always looked on you, Cook, as my second mother."

"Well, I am flattered, my dear, but is this not supposed to be a happy occasion? Just think of the future you will have instead of serving folk all your life until you get too old"

"I suppose so." conceded Sarah. "Anyway, I still have six more weeks to work here. Mr. Lennox said he would tell Forbes to start making arrangements to get another girl to take my place, but maybe some of you will know of someone suitable."

"We will think about that." they chorused.

Chapter 13

The following Sunday was quite a nice day. John suggested that he and Sarah took the children for a walk.

Once dressed, they all set off along the normal path they always took on such walks until they came to the crossroads. Instead of continuing on towards the canal, which was their usual Sunday walk, John took them on a different route.

"Where are we going? John." asked Sarah. "This is not the usual walk!"

"I thought we would go a different way today instead. When we go to the canal, we always have to hold on to wee Murdoch very carefully in case he falls into the water. He cannot get to run about much, so I thought today, we would come this way for a change and he could run off his energy!"

"Are you sure that is the only reason we are going this way today?" Sarah's suspicions were aroused. "Have you planned something?"

"Now why do you think that Sarah?" asked her husband with a little smile at the corners of his mouth.

"I am not stupid you know. I feel there is something you are not telling me. I know you too well, John Munro. Am I right?"

John grinned. "Wait! and you will see where we are going."

It suddenly dawned on Sarah that just maybe he was taking her to see the house and farm they had inherited. *Could it be?*

"John, are we going to see this house and farm we now own. Oh, do tell me we are...*please.*"

"Och! I cannot keep anything secret from you now, can I?

Yes!"… he confessed. "That is where we are going today." "Wonderful, oh wonderful!" gushed his wife. "I have been so longing to see this place. Thank you! Thank you! John, for thinking of this surprise for me.

I love you very much." All this being said with eyes and feet dancing!

With that she gave him a big hug and a kiss... secretly; John was glad there was no-one around to witness this outburst of affection... he would have been so embarrassed.

Eventually they arrived at their new home to be.

James answered John's knock on the door and welcomed them in.

The elderly James was very grateful to this young man... his new employer to be...for allowing him to stay on.

When old Mr. Edward had died, he had wondered what was to become of him. He had no living relatives and had devoted most of his adult life taking care of Mr. Edward.

"James, is it?" asked John. He couldn't remember if he had got this man's name right.

"Yes, sir, it is indeed and I am very pleased to welcome you to *Westcroft*."

"We are equally pleased to be here" answered John. "Allow me to introduce my family... this is my wife, Mrs Munro and these are our two children, Murdoch and John."

James gave a slight bow of his white head and murmured to Sarah; "So very pleased to make your acquaintance madam."

John continued; "Mrs. Munro would like to see round the house today if it is convenient. We will be occupying this house and farm and my parents and brother the property nearby."

"Very good, sir, would you like me to escort you or would you prefer to go round on your own?"

"We will just wander around on our own, thank you." replied John. "Have all Mr. Edward's personal possessions been removed from the house? Adding: "and will all the other contents be staying in place?" asked John, hoping the answer to both questions would be 'yes'.

"Yes, sir, Mr. Edward's personal items have all been removed and placed in storage, but everything else will remain, unless you wish replace them with your own possessions."

"No, no, that would suit us perfectly well if the contents remain." John hurriedly assured him.

Little did James know that except for a few second hand bits and pieces - they had hardly any possessions of their own at all.

All this time Sarah had not opened her mouth. She just stood there gazing around her ... unable to take in the fact that this lovely house was now theirs. It was unbelievable!

Little Murdoch was quite awestruck by the shear size of the place and stayed beside his mother...not making a move or saying a word. He was being the perfect little angel. Normally he was anything but!

James left them to their own devices...advising that after they had viewed the house, tea would be served in the drawing room.

When James left...once they were alone...Sarah came to life! Casting her arm in an all-encompassing gesture she exclaimed:

"I cannot believe that all of this is ours, husband!"

Then she, John and the children headed upstairs to begin the grand tour of their new home.

After examining the three bedrooms, Sarah decided who would go where. She would also have some of the furniture moved around a bit. Oh the fun she was going to have! She thought that the rooms could do with redecorating, but that would come later.

Coming back downstairs they viewed the drawing room, dining room, and finally the kitchen and pantry.

They found the Cook in the kitchen together with the young girl.

After introducing himself and his family, John spoke to the older woman. "Do you have a name or do we just call you Cook?"

"My given name is Mary sir, but Cook will do just fine thank you!"

"All right," agreed John... "Cook it shall be if that is what you prefer. He went on; "I believe you are married to our ploughman. What is *his* name?"

"John Gibson, sir."

Turning to the young girl beside Cook John asked "And what is your name young lady?"

The girl giving a little bobbing curtsy answered "Annabella, sir, but everyone calls me Annie"

"Is that what *you* prefer?" asked Sarah this time.

"Yes, madam" the girl answered with a faint blush in her cheeks.

"Thank you both." said John by bay of closing the conversation.

"We will not keep you from your work." With that, he and Sarah left the kitchen.

During all this, Sarah had hardly been able to keep from laughing but once out of earshot, she giggled.

"It sounds so ridiculous... you being called Sir and me being called Madam. If only they knew what we will be doing for the next few weeks before we are here permanently; they would be the ones to be laughing!" she chortled at the thought.

However, she should have remembered that servants were the biggest gossips on the face of the earth. When they met in various places round the village on their days off, they exchanged gossip about their respective employers... *nothing* was sacred!

The servants at *Westcroft* were no different... they *already knew* all there was to know about their new employers!

When John and Sarah returned to the hall, James reappeared and ushered them into the drawing room.

"Annie will bring in tea for you in a few moments. Would there be anything else, Sir?"

"No thank you James" replied John.

James left, closing the door quietly behind him. When he had gone, they studied the room more intently.

"It really is quite a grand room, John?" remarked Sarah, wandering around.

The Drawing Room was elegantly furnished and the decoration and soft furnishings were extremely tasteful, with colours blending beautifully to set off the whole scene

And so, as they enjoyed their first pleasure of ownership, Annie arrived with a tray of tea and little dainties to eat. John and Sarah didn't waste too much time over these and left very shortly afterward, advising James they would return soon.

As they headed down the road, Sarah enthused, "It is a beautiful house, John...the furniture and decoration are of the finest quality. Along with all the other things they have; doubtless there will be lots of linen at *Westcroft* as well."

She was very quiet for a while, which was most unusual for her.

"Is there something bothering you, Sarah?" ... Asked her husband... "You are very quiet."

After a moment, she replied.

"I was just thinking; I do not really know what will be expected of me when we go to live there permanently. What am I supposed to do all day? I cannot very well say *I will do the cooking* or *the cleaning*, now can I? What will I wear? I have one decent dress and that is the one I wore to our wedding. The rest of the clothes I have...not that I *have* very much... just will not do in that house. I will look like a servant instead of the mistress! How can I wear the same dress every day?"

John sympathised with her situation.

"My dear; I wish I could tell you to go and get some more dresses made, but we just do not have any money at the moment to do that. However...".....He promised... "Once we find out about the money situation regarding the legacy, then you can go ahead and get some nice things suitable for the mistress of such a grand establishment."

"But that will not do any good at the beginning, will it?" Sarah protested. "I do not want these people thinking I am as poor as a church mouse and not suited to be the mistress of that lovely house. It is alright for you, you will be out and about the farm all day, so it will not matter what *you* wear."

John could see that Sarah was nearly in tears and really quite upset about this. He felt sorry for her and at the same time, so inadequate. He simply could not give her the money to buy nice dresses. Knowing such things to be very important to a woman, he would need to think about this and see if he could come up with a satisfactory solution.

As they were passing *Eastfield* Farm, Murdoch spotted them on the road and shouted to them to wait a minute. He came hurrying down to meet them.

"Why do not you all come in for a short visit and let the children meet? Agnes would be so pleased to see you all together for once. Besides; I want to talk to you anyway, John."

"We would be pleased to do that, thank you Murdoch." replied his brother.

They headed up to the house where they found Agnes. and her children.

"Please come in Sarah, it is so nice to see you and the children, how are you all?"

"Very well, thank you...you are well also?" inquired Sarah.

"Yes, thank you, come away into the house and have tea...we can let the children all meet." said Agnes. She continued...

"You know; it seems so silly that although being cousins, and only a short distance away, they have not yet met.

"It is silly!" agreed Sarah. "I suppose the problem is that John and I have only one day off in the month and have to work such long hours. As such, it does not leave much time to visit." Secretly she thought to herself: *it" is all right for you Agnes, you have all the time in the world with nothing much to do, I have to work.*

Meanwhile their husbands had gone into another room. After closing the door, Murdoch opened a drawer in a desk and took out an envelope which he handed to John.

"Now before you get on your high horse about this: it is money to cover the two days you were off work when father was here. I told you I would take care of that in the meantime and you can pay me back when you move into your farm and find out about the money situation. It is NOT charity John; consider it as a loan... nothing more.

On Agnes's suggestion, I have added a little extra. She thought that Sarah might like to get some new dresses for her new home. I hope you and Sarah will not be offended about it or Sarah will feel that we think she *needs* charity; it is just till you get started. We know you do not have

a lot of money...so we hope you will accept our help with good grace."
He emphasised his offer... *please?"*

John did not hesitate

"I am *very* grateful, Murdoch, and accept your offering gladly.
You know I would not dream of asking you for money under normal
circumstances, but I am a little desperate at the moment.

You must be a mind reader...Sarah was quite upset on the way back
from seeing the house today... complaining that she did not have any
nice dresses to wear when we move there. I, in turn, was lamenting
the fact that I could not buy her any new clothes. I am sure she will be
delighted to know that now she will be able to go ahead and get what
she needs. It was very kind of Agnes to think about her... please thank
her from both of us for her thoughtfulness."

"I will do so." replied Murdoch. "but we will say nothing about this
just now in front of the ladies just in case they might feel embarrassed ...let
us go and join them for a little while."

While the adults chatted, the cousins had been playing together.
Finally Sarah announced that they needed to get her children home as
it was getting late. Goodbyes were said and John and Sarah took their
leave.

On the way home, John decided to tell Sarah what had transpired
in the other room when he had the talk with his brother. He did so with
apprehension, knowing full well that if there was anything Sarah hated
above all else, it was charity. He expected that when she got the full story
about the dress money, she would fly off the handle.

He began with;

"No doubt you are wondering what Murdoch wanted to talk to me
about? I am surprised you have not asked me yet!"

"All right then, what *did* he want to talk to you about, or am I not
supposed to know? Is it some kind of secret?"

"No, no!" John protested, "It is nothing of the kind, but before I tell
you, please do not cause a fuss about it in front of the children".

"All right" Sarah agreed ...but with a very suspicious look in her eye.

John began. "If you remember, I told you that Murdoch had offered
to give me the money for the days I had to take off work to see the

lawyer? He wanted it to be as a loan, not charity, to be paid back as and when I could. Do you recall me telling you this?"

"Yes, I do remember... so is that what it was all about then?" "Well, yes and no. He has given me the money for the two days wages I lost, but he also gave me some extra money. It is for the purpose of buying you some new dresses and things for your new home."

Before the expected retort from Sarah, he continued:

"This was Agnes's idea."… adding quickly... "and I think it was very kind of her to think about you. She did not suggest this to be charitable... she sees it as a loan; to be paid back when we get into the new farm."

John waited for the explosion that he was certain was about to erupt from his wife. He knew that if Cook had spare money and offered it to Sarah for new dresses, she would have accepted it, but not from Agnes!

Sarah was quiet for a second or two then responded.

"I think you will be expecting me to say *I do not want it, although it was kind of her to think along these lines.* Well, I will do no such thing! I *am* desperate to have some new things when we move, so I will accept it gladly. But!" she added... "only as a loan, mind you...that we must pay back as soon as we are able to do so."

John was so surprised he nearly fell over! *His Sarah taking what seemed like charity and thanking the donor into the bargain? She must be desperate indeed!* He certainly was relieved not to be having another row with her over this.

The time passed agonisingly slowly.

With Jean's help, Sarah chose material for her new dresses and Jean and Lizzie agreed to make them for her. Sarah was delighted and insisted on paying the girls for their work. She couldn't expect them to do all the sewing for nothing. She had a little left over from the money donated by Murdoch and Agnes and knew her friends would be glad of the extra money.

John told Sarah that when she had a spare minute or two, he was going to teach her to read and write...reasoning:

"You cannot possibly be the mistress of that house and not be able to read, now can you? For example, what if Cook made out a list of things she needed and asked you to look it over to see if everything was in order. What would you do? Tell her you could not read? I think not. So, whether you like it or not, you are going to sit down and concentrate on what I show you, tell you, and therefore learn!"

Sarah could see John's point of view and knew the situation he had described could turn out to be very embarrassing to her, so perhaps she would just do as she was told this time, without an argument!

"Alright, then, John, I will do my best to learn, but I think it will take longer than six weeks, do not you?"

"Depends on how much you concentrate and whether you go over and over what you have been taught when you have a spare minute to do so."

And so, Sarah applied herself to the task ... by the time the six weeks were up, she had learned the basic rudiments of reading and writing... *very* basic, but it was a start. She had made a huge effort and it showed.

John reminded her that even when they moved into the new home, she would still have to keep it up and increase her knowledge of the subjects... adding that he would help her whenever he had a few minutes of spare time. Inwardly, he knew he would have an awful lot of learning to do himself when Agnes came to teach him how to keep the books and pay the wages.

By the time the six weeks were up, Jean and Lizzie had finished two dresses... they looked really nice...Sarah was thrilled with them. Thanking both girls for their efforts, she paid them the money she had promised, adding that she was very grateful to them for having given up their leisure time to get the dresses finished. What with their work, keeping their own houses in order and looking after their husbands and children; leisure time for these girls was extremely limited.

While Sarah was excited about going to her new home, she was also sad to be leaving the people she loved and had known for so many years. To her, they had been like one big family.

And so, the time came for John and Sarah to leave *Kirkland*. For all the women, except Cook, the goodbyes were tearful. The latter tried to keep everyone cheerful by reminding them that this was a great opportunity for John and Sarah.

Sarah promised that once she was settled into the new premises, she would return and visit them. She also asked them to come and visit her so that she could show them what she and John had inherited.

Thus, promises were made and kisses exchanged. John gave the girls and even Cook, a hug and thanked them for all the kindness they had shown to him and Sarah.

Murdoch had said he would come and collect them and their belongings which did not amount to very much. He was waiting for them when they finished saying their goodbyes.

Then John, Sarah and family, plus their meagre belongings set off in Murdoch's trap for the new house. A new chapter in the lives of John Munro and his family had begun!

Chapter 14

*A*s soon as they arrived at *Westcroft*, James came out to welcome them and assist with their belongings.

The young boy appeared and took charge of the pony and trap until everything had been unloaded. Following this, Murdoch said his goodbyes, declaring he would see them all again soon.

Cook and the girl Annie, along with another woman, who was the farm manager's wife, were waiting in the hall, to welcome them.

Addressing the other woman John asked:

"I believe you are the Farm manager's wife, am I correct? "Yes, sir, I am", she replied

"What is your name and what exactly do you do?" asked Sarah "My name is Catherine, madam but I am called Kate. I do all the laundry, assist Cook when necessary, and also do a bit of cleaning"

"Thank you Kate" smiled Sarah, "That is fine!" then addressing the assembled staff:

"Thank you all for your welcome. We will not keep you from your work at the moment. We will get settled-in first and then perhaps we can have some tea a little later."

"Very good, madam," said Cook... Whereupon the staff melted away to carry out they are various tasks.

John, Sarah and the children went upstairs, followed by James bringing some of their luggage.

"Do you wish me to unpack your belongings, sir, and put them away for you?"

"No thank you, James, we will just leave that for the time being."

"Very good, sir," answered James and left.

James brought the rest of their belongings up to the bedroom, and informed them that tea would be served shortly, and if there was anything special they required for the children, to please let him know.

Little Murdoch was completely overawed by the whole thing, and clung to his mother's skirts. He didn't much like this place and all these strange people.

"Want to go home now." he said.

Sarah fully understood how her children must be feeling. She smiled and gently comforted the wee lad:

"This is your new home now, Murdoch. Do not you think it is so much bigger and better than the one we just left? Just think! When you and John get a bit older, you can each have your very own bedroom. What do you think of that now? Is that not just wonderful?"

It didn't work... "Want to go home now" was all the little boy would say. It was going to take some time for him to get used to the idea of being here permanently. After all, he was only a small boy of just under three years old. *Kirkland* and the people there was the only home he had ever known. No doubt he would eventually get used to his new surroundings.

Sarah looked out of the window and, lo and behold, a lovely Collie dog appeared in the yard. She urgently beckoned to her little son.

"Come quick, Murdoch, look what I see."

The wee lad hurried over and his mother held him up to see the dog. He was thrilled. His bright blue eyes lit up with excitement

"Oh mama! Can I go and play with that dog?" he asked.

"Well, not right now Murdoch, you will have to get to know the dog first and it in turn, will have to get to know you. Besides, I expect it will not be used to children and we will need to find out whose dog it is and ask them if you can pat it.

Just then she spied a movement behind the dog.

"Oh look Murdoch! I can see some cats as well. Look! a black one and a striped one." It crossed Sarah's mind that the cats and a dog here might just make her little Murdoch a bit more settled about staying.

Once everything was put away, the family went downstairs to have tea. Sarah asked James about the dog she had seen in the yard.

"Oh that will be Ben madam. He was Mr. Edward's dog. I think he is missing his master somewhat. It is a pity, since he is a really calm friendly animal."

"I was wondering: would the dog be all right with a child?" asked Sarah. "I do not expect it has been used to children and may not be too happy to be touched. Do you think my son would be able to get to know Ben?"

"I think, madam; if he was approached in a quiet manner, he would be all right with the little boy. As a matter of fact, he was used to being in the house with his master, but we thought it better to put him outside when you came, since you may not wish to have a dog in the house."

"Poor dog," said Sarah, "not only has he lost his master, but he has been put outside as well."

"I think it best to leave the dog outside in the meantime" suggested John. "At least until he gets used to seeing us around. Then, if he is quite happy to accept us, we might think about allowing him into the house some of the time"

"That would be a good idea, sir!" enthused the manservant. "Now if there is nothing else you require, I will leave you to enjoy your tea."

"Thank you, James; we will call on you if there is anything else we need"

When they had finished their tea, John said he would go and see the farm manager and find out what was happening around the farm.

After John left, Sarah took the children upstairs. Baby John was needing fed. When this was done, she would tuck him up in his bed to have a sleep and find some things for wee Murdoch to play with while she unpacked the remainder of their belongings.

As she had unpacked their clothes, she realised just how little they had... not even enough take up half the allotted wardrobe and drawer space available.

She had three dresses plus the one she was wearing. When she was working, all she had needed was her uniform, underclothes, and one dress for her day off.

John's situation was the same, as he too had mainly work clothes plus his one good suit and shirt for special occasions.

As for wee Murdoch, he did not have many clothes at all. He had been around the farm most of the time and didn't need a lot. He only had a few better items, worn during their once a month Sunday walk.

Baby John was different; he was just a baby, so it did not matter so much.

Something most definitely was going to have to be done about this situation. She would not have her wee Murdoch looking like some poor tinker's waif! She would need to speak to Agnes about where to get the things needed... Agnes would know. After all, they were sisters-in-law. Maybe in the future they might even become friends. Only time would tell.

When Baby John eventually woke up, Sarah decided to take the children for a walk round the farm and see who was about. It would let wee Murdoch see the place... maybe the dog would be around.

They wandered aimlessly about for a bit, until Sarah saw John speaking to a man beside the dairy. She wondered if this could be the farm manager that he had talked about. Just then, John caught sight of them; called them over, and introduced Sarah. Her guess was correct... it was indeed the farm manager.

I m pleased to meet you, Mr. Mackintosh. I met your wife earlier."
"Pleased to meet you Mrs. Munro; I hope you and your family will be very happy in your new home."

"Thank you." said Sarah- adding: "I will not keep you gentlemen, I will be on my way now and let you two men discuss business."

Sarah and the children carried on round the farm until they came across the dog Ben lying outside a barn. As they got nearer, the dog stood up and wagged his tail.

"Hello there, Ben." said Sarah gently extending her hand palm downward to let him have a sniff at it. "Come and see me boy."

Ben quite happily came over, wagging his tail furiously. Here was someone paying attention to him! He sniffed Sarah's hand noisily then looked up at her with bright, intelligent eyes. When all seemed well, she moved her hand slowly over his nose and gently patted his head between his ears. The dog narrowed his eyes and almost smiled... obviously enraptured.

"Can I pat him too? asked wee Murdoch.

"I think we should just be careful at this point" cautioned his mother... "and let him get to know us."

The dog sniffed round Murdoch's face and neck and appeared quite happy with this wee human. Murdoch gave a little squeal of delight at this.

"Now he knows us, so we will move on. We can let him get used to us a little bit at a time."

They left Ben standing there with his tail wagging and continued round the corner of the barn and were confronted by a stable containing horses. When Sarah looked round, Ben had followed them and was sitting behind them, watching.

With difficulty, since she was carrying baby John; Sarah hoisted Murdoch up in the crook of her free arm so that he could have a closer look at the horses which were Clydesdales

"Look! Don't you think that they are just the same as the horses that James has?"

"Same as James." Murdoch agreed, nodding his head as he echoed his mother's words.

Sarah then decided it was time to go back to the house to find out what the arrangements were for dinner that evening.

Arriving at the house, Sarah went to the back door and entered the kitchen. Cook and Annie were there preparing food.

"Good afternoon madam!" greeted Cook adding with a broad smile: "I see Ben has taken a fancy to you."

When Sarah looked round, Ben was sitting just outside the kitchen door with a hopeful look on his face while dusting the doorstep with his fine feathery tail.

"So I see!" she smiled. "What were the arrangements about the dog after Mr. Edward passed away?"

"He was fed in the kitchen as usual, but instead of going upstairs at night with Mr. Edward, as was his way; we let him sleep in here in the kitchen. However, James decided it might be better to put him in the barn at night and feed him there too, so that he would get used to it before you and the family arrived, madam."

Sarah thought for a moment before responding. Then:

"I think it would be much better for Ben if we go back to the previous arrangements. He can be fed in the kitchen as before and allowed to sleep in here at night too. It seems to me a bit cruel to put him outside when he was never used to that. Besides it will get very cold for him in the winter. He must miss his master, so no point in adding to his misery."

This decision obviously pleased the occupants of the Kitchen judging by the beaming smiles.

"That would be very nice for him, madam, we hated putting him outside. It made us feel terrible when he would whine to be let in at the kitchen door."

"We are both fond of animals." Sarah told her. "I know Mr. Munro will not object to these arrangements as long as the dog does not come upstairs at night. We would not want him in the bedrooms"

"Very good, madam, we will see he stays in the kitchen at night... and thank you for your kindness!"

Sarah suddenly remembered the purpose of her visit;

"I really came to ask you what arrangements you normally make for serving dinner at night. What was the routine in Mr. Edward's day?"

"Mr. Edward always dined around 7.30 at in the evening, and breakfasted at 7 o'clock in the morning."

"That will suit us just fine as well! Have you decided what you will be cooking for tonight?" Hastily adding... "We are not fussy eaters, so I am sure whatever you have decided on will be fine."

"Well madam; we always have soup first. This is followed by a meat dish accompanied by vegetables, and we finish with a pudding. I hope that will be suitable. What about the children madam? Is the baby weaned yet?"

"No!" replied Sarah. "Not yet, but I had planned to do just that perhaps next week. Wee Murdoch will eat a small amount of whatever we have, so there will not be a problem as far as he is concerned."

"Will you be having wine madam?" ventured Cook.

"Not for me, thank you, but I think my husband might enjoy a glass with his dinner."

"Very good, madam, I will inform James."

"Thank you Cook. I think that about covers everything for the time being, that will be all. I will get away now and let you get on with whatever you have to do."

On leaving the kitchen, Sarah took the children upstairs and had a look around the place once again to refresh her memory. She couldn't remember all of what she had seen the first time she was here; it was all so hurried. So she took her time and had a good look round. In particular, she was looking for a small bed...like the one she had in the attic at the Lennox farm. It had been for one person only. Such a bed would be perfect for Murdoch. If she could find one she would have it put in her bedroom beside the bed she and John would share.

Until now, Murdoch had shared their bed. It was different in the cottage, there was no room for extra beds and they all slept in the one big bed, but things had changed. Sarah planned that in the future the children would sleep together in the room next door. In this way, she and John would have a bit of privacy but that would be some time later. Meantime, baby John was still small enough to sleep in the basket at the side of his parent's bed. As for wee Murdoch: he would need to sleep with them until he got used to the place. No way would he sleep in the room next door on his own. Nor would it be fair to expect him to do so.

So many problems to be solved, thought Sarah, but no doubt solutions would be found in the fullness of time.

John arrived at that moment and wee Murdoch ran to him. His father lifted him up and swung him over his shoulder extracting great squeals of delight from his son.

"So, how did your walk go? Meet anyone?" John asked

"No, not a person...just a dog! We met a dog, didn't we, Murdoch. Tell your father the name of the dog.

Wee Murdoch nodded and said "His name is Ben, and he is a nice dog."

Sarah told her husband the full story.

"He was your Uncle Edward's dog. I patted him and he was very friendly. He followed us all round and seemed glad that someone paid attention to him.

I told Cook to feed him in the kitchen and that also he could sleep in there at night. Poor dog! I thought it would be better for him in the kitchen than sleeping in that draughty barn.

"That is fine by me." said John. "I will probably be out a lot anyway." He changed the subject.

"Douglas Mackintosh is a very capable Farm Manager and has been managing both farms for some time. It will be good if he is willing to continue doing so when my parents get here

Sarah then told him about the rest of her day.

"I asked Cook about the meal arrangements. She told me that dinner had usually been served at 7.30, so I said that was fine in the meantime, until we get some kind of routine going. Breakfast is at 7 o'clock but if you want to change that, I will tell her. I see no reason for it to be earlier. We were up so early at *Kirkland* to work, but it is changed days now, do not you think?"

John agreed.

"I As long as Douglas Mackintosh is there running the farms and overseeing the workers, I see no need to interfere, unless there is something he needs to talk to me about. You did not see Mr. Lennox up and out seeing to things early; he left that to his manager, so I will do the same."

Sarah had almost forgotten… "Cook also asked if we would like some wine with our dinner. I said not for me, but you might like a glass with your dinner.

Fancy us having wine with our dinner! Can you believe it, John and getting served at table? It seems like a dream."

"I know; it is going to take some time to sink in that we actually own this place and we give the orders, not take them. What a change to our lives."

With those remarks, John picked Sarah up and whirled her round and round, both of them laughing.

"This is unbecoming behaviour for the master and mistress, John Munro, put me down at once" she said, chiding him in a mock serious voice, while trying not to giggle.

After they calmed down Sarah asked him; "How did your talk go with Mr. Mackintosh today?"

"Very well indeed. He gave me all the books that he had in his safe keeping. They were given to him by the lawyer and had been parcelled up so that he could not look at them. I have not opened them yet, and am a bit apprehensive about doing so. I wonder what I will find there that I do not understand!"

"Why do not you leave them for now?" suggested Sarah. "You can always look them over when Agnes comes and she will explain things and show you what to do. It is really kind of her to offer to do this for you.

While she is here, I would also like to speak to her. I need to know the best place to get some more clothes; particularly for Murdoch. He looks like an orphan!" She laughed at the thought. "Besides; once you have looked at the books, maybe we will know how much we can afford to spend.

Talking of money...I take it the money to pay wages and accounts are in the bank. If so, you will probably have to go there and speak to them as well."

"There is another thing." said John, "I will need to get James to take me in the pony and trap and show me how drive the thing. I suppose I should learn to do that too. Then we can go out on our own if we want to."

Sarah's next comment summed things up.

"So many things for us to learn, John, but I think we are capable of doing so, do not you? Oh! and while on the subject of learning...I also want to keep up the learning of reading and writing. It was so stupid and stubborn of me not to concentrate when you tried to teach me before. I wish I had listened to you then!"

As John listened to his wife, he could feel her joy mixed with anguish.

161

"It iss never too late to learn, Sarah, and if you take up where you left off and keep up with your studies, you will be amazed at how quickly It will all come together. The big words and spelling of them will get a bit more difficult, but I know you are intelligent enough to eventually overcome all these trials."

At these words, Sarah was overcome with a feeling of warmth toward the man standing before her.

"You are the most wonderful husband, John, and I love you very much. You always make me feel more adequate than I am, but it is nice that you have such confidence in me."

"I know you are not stupid, Sarah, and you underestimate your own abilities, but I do love you such a lot."

John gave her a kiss and a big hug. Wee Murdoch piped up "I want a hug too'."

So they all hugged together.

When they sat down to dinner in the dining room that first evening, it seemed a strange affair.... John sitting at one end of the long table and Sarah at the other. They seemed so far apart.

A place had been set for wee Murdoch in the middle of one side, but Sarah told Annie to move his place down beside her.

Throughout the meal, they ate more or less in silence. It was a good sized dining room and Annie and James were in and out all the time as they served courses and collected the used plates and cutlery.

This was not what these Munros were used to at all. Wee Murdoch hardly ate a thing... he was not very happy about this situation. He was also very tired by now, so that did not help either.

As for baby John... he could not have cared less what was going on! He was fast asleep in his basket, and oblivious to the goings-on around him.

Sarah felt a bit sorry for Cook! After all her obvious efforts, they didn't eat very much and a lot of the delicious food went back to the kitchen. She conveyed her apologies via James... using the excuse that they were all very tired after the day's events. As for Cook; she must have wondered what kind of folk they were.

When dinner was over, they all went upstairs to the bedroom.

Baby John would sleep till early morning.

Sarah got Murdoch ready for sleeping then put him into their big bed. She and John sat, one on either side of him, talking quietly, until he fell asleep.

They both were very tired and decided to go to bed early. John went downstairs to tell the staff that he and his wife were retiring and would not require their services until the morning. They could just go off duty as soon as they had cleared up.

For everyone; this was an unforeseen, but welcome, early night off!

Chapter 15

Morning had the promise of a beautiful day to come.

Baby John woke first. Sarah fed and dressed him, while her husband and Murdoch slept on. Eventually everyone was up and ready to go downstairs for breakfast.

It turned out to be a more informal meal so the family enjoyed it much more than dinner the previous evening.

Sarah had decided to have a look at the other farmhouse and to find out what state it was in.

James told her that Mackintosh, the farm manager, had the keys to the property so she set off to find the man in question.

As soon as she left the house she spied the very person she was looking for. He and John were in deep discussion.

Approaching the two men, Sarah began by asking to be excused for interrupting their conversation.

"I wonder, Mr. Mackintosh, if I may have the keys to the other property that Mr. Munro Senior will be occupying?"

"Good morning Mrs. Munro! I certainly do have the keys and if you just wait for a few minutes I will go now and get them for you."

"Thank you," said Sarah. As she did so, she could feel that John was desperate to know why she wanted them.

Her feelings were proved correct. As soon as Mackintosh was out of sight, he asked that very question.

"I want to go and have a look at the house and perhaps open it up a bit and air it." She explained. "Having been closed for some time, it will probably be damp and stuffy. It is such a nice day today so I thought it would be best to take advantage of the good weather, and have a look... just in case your parents arrive sooner than expected."

"Good idea, Sarah!" said John. "I never thought about that." True to his word, Mackintosh returned with the keys.

Handing them to Sarah; he explained in great detail, which key opened which door. Sarah thanked him and went back to the house while John and Mackintosh continued their discussion

John would have liked to go to the quarry and see what was happening there, but didn't want to confront that most unpleasant man without someone being with him. However, since Mackintosh was on his way to the other farm - John decided to accompany him to see the work that was in progress there.

On the way, he asked his farm manager if the man, who currently managed the quarry was in charge of sales as well as the quarrying of the stone.

"I really do not know very much about the quarry Mr. John, I prefer to keep well out of the way of Neil McLachlan; he is a nasty bit of work! Having said that; he *does* know his job and handles everything very well. I suspect that was why Mr. Edward kept him on. However, I cannot imagine him being very polite to the customers. For that reason, I am sure Mr. Edward did all the negotiating and talking to the clients; taking them to the quarry to let them see the stone when necessary. Consequently, McLachlan had no face-to-face contact with them"

"Maybe that is just as well, or we would not have had any customers left" observed John with a wry chuckle.

"Fortunately, he lives somewhere locally, so goes home at night." said Mackintosh, laughing. "Could you just imagine him living in the Bothy with the other men? He would start a riot and have all the farm hands leaving!"

John thought; *I like this man. Father and I will get on very well with him. It is such an advantage to have a good farm manager for us to rely on!*

Meanwhile, Sarah and the children were heading off in the direction of the other farm... little Murdoch was running ahead and enjoying the freedom.

On the way, Sarah took time to admire the abundance of wild flowers that lined the route; pointing out to her little son, the names of the ones she knew. Soon they arrived at *Oatlands*... for that was the name of this other farm.

After a few minutes, Sarah managed to find the right keys to open the kitchen door. Swinging it wide open; she was met with a musty damp horrible smell.

"Poo!" exclaimed little Murdoch. "Bad smell here!"

Once inside; Sarah immediately went around the house -opening up the windows in every room, and leaving the front and back doors open; to allow the fresh country air to blow through the house.

Once the atmosphere had sweetened, she looked all round the house to see what furniture and linen was there. While doing so, it struck her that although it had been dank and smelly; it certainly was well cleaned and tidy. Either the previous tenant had left it that way, or Mrs. Mackintosh and Annie had been here after the people had left.

She found *Oatlands* House to be well stocked with furniture, linen, crockery, and all the usual things one would expect in a house of this size. From what John's father had told Sarah when he had visited her; he and his family did not have very many belongings in their croft up north. Even if they did have, they would certainly not be bringing any heavy furnishing with them, so the contents would be a welcomed extra.

Mrs. Munro will be well pleased with this! thought Sarah. Thinking about her in-laws concentrated her thoughts. She wondered what was keeping them from getting here? *They have nothing really to stop them leaving where they are, or have they? Were the owners of the croft they lived in demanding some extra payment for them leaving in a hurry?*

The thought also occurred to Sarah: *How were they going to get here? Had Murdoch given his father money for their fares? Perhaps he*

166

did, otherwise how could they afford it? Questions without answers... *and probably none of my business anyway!*

Putting her thoughts aside, Sarah decided she would keep the house aired until John's parents finally arrived. She would hang the bedding outside on good days... just to make sure it was not damp, as and when, eventually the older Munros *did* arrive. It would give her something to do, and help her plan her day.

Perhaps in the afternoon, when the children were otherwise occupied, she would get on with her reading and writing. She had vowed to make the effort... to keep it up and get better at it.

After making sure *Oatlands* House was secure, Sarah returned home.

When she arrived home and before entering the house, she noticed there was some soft ground near the front door. This gave her an idea! She would get someone to dig it over and then she would make some pretty flower beds. Her sister-in law Agnes had some nice flowers and shrubs at the front of *her* house, so why not? Besides, it would be something else for her to do. First in the planning and planting, then later on; the careful tending of the little flower gardens. Her thoughts concerning things to do continued.

There was a huge bookcase full of books in the study room. Perhaps some day soon, she would be able to read them.

The thing that amazed Sarah... which she considered the most incredible invention ever... was the gas lighting. It was fitted throughout her new house. It meant that when they went to bed John could read a book and she could practice her reading and writing. In addition... once the children were old enough to be left upstairs in bed alone, she and John could retire to the drawing room after dinner and read quietly. She must therefore learn to read quickly ...there were so many things to be learned from books. John's brother Murdoch had found that out when he got the books from Mr. Mitchell's library.

John returned soon after Sarah and they had a light informal mid-day meal. After the meal, Sarah took the children upstairs for their afternoon sleep and John went to the study to go over the books and see if he could understand any of it at all.

However wee Murdoch was rather reluctant to have a nap. He wanted to go and look for Ben, the dog, but Sarah tucked him up in bed and told him that if he couldn't sleep, he might just like to lie there and have a little rest. She promised they would look for Ben later on. This seemed to satisfy him and he settled down quietly.

Sarah then took out her writing materials and a small booklet in which John had written down the letters of the alphabet. She proceeded to study them and copy them out. Her husband had also given her a list of easy words to learn and so she carefully copied them also.

Breaking her concentration, she turned round to see what wee Murdoch was up to, and was pleased to see that he had eventually fallen asleep...she would now have peace to concentrate on what she was doing.

Thus, the afternoon passed quickly.

When the children awoke, Sarah took them outside to look for the dog as she had promised. They did not have to look for long.

Spying the children, Ben came rushing over to them, tail wagging furiously as usual... Murdoch asked if this time, he might pat the dog.

"All right then! But be very gentle... Do not rush at him. Put your hand out first like this. Let him sniff it. If all is well, then you may pat his head. But only his head." warned Sarah.

"Nice Ben" said Murdoch doing exactly what his mother had told him.

Sarah was surprised to see Ben licking Murdoch's hand and wriggling round him, tail wagging. He seemed to have taken a shine to the little boy.

"He likes me", said Murdoch.

"He certainly seems to like you very much, but remember always to be careful and not to startle him. Dogs do not like to be rushed at or to be roughed-up too much. They have very sharp teeth and can give you a very nasty bite if they get frightened."

Murdoch will be careful" he answered.

Thereafter, Ben followed them everywhere, sticking to Murdoch's side like glue. Sarah thought *this dog will possibly be a great companion for Murdoch and watch over him, given time.*

John poured over the farm books... some of which, much to his surprise, he actually understood. Maybe all his worries had been for nothing?

There were a few bits he was unable to fathom but perhaps Agnes would be able to advise him regarding those.

The next thing he would have to do would be to go to the Bank and consult the Bank Manager. Doubtless there would be papers requiring his signature. Most important though: he would have to have it verified that he was the new owner of the property. This would enable him to have access to any available funds.

He would have to draw money out to pay the wages of his own men, but what about his father's farm hands? Until Murdoch senior arrived and made his mark in front of witnesses, authorising John to look after the affairs of *Oatlands;* John would not be able to touch any funds available for the running of his father's property.

All these thoughts passed through his head as he sat there thinking. Most important, he thought - *I must make a list of things I have to do and see to, or I will forget something!*

Finally, John had had enough of books for that day. Leaving the study, he went to see what Sarah and the children were doing.

He met the three of them at the side of the house with the dog still in tow and firmly attached to little Murdoch.

Sarah greeted her husband with... "Ben has taken a liking to Murdoch and is following him everywhere"

John had a quick look at the animal.

"He seems to be quite a young dog, and as far as I know, young dogs like young people...maybe that is the answer?

You will need to be careful that the boy does not get over-enthusiastic... just in case the dog nips him."

"Oh I have already warned him several times to be careful and not upset the dog." Advised Sarah. "I think he understands the warnings very well. Sure you do Murdoch!"

Murdoch nodded vigorously. "Ben likes me, father."

"That is nice son." smiled John. "Now you now have your very own special friend here."

Turning to Sarah he asked;

"So what have you all been doing this afternoon?"

"Well: we went upstairs first, and both the boys had a short sleep while I practiced my reading and writing." Adding: "You see; I am being a good girl and doing what you told me to do!"

"That is good, Sarah! The more you practice the quicker you will learn. Tonight we will sit together and I will find out how much you know. I will also give you some more words to learn. We have to keep it up every day."

Sarah then countered John's original question with:

"So, how did you get on with the books this afternoon? Did you learn any more and do you think it will be as difficult as you thought it would be?"

"Fine!" exclaimed her husband. "In fact, I understood quite a bit of it, but there are still a lot of questions I have for Agnes when she comes over.

The men will require wages soon, so I will need to go to the Bank and get money to pay them. I do not know how Edward actually paid out the money...if he had them collect their wages or he went round and gave them the money in their hand.

According to the books, they all get different amounts, depending, I think, on their age or how long they have been here. I am sure it will not matter to the men how they get their money, just so long as they get it. Maybe James will know. He is a very useful source of information." adding - "I am so glad he did not leave!"

Dinner that night was not quite as formal an affair as the night before. Sarah had decided it was ridiculous for them to sit at opposite ends of such a long table, so she told Annie to set three places at one end and they could all sit together. If that was not quite protocol, who cared? There was no-one else around to see them anyway.

Next morning, John's brother Murdoch arrived with Agnes in tow. He wanted to talk to John about the Bank situation before Agnes and John got together over the farm books.

While the brothers talked, Sarah used the time to ask Agnes a few things.

"Agnes, where would be the best place to buy clothes? I am not much of a sewer but I need things for little Murdoch and his father. I also need a few small things for the baby and myself.

I also wanted to ask your opinion about plants. There is a little piece of soft ground at the front of the house and I would like to make it into a flower garden. What do you think?" She hastily added: "I hope you do not mind me bothering you with all these silly questions!"

Agnes was exceedingly pleased that Sarah was seeking her advice.

"Not at all Sarah! It is good of you to ask.

Actually there is a good place in the village I know of. I sometimes go there myself for small items of clothing. In fact, I will be only too happy to go there with you if you like?

As for the garden while these two men are gossiping, let us go outside and have a look at the place you talk of."

The Sisters-in-law went out the front door and looked over the site for the flower garden.

Agnes had a good look at the place - saw the potential and exclaimed:

"That is a perfect piece of ground for maybe two flower beds. I tell you what; if you get one of the men to dig it up and turn it all over for you, I will bring you some plants. Sometimes the ones I have get too large and I have to thin them out. In consequence of which I am left with extra plants I do not need. You can have those to get you started. How would that suit you?"

"Absolutely perfect!" exclaimed Sarah. "Thank you very much indeed. I value your opinion very much Agnes. You and Murdoch are being so very helpful to John and myself."

Changing the subject, Agnes asked:

"Where are the children today?

"Annie the kitchen girl said she would watch over them until I spoke to you. Would you like to see them?

"I most certainly would but I am so short of time to day. When the men have finished their conference, I would really like to get on with looking at the farm books and see where I can advise. After that, I would love to see the children and perhaps take tea with you!

"That will be splendid! Is Murdoch going back to *Eastfield* after talking to John?"

"Yes he is." confirmed Agnes. "But he will come back later on to collect me."

Sarah had an idea.

"Perhaps James could take you home in *our* trap and that would save Murdoch having to come all the way back for you?"

"How thoughtful of you Sarah that would be splendid!"

"I will tell James of the arrangement then" said Sarah. "and we will tell Murdoch not to bother coming back later on."

It was thus arranged. Murdoch went back to *Eastfield* while Agnes and John disappeared into the study to start looking at the books.

Meantime, Sarah retrieved her children and set off for *Oatlands* to air the farm house once more.

As she wandered along the road, her thoughts turned to Agnes. She was being very helpful, and agreeable, of that there was no doubt. However she did not fool herself for one minute that the two of them would become close friends. Agnes was being nice and helpful because John was Murdoch's brother, nothing more. Sarah knew that she and John would never be invited to socialise with the other Munros or their friends. And she would certainly not be asked to join an afternoon soiree with Agnes and *her* friends. *Ah well! So be it.* In the meantime, Agnes was being most generous in giving up her time to assist them. As an individual, she was really a very nice and kind person.

Sarah once more opened up *Oatlands* House to the fresh air and then she and the children played a game in the yard.

As they were playing, who should come creeping round the corner, but Ben the dog. When they had left *Westcroft*, he had followed them at a distance... not quite sure if he was meant to be there. However, as soon as wee Murdoch saw him he squealed with delight and shouted to the dog to come. Ben obligingly came rushing up to him, tail nearly wagging itself off in his pleasure.

Baby John - who was sitting on the ground - was not so sure about the dog. After all, until that moment, he had only seen Ben from up in his mother's arms this was different!

Spying the baby; Ben went over and gave wee John a lick, which made him chortle with laughter... no sign of fear... he was not in the least afraid of the dog.

Sarah found a stick which she threw for Ben. He brought it back, retreated a few paces then sat beautifully tongue hanging to one side and looking alternatively at the stick and then up at Sarah. Dog language for "once again please!"

This antic kept the children amused for some time - until Sarah got tired of throwing the stick and declared it was time to close up the house and go home.

Later, Sarah got one of the men to dig over the patches she wanted for flower beds. When they had finished, she edged the patches with white quartz stones. All she needed then, were some plants to plant in them.

Sure enough and as promised: three days later, Agnes arrived, laden with plant cuttings and a few nice mature plants.

She advised Sarah as to what kind of plants they were and how to look after them. Leaving the final position of the plants to Sarah, she then went inside with John to continue going over the books.

As before, Sarah made arrangements for tea to be served and for James to afterwards take Agnes back home to *Eastfield*.

When Agnes was finished instructing John, she asked Sarah if she would like to go shopping with her the next day. John was meeting Murdoch in the morning and they were going to see the Bank Manager. She thought that if Sarah came to the village with John, the two women could go shopping while the men discussed business, then John would be able to take Sarah home again. Sarah was delighted.

"That is a very good idea, Agnes, I would be most happy to meet you tomorrow morning. I can get Annie to look after the children for a few hours. Thank you for the suggestion and for offering to accompany me. Oh I nearly forgot... thank you very much as well, for the plants."

Just then, James came round with the trap and Agnes and he left for *Eastfield*.

Over the mid-day meal, Sarah asked John how he had progressed with the books that day.

"Agnes said she thought I could now manage on my own and that I had got a good grasp of the situation. She left lots of written instructions in case I got stuck and said she didn't need to come back. She told me that if I had a problem, to let her know and she would help."

"That is good, my clever John Munro! You have certainly got to grips with these books." Then she changed the subject.

"Did you see the plants Agnes brought me today? Lots of different things to get my garden started. She also mentioned that you are meeting Murdoch in the morning to go to the bank, so suggested I went with you and she and I would go to a place she knows to buy some clothes."

This news gave John an idea.

"She really is very kind to give up her time for us. Maybe we could all become friends and perhaps have them to dinner sometime, what do you think?"

Sarah declared her previous thoughts on the subject.

"Oh John! do not be so silly. Of course they will not want to socialise with us. We are not their *cup of tea*. We will never be asked to anything at their house, apart from perhaps an afternoon visit if we are in the area. They...particularly Agnes...are really above our class. I think she is helping us because you and her husband Murdoch are brothers." she hastened to assure him.

"Do not get me wrong, I like her. She is certainly a very kind, thoughtful really nice person. But believe me; we will not be asked to mix with them socially."

John felt really put out at this. However - although he was not going to admit it to her - inwardly; he had to admit that his wife was more than likely right

Next morning John and Sarah went into the village to meet Murdoch and Agnes. The men went to the Bank and the women to the village shops.

At the Bank, the men attended to the details concerning the farms changing ownership.... signing papers to that effect. As proof of their entitlement to the properties in question, they presented the papers they had received from lawyer Beaton. They explained that their father... Grandpa Murdoch...would come to see them when he eventually arrived from the North to take possession of his property. Meantime, the women went shopping.

Sarah managed to buy most of the things she wanted and was quite pleased with her purchases.

Although she saw some very nice things while there: at that moment, she wasn't sure just how much she was able to spend. However, now that she knew the location, she could come back again herself when she *did* have the money.

Business at the Bank and shops being completed, the Munros made their respective ways home.

When they arrived back at *Westcroft,* John confessed to Sarah that his mind was in a turmoil with all the information he had to digest. He told her that The Bank had not been a problem. Everything had been sorted out for *their* farm, but they would have to wait until his father arrived to get the *Oatlands* finances in order. Meantime neither he nor Murdoch could touch that money.

The Bank Manager had assured them that arrangements would be made for the *Oatlands* wages and farm accounts to be paid, and that a representative of the Bank would visit Mr. Mackintosh for that purpose.

John was also getting to grips with the books, but there were still things he was not sure about. His big worry was the quarry. He had seen in the Quarry books that there had been some fairly large orders from various builders in the past and wondered if the same builders might just be turning up quite soon to order more stone. Because a lot of building work was going on now in Kirkintilloch and Lenzie. The area was beginning to develop quite quickly. One or two very large houses had already been built for which their quarry had supplied the stone. He discussed his thoughts with Sarah.

"I really do not know what to say or do if a builder turns up wanting to order stone. I know nothing about quarries and I dare not let that ill- mannered manager deal with a customer. He would chase them away for ever.

A prospective customer would want a price too, and I have no idea as to the pricing of stone."

Sarah thought before replying…

"Will it not be recorded in the books how much was charged? Might it be priced at so much per ton, or whatever and who it was sold to?"

"Yes of course!" exclaimed her husband. "I think that is how they work it, but there are probably different prices for different kinds of stone. This is where I would not know what to do.

While I want builders to come and buy our stone, I hope no one wants any till my father shows up!"

"Let us have something to eat and forget about business for a little while. I am sure things will work out fine at the end of the day" said Sarah.

Just after they had eaten, the farm manager came to see John and to tell him that the hay had all been cut and stacked. Douglas Mackintosh told him:

"A farm in Bishopbriggs usually takes our excess hay for their cattle and the manager from that farm will be showing up in the next few days to collect it, so you will need to give him a price for it.'

"Do you know if the price is the same each year, or is it increased a little?" asked John.

"I really do not know as Mr. Edward always did the negotiating for this. Sorry that I am unable to be more helpful Sir, but maybe if you look

back in the books for two or three years, you will see what he charged."
thought. "I will do just that, thank you, Mr. Mackintosh." He had a

"What do they do with the hay from *Oatlands,* the other farm my
parents will be occupying?"

"Sorry again." apologised Mackintosh. "But the people who occupied
that farm did all their own business and just paid a rent to Mr. Edward."

"Is there a lot of hay on that farm?"

"Quite a lot, but not as much as ours" was the reply. John thought
foe a moment before continuing.

"If this hay is also ready, I will wait a little while in case someone
turns up wanting it, and if not, maybe the farm in Bishopbriggs would
want to buy some more. Would you agree with that?"

"Good idea, when the manager arrives from Bishopbriggs, I will ask
him if more hay was available would he want it, how would that do?"

"Fine" said John, "that would solve that problem. Unfortunately, I do
not have the books for that farm, so I do not know how things worked
there. The Bank Manager is keeping them until my father shows up."

Douglas Mackintosh felt a bit sorry for this young man who had
been thrown in at the deep-end on his own and was obviously trying
very hard to handle everything properly. Maybe the burden on him
would be eased a bit when his father showed up. In the meantime he
would help him as much as he was able.

Sarah started planting her garden that same afternoon.

The children looked on and, of course, Murdoch wanted to help. She
gave him an old spoon to dig with which kept him happy. Baby John sat
in a small chair watching what they were doing.

In mid afternoon a pony and trap came to the front of the house and
a very prosperous looking gentleman climbed down. Davie appeared
and held on to the pony then James approached the man.

"Can I help you, Mr. McLeod; do you wish to see the master? He
queried. name?"

"Yes, James, I would like to meet the new owner, what is his "His name is Mr. John Munro, sir. I will call him for you. If you care to step into the drawing room and have a seat, I will fetch Mr. Munro. If you will please follow me, sir."

Sarah was listening to all this and thought *James, you are really very classy and make us sound like the upper class!* She had a bit of a laugh to herself over that.

When James found John and told him about the gentleman to see him in the drawing room, John's heart gave a severe lurch. *Did the man want to order stone? Heaven forbid! Was this his nightmare coming true!?*

Entering the drawing room, John introduced himself. The man confirmed that he was a builder and that his name was Thomas McLeod. He advised that he had always dealt with Mr. Edward Munro and hoped that he and John could do business.

By his soft, lilting accent, John recognised that this man came from up North, so he spoke to him in the Gaelic - the old tongue of Scotland:

"*Co` a`s a tha thu?*" (Where are you from?)

"*Tha mi a` Ulapul*" (I am From Ulapool) answered McLeod in the same language.

Both men were delighted to hear their native tongue spoken; it had been a long time since either of them had conversed in The Gaelic. And so, they chatted on for quite a while in that language.

John told him his family story - about originally being from inland Sutherland until The Clearances. Then being moved to the East Coast just north of the Black Isle.

"These were bad days." said McLeod. "We were also moved for their sheep, so I came South many years ago to start a new life and I have been very successful."

"My father," said John," was first cousin to Edward Munro. His name is Murdoch Munro. His cousin left all this land to him, my brother Murdoch and me

"Is your father here then?" asked McLeod.

"No. My father, mother and younger brother have not yet arrived to take up the other farm and the quarry. Talking of which - how can I help you? Is it stone you are needing?"

"It certainly is! I ordered sandstone from here before and it was very good quality material."

"If you could just give me a minute until I get the books and I can then see what you ordered before."

John left the room to get the Quarry book...hoping that this man was as agreeable as he seemed to be. *At least he was from the North so maybe that would help.*

He returned shortly with the book and looked up the record to see what Mr. McLeod had previously ordered. He found it fairly quickly and was pleased to note it was a rather large order.

"Ah here we are, Mr. McLeod! Would it be the same kind of stone you are wanting again?"

"Yes." confirmed the other. "The last time I had it cut for cladding, but I am sure your manager will know what to do with it. This time I want twice the quantity I had before, and all cut the same way. Shall we go to the Quarry and speak to the manager

This was the part John was dreading, but he decided he was not going to let this rude manager spoil the sale.

However, when they arrived at the quarry, the man in question remembered Mr. McLeod and was reasonably civil.

McLeod spoke in English for the benefit of the Lowlander in front of him.

"I want the stone cut for cladding. Just exactly the same as you did with my last order. It will be rather a large order. Will there be any problem with this??"

"No problem at all, Sir. Will you be collecting it in two or three lots then?" the manager asked.

Turning to John, McLeod answered.

"Yes, if you can let me know as each lot is ready for delivery, I will send people to collect it. The first lot will let me get started. Then you can let me know when the next lot is ready, and so on, till the order is complete."

"That sounds just fine by me", agreed John. "Shall we now go back to the house and discuss business?"

John had noted the previous price in the record book, but thought it should be a little more expensive, as it was quite some time since the last order had been delivered.

He and Mr. McLeod discussed this in a friendly manner, while speaking Gaelic all the time. They finished by shaking hands on reaching a mutually agreed fair price.

Having concluded the business, John ordered tea and they went into the drawing room and talked for a while of the days when they were up North.

Mr. McLeod had left many years ago, but was interested to hear about how John and his family had fared and how things had been for them. They both thoroughly enjoyed their chat. Eventually the builder left.

After he had gone, John went back up to the quarry and told the manager how much stone Mr. McLeod wanted - reminding him to be sure and let him know when the first lot was ready for delivery. The man just grunted a reply, turned and walked away. *Fine*, thought John, *have it your own way at the moment, my man.*

Next, he went to see Sarah at her gardening to tell her what had happened.

"I told you not to worry, that things would work out fine in the end, and was I not right? She asked.

"As always, my love." he said; joking with her. Then he changed the subject.

"Have you been keeping up your reading and writing? We must go over more tonight after the children have gone to bed"

"Yes." confirmed Sarah. "Every day I have been practicing and have learned quite a few more words today."

Chapter 16

At last! A great day for celebration arrived in the form of Grandpa Murdoch, Grandma Janet, and son Dugald.

They arrived at the station in Lenzie and asked a local boy to go to *Eastfield* Farm and tell Mr. Munro that his family were waiting at the station.

Eventually, Murdoch showed up with the pony and trap. What delight Janet had in seeing her second son again after all those years. She wept tears of joy just to see his face. My, how he had grown up from the young boy he had been when he and John had left home.

"Och I am so happy to see you again", she laughed through her tears, standing on her tip-toes and giving Murdoch a big hug.

"It will be so nice that we are all in the same place again at last.

How are your wife and children?"

"They are all fine, mother, and I too am so glad to see you again, it has been too long. And how is my little brother?" Murdoch asked, turning to Dugald.

"I am so happy to see you again too. My! Just look at you. What a braw lad you have turned out to be!

And Father...well it is not so long since *we* last met. Did you all have a good journey?"

"We did indeed, and so many interesting things to see." replied his mother "I never realised how big Scotland is, never having been out of the Highlands before. Oh, so much to see, it was wonderful."

"You must be tired after your journey." said Murdoch. "I will take you straight to John's and you can meet my Agnes and our children another day."

With that, he helped them into the trap with their bits and pieces and set off for *Westcroft*. John was going to get quite a surprise!

As they came up to the front of the house, James appeared immediately. Meanwhile, Janet and Dugald were totally stunned by the size of the house and farm. Janet just could not believe her son and his wife and children were actually owners of this place. She was speechless.

"Good day, Mr. Murdoch, how are you?" James asked. "And you, Mr. Munro Senior! I had the pleasure of meeting you sir the last time you were here."

"Yes, that is right James." answered Grandpa Murdoch - introducing the rest of the family. "This is my wife and my other son Dugald."

"Pleased to meet you madam... I trust you both had a good journey sir?"

Grandpa Murdoch answered; "Yes, thank you, James ... we certainly did.

When the formalities were over, Murdoch spoke.

"Let us all go inside now." But before they entered the house, he issued orders to the manservant.

"James, please find Davie and have him unload the trap and look after the pony untill I am leaving."

"Certainly, sir", James answered, going off to get Davie.

He was back in a minute with the boy, and the two of them started unloading the trap while Murdoch went inside to join the others.

Annie had come out of the kitchen on hearing voices. Taking in the situation at a glance, she went to fetch Sarah who was upstairs with the children. At the same time, James went off in search of Sarah' s husband, John.them.

Sarah came running down the stairs, her face full of joy to see

"How wonderful to see you all!" she exclaimed - adding; "Come into the drawing room and have a seat." Turning to the maid she said "Annie, please bring some tea and something to eat for the master's family."

Janet Munro stared around her in astonishment... "What a wonderful house" she murmured.

Her daughter-in-law recognised the bewildered look on her mother-in law's face and broke the silence:

"Forgive me for my bad manners. I am Sarah, John's wife and I know of course who you are Mrs. Munro. "and turning - "This must be my wee brother-in-law Dugald. I am so happy to meet the two of you at last.

John will be over the moon when he sees you. He is been hoping you would be here soon and that nothing was preventing you from getting here."

At that moment John came rushing through the doorway; straight to his mother, who he lifted high and hugged tightly, his wide, laughing smile emphasising his pleasure. Janet wept once more... this time to see her first born once again... to see the big mature, well-dressed handsome man he had become. Sarah - not to be out-done - joined in with her tears of joy.

Putting his mother back on the floor, John shook hands with his father, at the same time, telling him he was pleased to see him again. Then turning to his wee brother; he grasped him by each shoulder and, looking him up and down, exclaimed "My goodness, how you have grown and developed into quite the handsome young man. Good to see you again Dugald."

"Likewise big brother", agreed his sibling...a broad admiring grin lighting-up his face

Just then, Annie and Cook came in with trays laden with tea and all kinds of eatables. The travellers were really hungry and did sound justice to the amount of food supplied.

After they had eaten, Sarah asked Annie to bring the children to meet their grandparents and uncle.

When they were eventually brought before the assembled company, Sarah introduced them to the company.

"This is wee Murdoch and his wee brother John. " and to wee Murdoch: "This is your Grandmother, your father's mother; say hello to boy at all.

That complicated explanation did not seem to confuse the boy at

"Hello Grandmother my father's mother" he said dutifully. This brought loud laughter from the adults but wee Murdoch ignored it and continued. Pointing to baby John, he finished with

"That is my baby John."

Putting on a solemn face; Janet took the wee lad's hand and shook it twice.

"Well, I am very pleased to meet you Murdoch. So this is your little brother John?"

"Yes, and there is a dog called Ben and he likes me." ventured Murdoch.

"Oh I am sure he must do." retorted Grandma Janet.

Turning to Grandpa Murdoch Sarah asked: "Do you remember your grandfather - he stayed with us at *Kirkland?*"

"No." was the emphatic answer to that one.

"Well, say hello anyway and shake hands, please." said his mother. Again, Murdoch did as he was told.

This was followed by the same procedure with his new uncle Dugald.

It occurred to Sarah that although wee Murdoch was polite with all the adults, he seemed more inclined towards his grandmother and was quite happy to talk to her.

Probably because he had spent most of his young life with females.

The introductions being completed, Sarah announced... "Now that we have all had tea and you have had a bit of a rest, we will all go over to *Oatlands* and you can see your new home for yourselves. I have been going over there every dry day and opening the doors and letting it air, so it should not be damp. After that, John and I would be very pleased if you all had dinner here with us and stayed overnight. It will give you a chance to have a rest. Tomorrow morning you might want to go to your new home and take stock."

"That would be very kind of you Sarah, but would we not be putting you out of your own beds?" asked Janet.

"No not at all, mother." replied John. "We have three bedrooms. However, for the time being; until Murdoch gets used to the place - he sleeps in our room along with John, so there will be no problems with sleeping arrangements. You and father can have one room and Dugald the other. We would really like that and we can all catch up on all our news at dinner."

"Well, if it is not a problem for you to have us, we would be pleased to stay, would we not Murdoch and Dugald?"

"Yes indeed" answered grandpa Murdoch.

Up to this point Dugald had hardly opened his mouth. He was completely overawed by this house. He just could not take in the fact that this all belonged to his big brother. It was going to take some getting used to. He would manage!

"Yes indeed!" Dugald echoed his sire.

Sarah excused herself and went in search of Annie and Cook. Luckily Kate was there in the kitchen when she got there so she asked Annie and Kate to make sure the other two beds upstairs were made up for the guests. She also informed Cook that there would be three extra people for dinner that night and just to make something simple.

Cook told her what she had in mind for dinner that night and Sarah agreed it would be perfect. She also told Cook to tell James that wine would be required.

How grand Sarah felt. She had always been at the receiving end of orders...it was very nice to be giving them instead of taking them!

And so, they all trooped over to *Oatlands*...the other farm, which was to be Grandpa Murdoch and Grandma Janet's home for many years to come. Although it was a dull day, at least it was dry and quite mild.

At her first sight of *Oatlands*, Janet could not believe this was their very own property, it was so grand. She had worked hard all her life with little reward, except to see her children grow up and make a good life for themselves and had always had to try and make ends meet and live very frugally. Now; here she was in this grand house, which was all theirs... which nobody could take away from them or put them out of. What a feeling!

Grandpa Murdoch had seen the house before... he was more interested in the farm and quarry.

Dugald, although interested in the house, went with his father and brothers to see the farm and quarry.

Meanwhile, Sarah and Janet looked round the house to see if anything was needed. Her mother-in law was content with what they found.

"There is more in this house than I have had in my whole lifetime. I cannot for the world, imagine what else I would need to stay here."

"I know exactly how you feel." agreed Sarah. "When I saw *our* house for the first time, I nearly died of excitement. It had so many nice things in it... more than I ever thought John and I could have afforded in a lifetime. Do not get me wrong, Mrs. Munro; I was very happy with John in our little cottage on the Lennox farm. He is a good man and has been a wonderful husband and father, and the same goes for Murdoch with Agnes and their children. All credit goes to you for bringing them up to be caring about others."

Sarah felt she had given a rather long speech, but she had wanted John's mother to know that all the material things they now had were not as important as having a good husband. She sincerely meant every word she had said.

Janet responded to these words of praise

"It was very nice of you to say that about my boys and I am glad you and John are happy. I think, Sarah, that you and I are going to get along together very nicely." quarry.

When the men returned, Sarah asked them if they had gone to the

"Not today." answered Grandpa Murdoch. "We did not want to get into an argument with that lout of a quarry manager. We will go another day.'

Murdoch then took leave of them; promising to see them all again soon.

After he had gone, Sarah showed her guests their rooms, telling them, if they wanted to have a rest, she would call them all when it was near dinner time.

Dinner was quite a lively affair, with lots of talking going on. When James poured a glass of wine for each adult, Sarah decided to have some too since Baby John was now weaned onto solid food.

John had tasted the wine before, but, like his father and Dugald; was not all that enamoured with it.

Sarah sipped hers along with the food but secretly thought a glass of water would be just as nice!

Grandma Janet took one sip of the stuff then screwed up her face.

She caught Sarah's eye and they both laughed.

"I do not really like this at all." admitted Janet. "It is really not to my taste."

"Just you leave it then mother." suggested John. "I am sure you will enjoy a glass of *Westcroft* vintage fresh water instead." Everyone laughed at the thought of it.

With the dinner underway, John looked around the assembled company. Everyone was relaxed and enjoying each other's company. He felt proud of Sarah... instructing servants and being the perfect hostess. She was handling all this as if she had been doing it for years and obviously enjoying every minute of it! Quite the grand lady!

The gas lighting totally intrigued the visitors. It was indeed a wonder to those from the north... something not quite understood, but fascinating nevertheless.

Everyone spoke English while Sarah was present. She could speak Irish Gaelic but did not understand the Scottish version.

John told his father about his initial fear of someone showing up for stone and his lack of knowledge concerning the quarry operation.

"I was dreading it... I know nothing about stone as you know but my fears were unfounded.

A man called Thomas McLeod arrived at the door one day looking to buy stone. It turned out he was from Ullapool, so we spoke most of the time in The Gaelic. It was so nice to hear our language again.

We got on very well and he gave me a huge order for sandstone.

He is a builder and used to do quite a bit of business with Edward.

McLeod was also telling me that many people are now having houses built in the Kirkintilloch area and that Lenzie is also developing quite rapidly, so that will be good for us."

"How did he get on with the quarry manager?" asked Grandpa Murdoch.

"Actually, quite well. The man knew exactly what Mr. McLeod wanted and said he would get on with cutting the stone right away. He wasn't exactly pleasant to him, but he kept a civil tongue in his head. I think he knows his job and the workings of stone very well, so maybe we should think again before getting rid of him."

"Ah well now!" exclaimed his father. "We will be seeing about that later." He changed the subject.

"Are there any pressing matters I need to attend to?

"Not right now father" John chuckled. "But we will have to go to the bank as soon as possible to get money matters sorted out and for you to present your title deeds."

A load had been lifted from John's shoulders.

Now that his father, mother and brother were there, they could look after their own farm themselves.

He would have to teach his young brother about the *Oatlands* account books, but he did not doubt that Dugald would learn quickly.

At last, Sarah excused herself, saying that she would put the children to bed.

"Say goodnight to everyone - Murdoch. Maybe your Grandma would like a hug as well?"

Murdoch was quite happy to give his Grandma a big hug and say goodnight.

Janet was thrilled that her little grandson had taken to her so quickly. She responded by giving him back a big kiss and then giving baby John a big kiss for good measure... she was a very happy elderly lady!

Sarah then reminded the wee lad. "Say goodnight to your grandfather and Uncle Dugald too'

Murdoch again did as he was told.

These duties performed, mother and children left, bound for bed.

After Sarah had left the room, the remaining occupants lapsed into The Gaelic. Lots of stories were exchanged.

The new arrivals were curious about their new home and the surrounding area and John answered their questions to the best of his ability.

When Sarah returned to the company a little later, the Highlanders politely resumed speaking English for her benefit.

Eventually everyone was tired and decided to go to bed; agreeing unanimously that *there was always tomorrow and lots of other days ahead for talking.*

Next morning they all went over to *Oatlands*. There, Sarah and Janet discussed what would be needed as far as household supplies were concerned. Once they had made a list of essentials, Sarah said she would get one of her people to bring an initial supply from her own larder. This would be sufficient to tide Janet over until she had made a proper list of her requirements.

Janet thanked her daughter-in-law for her kind consideration, adding: "I suppose you know I cannot read and write, but I will get Dugald to make out a list of things I will need and maybe you could arrange for them to be delivered here. Once my husband gets to the Bank, we will be able to get some money to pay for things."

"Do not you worry about a thing until you get settled in and used to your new surroundings Mrs Munro!" Sarah protested. "I will get Cook to arrange for this to be done. She is usually the one who handles the food and cleaning supplies in our house."

The problem of consumable supplies being solved; they wandered round the house taking stock of linen supplies, crockery, cutlery, etc.

This gave Janet an enormous amount of fun. All these wonderful things she had never been able to afford were now hers.

"Would you be wanting a Cook or any other servants, Mrs. Munro?" asked Sarah... "Because if you do, I can have that arranged for you as well."

"No, I do not think so, Sarah, maybe just a woman to help do the laundry and clean a bit. I would rather do the cooking myself and part of the cleaning; otherwise what would I do all day. I have been used to working hard with little help all my life, so idleness would not suit me at all."

Sarah made a suggestion...

"Kate comes in to us some days, but not every day... maybe she would welcome the extra money for say; two days a week. I can speak to her if you like? Failing that; if Kate doesn't want any more work; she or Cook might possibly know of a young girl who may be looking for work and would be available."

"That would be splendid." replied Janet. "Even two days a week would be fine. I am not so old that I cannot do some work myself." "she laughed. "It is different for you as you have the children to care for and they no doubt take up quite a lot of your time."

"They certainly do." agreed Sarah. "and of course Murdoch is getting to the stage where he wants to explore everything, so I have to keep my eye on him and watch that he doesn't wander too far off."

Her Mother-in Law changed the subject.

"I was thinking that once I have some money, I will need to buy a few more items of clothing. Grandpa Murdoch and myself do not have very much. All we did was work. The only decent clothes we have are the ones we wear to Church on Sunday, and we are wearing them now."

"I know of a good place in the village where we can get things." suggested Sarah. "Agnes took me there one time. It has quite a variety of things; you can even have dresses made for you if you wish! I will take you there whenever you want to go."

"That would be very kind of you, Sarah! I am glad you are here and willing to help me. I would not know what to do."

"Och! Think nothing of it. I was very grateful to Agnes for putting *me* right about things." She went on;

"Agnes has been very kind to John and myself in many ways. The plants in front of our house were given to me by her, and she helped John understand the books." She hastily added:

"Even although she is much more upper class than we are; she is never-the-less, a very kind person."

"Is Murdoch happy with her?" asked Janet.

"Absolutely!" exclaimed Sarah. "He thinks the sun rises and sets on her and their children. The house they have is very grand; much bigger and grander than ours, but then again it is Agnes's father's house and farm. When Mr. Mitchell is no longer with us, all the property will be left to Agnes and Murdoch."

Sarah carried on speaking - warming to the subject.

"Here, we too are fortunate, in that that Edward left this property to us, are we not? No way would we ever have been able to have something like this.

We have often said a little prayer thanking Edward for his kindness in leaving this property to us all."

Janet sat in silence. She understood that her Daughter-in-Law was excited and that talking was her way of calming down.

Sarah continued:

"Murdoch, of course, collects the rent from the third farm which he now owns, but he is quite content to let the people stay there in the meantime." adding: "I recall Mr. Munro saying there was no way he would want to evict the present occupiers; since he had seen enough of that in the Highland Clearances."

Sarah finished speaking - almost breathless with the effort

"Yes." agreed Janet, "It was a bad time. John was only three; Murdoch just under two, Angus was six months old, and I was also pregnant again with Catherine; so it was a dreadful upheaval for us."

Lowering her head and shaking it from side to side and with eyes closed, she continued:

"But that was then, and I do not want to think about it now. I prefer to look to the future which has a much more promising outlook."

Sarah felt so embarrassed. She had really put her foot in it this time big style!

"I am so sorry, Mrs. Munro, I really didn't want to upset you, I feel so stupid bringing up the subject."

As before; Mother-in-Law Janet understood

"Do not you worry about it, lass, I know you did not mean to upset me at all and no offence has been taken."

Chapter 17

few weeks after John's parents and brother had arrived, Sarah announced that she was pregnant again. She was delighted and secretly hoping that this time, it would be a girl.

Agnes was also pregnant, so the news of the pregnancies was received with delight by the grandparents.

The *Westcroft* and *Oatlands* Munros were finally invited by Murdoch and Agnes to visit them in their home for afternoon tea.

To Sarah, it seemed they had taken their time over this, until it transpired that Agnes had not been very well over the first few weeks of her pregnancy.

As previously arranged; Sarah had accompanied Janet on a shopping expedition to the village. There, the latter had purchased a few things she and Grandpa Murdoch needed. Janet had also found a dress she liked. It was not flamboyant or anything fancy, but more in the practical line. She liked it so much that she had asked the shop owner to make two more of the same for her.

Thus, when the day arrived for this first visit to *Eastfield*, all the visitors felt reasonably well dressed for the occasion.

Janet and Dugald were extremely impressed with *Eastfield* House. Janet in particular, could hardly believe that both her first born sons had done so well.

After all the formal introductions and greetings, Murdoch brought in his children to meet their grandmother and uncle. They, being very polite well mannered children, performed the duties of kissing and shaking hands like little adults. They stayed with the adults for a short while, and then were whisked away by the governess.

Sarah was quite shocked by the physical appearance of Agnes. The latter looked quite ghastly... pale and drawn. However she made light of it.

"We hear another little Munro is on the way and that you have not been so well. Are you feeling any better now?"

"A little, thank you Sarah. I apologise for taking so long to have you all visit, but I was not feeling up to it and spent a lot of time in bed, however it is very nice to see you all now."

Agnes was most definitely not herself at all and was making an effort to be polite and welcoming. Truth be known; she was wishing this visit would be over soon.

Poor Agnes! Sarah could almost feel her anxiety and decided within herself, that they should not stay very long. The fact that Agnes's children had been taken away and not allowed to stay and play with *her* children suggested that Agnes was feeling worse than she was letting on.

They all chatted for a little while longer until tea was served.

However, as soon as tea was over, Sarah suggested they should all leave and let Agnes have a rest.

Despite polite protests, Agnes was grateful to Sarah for understanding how she felt and taking the situation in hand.

When they arrived home Sarah remarked quietly to John that she thought Agnes looked terrible. He agreed with her.

"Did not she have a bad time with the last baby?" asked John. "Indeed she did. Maybe they should just forget about having more children if she is going to be so ill every time. I suppose it just happens, what can she do about it?"

"That, I am afraid, my dear wife, is a woman's luck!"

Sarah thought about that then announced her solution

"If I was as ill as her every time, I would ban you from my bed, John Munro, and send you to the other bedroom to sleep with the children so there!" This said with a laugh... knowing fine that would never happen in their case.

Sarah's pregnancy was proceeding without a hitch. She was thankful that she did not feel as bad as her sister-in-law looked. It crossed her mind that Murdoch and Mr. Mitchell must be somewhat worried about her.

Grandpa Murdoch, Janet, and Dugald had settled nicely into *Oatlands*. Janet spent her early days cleaning everything and enjoying every minute of it.

She had changed lots of furniture around and the place now had a lived-in look... really very comfortable. This was her reward for all the hardship she had put up with during all the previous years. Now, she was grateful for having all this luxury to enjoy in her older years.

The farming side was running well. John had taken his young brother Dugald in hand and was teaching him to understand the account books. Soon Grandpa Murdoch and Dugald would be independent and able to run the whole farm themselves, leaving John to attend to his own business. This would be a load off his mind.

Douglas Mackintosh had again been very helpful to Grandpa Murdoch showing him all the ropes about running a farm. The latter may not have been able to read and write, but he was not stupid and quickly picked up the knowledge that Macintosh imparted to him.

Things on both farms were going very well. Kate was quite happy to go to Janet two days a week to help with the cleaning and do the laundry. She and Janet got on well together, but then again; Janet was the kind of person who got on with everyone.

One day, sad news was received from Murdoch at *Eastfied*. Agnes's father, Mr. Mitchell, had suddenly dropped dead with a heart attack. The news was so unexpected, since the man had always been very healthy and never seemed to have any illness.

"This will devastate Agnes", Sarah commented to John. "She wasn't very well herself and this will be a dreadful blow to her. She and her father have been very close all those years.

For a long time...until Murdoch came along... she had no one *but* him. I wonder how this is going to affect her and this pregnancy?" "Very badly, I would think." replied John.

"We must find out when the funeral is and attend. Do you think we should go and see Agnes and pay our respects now?"

"I do not think so at the moment. Can you imagine how she is feeling? I think we would be intruding. I will go along and see Murdoch and ask after Agnes. I can then find out if he thinks it wise for us to go and see her. Do you think that is the best way?"

Sarah thought for a moment then answered. "Yes, I think you are probably right."

John went over to *Eastfield* and had a word with his brother concerning the death in the family.

As Sarah had predicted; Murdoch thought it better to leave Agnes in her sorrow for the time being and wait until the funeral before offering her comfort. As for the funeral arrangements, Murdoch said he would like John to be there with them on that day.

Without hesitation, John replied.

"Of course I will be beside you and Agnes!" adding; "If there is anything either Sarah or myself can do to help just let us know."

Eventually the funeral day arrived. Fortunately for the mourners, it was a dry but cold.

John, Sarah, Grandpa Murdoch and Janet attended and gave support to Agnes in her hour of grief.

Young Dugald stayed behind at *Oatlands* to look after things there. In any case, he didn't really want to go, as he had not known Mr. Mitchell. Besides; being young - funerals depressed him!

During the funeral service by the grave side, Sarah had to almost hold Agnes up. If Sarah had thought the latter looked bad on the day of their previous visit, she looked much worse on the day of her father's funeral.

Since her father had died and until the day before the funeral, Agnes had not stopped crying. Now, she was all cried-out and did not shed a single tear at the grave side. Unaware of this, but for Agnes's sake, - Sarah also held her emotions in check throughout the service.

After the funeral, the immediate family and John Mitchell's closest associates returned to the house for drinks, tea and food.

Sarah was sure Agnes just wanted to go to her bed and leave everyone, but protocol did not allow her to do that. Therefore Agnes elected to stay there and accept condolences from all those who had turned out to show respect for her father.

As she sat politely...robot-like ... uttering *thank you* to each and every utterance of *"so sorry."*...there seemed to her a never ending number of them.

When most of the people had departed and only close family members remained, Sarah took charge.

"I think Agnes has had enough today and should now go to bed. Do you want me to assist you, Agnes?"

"Yes please Sarah, that would be kind of you."

Without another word; they both headed upstairs and Sarah helped Agnes into bed.

Having seen Agnes settled, Sarah returned downstairs and re-joined the family.

"I am really worried about Agnes." declared Murdoch to no one in particular. "She just cannot seem to be able to rally at all. I know she hasn't been well with this baby. Her father's death has been a terrible blow to her. Goodness knows how she will be. She doesn't even want to see the children! It is not fair on them - poor wee souls. They do not understand. I suppose all I can do is try and encourage her to eat and get better. Only time will tell."

Everyone felt sorry for him; he was so worried.

To add to his worries; he now had the farm to run by himself. Not only that; if Agnes didn't get better, who would keep the books and pay the wages?

Murdoch knew nothing about the account books but he would just have to get on as best he could till his wife recovered.

Fortunately, there was no urgency in that direction. The crops had been gathered-in and threshed and were ready for selling. The men had been paid... most of them having been paid off, so there was not so much to do now.

"If there is anything any of us can do to help, please let us know." offered John.

Murdoch appreciated his brother's offer of help, but he was stubborn and independent.

"Thanks for that brother... I will let you know how things are going."

Chapter 18

*J*ohn had finally decided to get James to teach him how to handle the pony and trap. He practised all round his own farm and on trips to and from his father's farm.

Very quickly, he got the hang of it and really enjoyed the freedom it gave him... to be able to go anywhere he wanted *when* he wanted and not always having to rely on James.

Sarah went about her daily duties, looking after the two children, going to see her mother-in-law some days, and tending her little garden plot on others.

She had dug up all kinds of wild flowers and bedded them in her plots. They had all taken very well and her little gardens were looking quite nice. They would look even better when the spring and summer came. She was feeling very well and looking forward to this next baby arriving.

It was now time for Murdoch to move into the other bedroom and he seemed quite happy and excited about it. Sarah had thought she would need to get a smaller bed for him, but then changed her mind and decided to put both the boys in one big bed together. This would make wee Murdoch feel less lonely. Baby John was old enough now to be in the big bed next door with his brother.

At a mealtime, she told John what she intended to do... he was all for it - it suited him fine. He was fed up with both the children being in the room and wee Murdoch being in with his parents. They had all this space, so why not use it and give themselves a bit of privacy.

Consequently, Sarah told Annie to make sure the bed in the room next door to theirs was clean and not damp as she would be moving the children in there the following night. No doubt, she thought, there would be protests and she wasn't sure if they would settle, but she was determined this was the way it was going to be - protests or otherwise! She had decided!

The following evening, as bedtime approached, she explained to the children that they were going on a big adventure next door. Telling them that it was going to be great fun for the two of them to be sleeping together in the same big bed!

This information was met with a stare from wee Murdoch, but baby John was too young to bother. Never-the-less, she put them to bed and stayed with them for a while singing little Irish lullaby songs until they finally fell asleep. She hoped they would sleep all night, but just in case, left their door open, so that if they wakened and were afraid, they could come into her room.

As it turned out, they *did* sleep all night and did not seem to be bothered about sleeping together at all.

Next morning, Sarah moved all their clothes and toys and little belongings into their new bedroom. This had the effect of making the room look more like a children's room rather than just a spare room next door. All then was well. Mission accomplished!

One day, Murdoch came clattering into the *Westcroft* farm yard in the pony and trap. He brought more bad news! Agnes had had a miscarriage almost a week previously and was in a bad way. He told John and Sarah that her problem was more of a mental nature than a physical one.

"What can we do to help?" asked Sarah. "Would she want me to go and see her do you think?"

John quickly replied… "At the moment, I think not, but I thought I had better let you know what was happening.

As you know, she wasn't well anyway to start with. I am sure the grief of her father's death has aggravated the situation and brought this on. Maybe once she gets over this, she will make a bit of headway with her health and get much better.

I am hoping this will be the case anyway."

"We are really sorry to hear of this, Murdoch." sympathised John. "Poor Agnes... so soon after losing her father... now this! It has been a very bad time for you both. As Sarah said, if there is anything we can do, just let us know."

After Murdoch had left, John said "We will wait a little while until Agnes gets over this, then go and see her and give her a bit of support."

"Maybe she will be upset that I am still pregnant...maybe I should keep out of the way meantime?" volunteered Sarah.

John dismissed the idea.

"Don't be daft! She knows perfectly well that you are having another baby, and if you do not go and see her, she will think you do not want to.

We will wait until Murdoch tells us that she is recovering, then we can go and pay her a visit."

"Yes, I suppose that is best." conceded Sarah.

Grandma Janet and her daughter-in-law spent quite a lot of time together chatting about all sorts of things. They enjoyed each other's company, and Janet particularly enjoyed being with her grand-children.

To her great amusement and delight, wee Murdoch was quite the little chatterbox and talked away to his grandmother all the time. Baby John was beginning to say a few words and tried to copy his brother.

The two of them were very well behaved, since their mother Sarah would stand no nonsense. Her word was law; yet she had lots of fun in her, and often spent time playing games with them. She simply adored her children.

It was quite some time before Murdoch came back again to give the family an up-date on the health of Agnes.

He told them she had improved slightly but still would not eat very much and just sat in the drawing room staring into the fire.

She still would not see her children but merely asked the governess if they were all right.

Even the staff... some of whom had known her most of her life...were very worried about her.

Cook had tried her best to tempt her with small tasty appetising amounts of her favourite food but to no avail. Agnes just picked at it then sent it back.

Conversation with her was impossible. Seemingly, nothing Murdoch said or did made any impression on her. She did not want any conversation.

He had even tried to get her to take a slight interest in the Account Books...explaining to her that he needed to pay the wages and keep the books up to date. He may as well have been talking to the wall.

She wouldn't see any of her friends. When she was told that *Miss* or *Mrs Whoever* was there to see her, she would tell them to go away; she did not want to see anyone.

Murdoch was at his wit's end and didn't know what to do.

Sarah listened to his woes then asked:

"Do you want me to go and see her? Maybe she would see me, being that I am a relative? What do you think, Murdoch?"

"If you would be willing to give it a try, I would be much obliged. I think we have to try anything to get her out of this state she has got herself into. She doesn't even cry any more... In fact - I think if she did it would help."

Sarah did not hesitate;

"I will come with you right now. I will get Cook or Annie to take the boys to their grandmother. She will be more than happy to look after them. Whoever takes them can also explain to Grandma Munro where I have gone and that I will collect them as soon as I get back" Turning to her husband she asked:

"John, will you come also?" Adding; "If it is not convenient to you at the moment, send James for me in about two hours."

John felt his brother's anguish.

"Of course I will come with you... and keep Murdoch company for a while. I will see if I can help with the books while I am there."

Having arranged for the care of the children, the three of them departed for *Eastfield*.... Murdoch in his own trap and John and Sarah in theirs.

On arrival, Sarah told the girl that she was here to see Mrs. Munro. "I will tell her, madam, but I do not think she will see you. She is not seeing anyone these days."

"We will see about that", said Sarah firmly; determined she was going in there to see Agnes by hook or by crook.

Predictably; the girl came back saying that Mrs. Munro would not see her today.

"Fine!" exclaimed Sarah. "Is she in the drawing room?" "Yes, madam, she is."

"Right, then I will just go in and see her myself. I am not taking no for an answer."

With that remark, Sarah boldly swept her way into the drawing room, closing the door behind her.

"Hello, Agnes!" Emphasising her words, she stated: "*I* decided *I* wanted to see *you* and *I* am not about to be put off.

What is the matter with you? Where has your spirit gone?" continuing..." This is not the Agnes I know.

I am told the Doctors say your health has improved a lot and that you should now be in much better health than of late. So tell me, why are you sitting here day after day, worrying everyone in this house?" Not waiting for an answer - she continued...

"Cook and all the servants are extremely worried about you, Murdoch is at his wit's end and your children are wondering why their mother does not wish to see them any more. This is just being utterly selfish and not like you at all." Sarah had to draw a big breath at this point.

Agnes looked at her in bewilderment. *How dare anyone speak to her like that?* Finally she spoke:

"You have no idea what I have been through, have you? I have lost my father and a baby within a short space of time. It has been agony for me and I sometimes feel I wish I was dead."

Sarah's Irish *dander* was up. She was not going to be fobbed-off with excuses. She knew instinctively that in this case, to be cruel was most certainly going to be kind. Closing her eyes briefly she opened them and let them flash at her sister- in-law... a daunting sight!

"If I am not wrong, you love your husband and children very much yet you are putting them through this torture. That is not fair. None of this is Murdoch's fault but you are acting as if it were. Other women have lost babies and got over it. You will just have to do the same.

As for your father... you were lucky to have him so long. Even when you married, you were still able to stay here and be with him. That was lucky in itself. Do you think for one minute that he would want to see you like this? I think not. My guess is; he would want to see you happy with your husband and children as you all were when he was still alive taking care of the farm's books, the way you always have done. There now, I have said it! So Agnes; give yourself a shake and think about what I have said."

Agnes had been sitting there apparently not listening to her. Suddenly, she burst into tears and cried and cried uncontrollably.

Sarah was taken completely by surprise at this outburst of anguish. All she could do was put her arms round her sister-in-law in a tight hug and let the poor woman's tears flow. This was just what Agnes needed to let all her grief come out.

Eventually, Agnes stopped - dried her eyes and looked up at Sarah.

"I know that all of what you have said is true... I suppose I *am* being selfish, I have just felt so miserable and had no-one to talk to about it. A man does not understand and all the friends I have are casual.

They would never have burst in here and said the things you did. Perhaps I needed that." She continued: "Thank you for that Sarah; I promise you, I *will* try to get better for everyone's sake, but it will take time, I think."

Sarah felt elated. Obviously her outspokenness had had the desired effect. She offered a little advice.

"Every day you will feel a little better and brighter, but you have to make the effort yourself and you also have to start eating better again. Cook has been trying hard to please you and is so disappointed when you send her offerings back. She feels she is failing you, so please do make an effort... just a little more each day ... You will feel much stronger if you do." "Thank you again Sarah for coming here to see me. It took a lot of courage for you to say what you said to me today."

"I only want to help you Agnes. You have been so kind to us, so I felt I had to try and make you see sense.

Take your time getting better, there is no rush... just a little bit more each day will do the trick. I will leave you now; you must be tired after listening to my tirade!"...This said with a little chuckle... trying to put a little lightness into the situation.

She finished with..." I will come back again another day and I WILL expect to see a little improvement in you. Just let the tears flow as often as you feel like it, it will do you good."

Sarah then left the room... feeling almost drained herself. *What a cheek!* She thought, *bursting in like that*, but it seemed to have worked and shaken her sister-in-law up a bit. Hopefully she would rally and think about what Sarah had just said.

That particular summer had been a bumper year for the crops. The weather had been extremely kind, with just the right amount of sunshine and rain. All the farms in the area had done very well and profits had been made.

The Munro farms had the added advantage of having the quarry, which was doing great business. John had talked to his father about the quarry manager. They decided that in Murdoch Junior's absence, they would leave things as they were meantime. With Agnes being ill, Murdoch had enough on his plate to worry about. There was little doubt that the quarry manager knew his trade very well, so they concluded they would *let sleeping dogs lie.*

Mr. McLeod had paid his bills promptly for each consignment of stone, so things were going very well.

Eventually there was better news came Eastfield.

Agnes had improved quite considerably and was now spending a little time each day getting the books in order.

Chapter 19

Sarah was beside herself with excitement. Christmas would soon be upon them and she planned that this one was going to be a great one for everyone. This was the first time she would have the money to arrange a few presents and have a nice Christmas dinner.

She was very careful about the presents she bought. She and John had worked hard and were accustomed to being very thrifty as far as money was concerned, so she was not about to start throwing it around just because they had more in the bank than she would ever have thought possible.

The weather steadily turned colder and then the snow came. The children had great fun playing in it with Ben, the dog.

The snow lasted until Christmas and although it was very cold, the countryside looked beautiful in its silent white mantle.

Then the wonderful Christmas Day Sarah had planned for finally arrived.

All the family including Grandpa Murdoch, Grandma Janet and Dugald gathered together round the big dining room table. Everything transpired exactly as Sarah had planned it and they all had a lovely time.

Sarah had told the staff that as soon as the family had been served the last course, they were all to go into the kitchen and have their Christmas dinner. She told Cook that she and her husband, John the ploughman and their son Davie were also to join the rest of the staff in the kitchen.

Kate and her husband Douglas, the farm manager, would not be present. They had gone to spend Christmas day with their married daughter, who lived in the village.

Sarah had finished her orders by telling her staff... "Have some time off to yourselves and enjoy your Christmas dinner. Dishes can wait, I think, do not you?"

What she did not tell them was that she and John, and John's Mother and Father had decided to give the staff a little surprise!

As soon as Annie had served the last plateful and the dining room door closed behind her, the four of them quickly got up and donned coloured party hats which they had hidden. Then they went out the dining room door into the hall then out the front door and round to the back of the house. Dugald volunteered to keep the children amused while the others were away.

At the back of the house, Sarah looked through the kitchen window and spied Cook in the pantry, just inside the kitchen door. Quietly, she opened the back door, but not quietly enough. Cook turned round and saw her and was about to speak when Sarah - with a broad smile - lifted her index finger to her lips indicating be quiet. Cook instantly knew some fun was at hand and obeyed.

Sarah whispered in her ear...

"Away you go through and join the others at the table. It is our turn to serve all of *you* at table. This is our way of saying *thank you* for all your hard work this last year. Now away with you and I will hear no argument."

When the Master, his wife and the elder Munros - all wearing party hats and aprons - marched into the kitchen, the variety of expressions on the faces of the staff members round that kitchen table were a joy to behold. It would be a story told with relish round the local neighbourhood for many a year to come.

After the first shock of amazement, the Master and Mistress proceeded to dish up and serve the various courses much to the delight of the staff. This had never happened to any of them before and was such a treat!

After Christmas was over, Sarah said to John "I think we should take the children and pay a visit to where we met at *Kirkland*. Cook and the girls there were ever so kind to us in many ways and I promised them that one day, I would come back and see them. Would you agree with that?"

"If that is what you want to do, then that is what we will do." answered her husband. "The children would love to go in the trap for an outing and the pony could do with some exercise anyway." And so it was arranged!

Sarah had bought a few very small items to take to them and so, one bright morning they set off.

When they reached *Kirkland* - the Lennox farm - Jean saw them arriving. With squeals of delight, she came rushing up and gave Sarah a big hug. This was followed smartly by Lizzie who was right on Jean's tail.

Cook came to the door to see what all the fuss was about; then her face broke into a big smile when she saw who the visitors were.

"Well, if it is not the toffs arriving with their pony and trap." she exclaimed. "Come here both of you *and* the children and give old Cook a big hug!"

"My how the boys have grown in the short time you have been away." observed Jean with a laugh "Murdoch is a big lad now, isn't he? And just look at baby John, quite the little boy and not a *baby* anymore."

Sarah proudly showed off her brood.

"John's two now and Murdoch is four... and before you say it...I suppose you will have noticed I am pregnant once again." adding. "It would be nice if it was a girl this time."

"Come into the kitchen and get warm." invited Cook. "It is freezing out here. You can tell us all your news in comfort."

They all trooped into the warm kitchen and sat down. "So where is Catherine today" asked Sarah.

"This is her day off; she will be so sorry to have missed you. She has gone to visit a friend" said Cook.

"We brought a small present for each of you including Catherine, so you can give it to her tomorrow.' Sarah said; handing the presents round to Jean, Lizzie and Cook.

"Och you shouldn't have gone to all that expense!" exclaimed Cook. "but we thank you for your kind thought."

"I think I will take the children round to see James and the horses and let you women gossip for awhile" said John. He did not want to sit there and listen to all the tittle tattle of four women and he knew the boys would get restless so he took his leave saying he would be back shortly.

John stayed out of the way as long as possible, taking the opportunity to have a great, long conversation with James. They had plenty of time to talk since there was nothing much to do at this time of year until after New Year when, weather permitting, the ploughing would start.

James was delighted to see his old work mate.

"So, John; how are you finding managing a farm instead of working on it? Big difference, I would think?"

"It certainly is, James, but I think I have got it under control now. The biggest problem was doing the books, but with the help of my sister-in- law, I have managed to get the hang of that too."

They chatted on for quite a while, and James put the boys up on the back of one of the Clydesdales. Murdoch thought this was brilliant but wee John was a bit apprehensive and started to cry, so his father lifted him down again.

"I have a dog at our house" volunteered Murdoch.

"Do you really?" asked James, "and what do you call this dog?" "Ben" was the short reply.

"What kind of dog is he, do you know?"

"What kind of dog is Ben, father?" asked the little boy.

John smiled. "He is a Collie and a very good dog too, isn't he?" "Yes, he is my friend." was the solemn reply.

The two friends continued pleasantries and resurrecting old stories for a little longer, and then John decided it was time to go. He said his goodbyes to James and went off to find Sarah. He knew full well she would have stayed there all day talking, but he wanted to get home before the midday meal.

Even before he arrived back at the kitchen, he could tell by the giggles and shrieks of female laughter that the girls were having a great time. No doubt Sarah was passing on some of the funny occurrences at home. Sure enough, he found her holding court ... talking ten-to-the-dozen.

His news that he wished to leave was received with protests... could they not stay a little longer?

Regretfully Sarah had to agree with John. She knew he would not have cut short the visit without reason. And so they got ready to leave for home.

More hugs were of course the order of the day with a promise from Sarah that she would come back soon and that maybe they could come over to see her in her new house since she would love to show it to them.

Ploughing began on all the farms after New Year and the ritual of farm life started all over again.

Spring came quite early and the plants in Sarah's garden started to show their heads above the soil. It also brought the arrival of a new wee human being – the daughter that Sarah had hoped for.

Again Sarah had a pretty easy time of it and was up and about in no time at all. At least she did not have to go back to work.

John was completely enamoured with his little daughter and wanted to call her Sarah after her lovely mother. After all, his first born had been called after his father, and their second son was called after himself, so he reckoned this first daughter should be called after her mother. He did not want her called Susan after Sarah's mother, which was the usual way. He did not like the name. On the other hand, Sarah wanted to call her Janet after John's mother, but he went against this, saying that it would mean that all the children would be called after folk on *his* side of the family. So Sarah it was.

Little Sarah was a pretty little baby and her brothers thought she was just like a wee doll.

Time rolled on. The farms were all doing well. The quarry, which was a big money maker, was also doing extremely well but John and his father felt they needed to know more about the business. They approached the manager and told him they wanted to know all about the running of the quarry, in particular, the different kinds of stone and how certain pieces of stone were cut.

The manager was not a bit pleased. The quarry was *his* baby and he didn't want to share it with anyone. However, he did as he was told and informed them as briefly as possible about the running of things. However, as a result of the man's intransigence, they were left with no alternative but to go and talk to the other quarry employees...the men who actually worked the stone. They were far more cooperative, and like most working people: they were only too eager to talk about their work. They gave their employers lots of very useful, detailed information - information which John and his father stored in their heads for future reference.

Eighteen months after little Sarah was born; another daughter was born to Sarah and John. This time, they agreed upon the name of Janet for their new bundle of joy.

Grandma Janet was delighted to have her precious new granddaughter named after her.

John and Sarah's family was growing quite rapidly now; two boys and two girls.

As for Murdoch and Agnes... their life was back to normal. Agnes was in good health, but no more pregnancies occurred.

Their social life of entertaining and being entertained was pretty hectic. Their children now had a tutor to teach them to read and write.

Although young; their daughter Agnes was a clever little girl and had no trouble keeping up with her brother who was two years her senior.

As well as his parents and other brother, Murdoch had visited John and Sarah a few times. They in turn, had gone occasionally to see him and *his* family but they still felt like visitors rather than kin-folk.

Young brother Dugald had met a nice girl and was *walking out* with her whenever they could meet.

Sarah was really intrigued by this romance and pestered her husband to do some investigating on her behalf. She could not bring herself to ask Dugald outright but her woman's curiosity would not be satisfied until she knew the full story. John promised to find out all he could.

An opportunity to do so arose fairly soon after; when the brothers met at their father's house. John opened the conversation, casually, or so he thought.

"That seems a nice lass you have taken up with brother. You have been seeing quite a lot of her these past weeks. When do we get to meet her?"

Dugald suddenly found something in the distance to take his attention and did not reply. John tried again.

"So, Dugald, do you have some plan in mind then, or is this just a casual friendship? If you say it is, then I won't believe you. It has been going on too long. So what is in mind?" enquired John.

Dugald blushed.

"Not that is any of your business, big brother, but we do not have anything in mind as yet.

I will let you know in good time if there are any plans, never fear."

He was not about to tell John anything at this stage. His parents did not ask questions, so why should his brother who was just being nosey!

Murdoch had been thinking that it was time he employed a farm manager at *Eastfield*. He felt it was not quite right for him to be the owner, or part owner with his wife, and also be the manager. It would give him some spare time, which seemed to be in short supply. He broached the idea to his wife,

"I was thinking of hiring a farm manager to run the place, Agnes... giving me more time to spend at home with you and the children. Would you agree to that?"

"Of course!" she agreed. "if that is what you want to do. My father hired a farm manager at the beginning to oversee things, so why not you? I think it is a very good idea. It is not as if we cannot afford it. Just go ahead and find someone."

Murdoch was relieved.

"I think it would be a good time to do this now before the busy time starts, so that he can get used to the work, so I will go ahead and look for someone."

He did not tell Agnes that the real reason for hiring a manger was that he felt as if he was completely abandoning his brothers and parents. He just did not have time to visit them much or keep in touch. His conscience was bothering him a bit about this.

He knew perfectly well that for some reason, they were not too comfortable visiting *Eastfield*.

It followed that if he hired a manager, he would have time to go and see John and the rest of the family while Agnes was entertaining or going to visit her friends.

While she respected the fact that they were Murdoch's relations; she would never suggest going to see them.

She had done her bit in teaching John about the books, and appreciated Sarah shaking some sense into her when she was feeling very low; there it ended. In truth - apart from her husband; she did not consider the Munro family to be of her social class and that was that. They would just not fit in with her friends.

A few days later Murdoch turned up to visit John.

John greeted him with... "Well, well, at last you have come to see us. Is everything all right at home with Agnes and the children? We were wondering how you were all getting on. I was thinking of coming to see you soon to find out if all was well. I suppose you have been busy."

Murdoch did not miss the slight sarcasm in John's voice.

"It cuts both ways, big brother, and I do not have a farm manager to run things as you do, so I am always very busy."

"You are forgiven" said John laughing, "and take the frown off your face, it doesn't suit you!" he teased.

"You are all well I hope and mother, father and Dugald also?" asked Murdoch.

"Yes, they are fine and working hard. You know of course that Sarah had another daughter and we are calling her Janet after mother. She is a sweet wee thing, and little Sarah and the boys are thrilled with her. Come on in and let us go into the study and have some proper conversation. You can tell me how everything is with you and Agnes and I will give you all our news. We have lots to catch up on."

The brothers chatted for a long time - catching up on all the latest events that had been happening in their lives.

"Where are Sarah and the children today?" Murdoch asked.

"She took them and Ben to see mother and father for the afternoon. Mother loves to see the little ones."

"Who's Ben?" Murdoch enquired.

"Not a who but a *what!* Ben is the dog. You will remember - he was Edward's dog, so we kept him and he is now wee Murdoch's shadow. Where he goes, Ben will be beside him.

"I didn't see him the last time I was here, maybe he was outside then."

The two brothers then discussed the quarry.

John told Murdoch that he and their father had decided that since the manager certainly knew the business they would leave him in his post in the meantime. He also told him about their fact finding trip to find out in detail how the place was run and that this was done with a view to eventually taking over the running of the place. John hastened to explain; that at the time this was going on, they had thought Murdoch had too many worries already so didn't want to add to them.

Murdoch had been listening intently. Rather than being peeved at his exclusion from the quarry discussions - he made a suggestion

"I came up with a thought recently and made some enquiries about it. It was to do with grindstones... you know...sharpening stones! I had the idea that if we had the proper kind of stone in the quarry...why not sell some of it as grindstone? After all, lots of it is used for sharpening tools and knives. There must be a huge market for it. I have some contacts that could possibly do business with us. What do you think? Would you be interested in setting up some kind of outlet for this? It would be another way to make more money and I could become the merchant for it. Besides, I will have time to devote to it now that I have decided to get a farm manager to run the farm. Such an enterprise …marketing and selling grindstone would certainly add another string to our bow, and generate more income for us."

"That sounds like a good idea to me, Murdoch, we will talk to father about it when we go to *Oatlands*"

They decided there and then to go over there and see their mother, father, and wee brother Dugald.

On the way over, they discussed their young brother Dugald.

"Dugald is walking out with a very nice girl from the village…I was teasing him the other day about his relationship with her. I was asking him: *is this a serious affair or what.* He would not tell me."

"Time he had a nice girl and got married, do not you think?" asked Murdoch.

"I suppose it is up to him, he is old enough anyway.

There is plenty of room at the farm for them to have accommodation there, if that is what they would want. There are no farm cottages on that farm."

The boys, little Sarah and the dog were all outside playing when John and Murdoch arrived.

The boys were happy to see Uncle Murdo, as they called him, but little Sarah ran into the house for her mother.

In less than a moment, Sarah senior and her mother- in law came hurrying out to see the men-folk.

Murdoch thought his mother was looking really well and the lines of worry and hard work had left her face. She looked far younger than when she had arrived here and also had the appearance of being completely calm and happy. She had a nice home and money to spend without having to scrimp. Life had taken a wonderful turn for her.

Sarah was looking blooming and healthy, content and happy too. After hugs were shared, and questions asked as to Agnes and the children, Murdoch joked…

"You have lovely children Sarah, the girls look like you; unfortunately the boys look like their father!"

"If they grow up to be as good a man as their father, I will be well pleased" answered Sarah. "But perhaps they *could* be better looking, do not you think?" she laughingly teased.

"They couldn't possibly be more handsome than their father!" John retorted with pseudo solemn certainty. Having said that, he went away to look for his father and Dugald; hoping they could both take a little time off work to come and see Murdoch.

Grandpa Murdoch was pleased to learn that his son Murdoch had come to see them. It had been some time since they had been in each other's company.

On the other hand, Dugald decided to keep working. He wasn't particularly interested whether he saw his brother or not.

He felt that Murdoch had become a bit of a snob, and did not feel comfortable in his house or with his wife.

His Sister-in-Law was polite enough to him but he had the distinct feeling that as Murdoch's family, he and they were tolerated rather than welcomed.

Being able to see the house from where he was working: he would wait until he saw them as they were leaving. Then, he would hurry over and say hello. If he did not do so, his mother would think he was being very bad mannered by not appearing - despite knowing they were there.

Chapter 20

Things were going very well for all three farms. They were making good profits.

The quarry was also making money on a grand scale. More large houses were being built in the Lenzie area and demand for stone to build them increased almost daily.

Mr. McLeod the Builder was a good customer. He, in particular, ordered a lot of stone and more to the point; paid on time, which was a God- send.

As promised; Murdoch, through his various contacts, had investigated the possibilities for a grindstone outlet and was pleased to learn that there was a good market for them. He consulted with John and his father and they decided to go ahead and set-up a business making and selling grindstones of all shapes and sizes.

The Quarry Manager was not a bit pleased about this, since it meant more work for him and his men. He moaned about it at every opportunity. However; Grandpa Murdoch had no intention of letting this *upstart* -as he liked to call him - brow beat him or get the better of him in any way. Old Munro had a very strong will and a temper to go with it, and laid-down the law as he saw it. As far as he was concerned; this was the way things were to be! It was the Munro quarry and not the property of manager McLachlan!

There was dreadful animosity between these two men on several occasions, John had had to calm things down between them.

Since his father had accumulated a great deal of quarry information in the previous two years; John hoped this unpleasant character would decide to leave, and then his father could take over as Quarry Manager. He mentioned this casually to his mother. However, she was not too pleased about the idea at all.

She felt that her husband would be trying to do too much. Running the farm took up most of his time and he was not getting any younger. She spoke of her fears to John and Dugald, so John suggested a compromise.

If his father took on the quarry, which he seemed hell bent on doing anyway... and Dugald took on the management of the farm. Then they could employ someone else to take Dugald's place.

This arrangement seemed to ease Janet's mind while Dugald quite liked the idea of becoming a *manager. However...* they still had one major hurdle – Maclachlan! How to be rid of him?

Shortly after, the matter was completely taken out of their hands.

Cook approached Sarah one morning.

"I am a bit worried about Annie." she said. "She is not her usual self at all and I have asked her if there is anything wrong, but she just hangs her head and says nothing. On several occasions, I have tried in every way I know how to find what is wrong. Kate has tried her best too but we cannot get anything out of her. I thought you should know, and that maybe she will speak to you."

"You were quite right to tell me Cook. I do not want any of the staff unhappy or feel there is a problem they cannot share. I will speak to her and see if I can find out what the problem is."

Later that day Sarah asked Annie to come and see her in the drawing room. asked.

"How are you Annie and are you happy working here? Sarah "Oh yes, madam, I like it very much thank you."

"Cook tells me you have not been yourself of late. Is something bothering you? If so, I would like to help you if I can. Would you like to tell me what is amiss?"

Annie cast her eyes down and carefully studied the area of floor directly in front of her. Then she answered reluctantly.

"Not really, madam, I do not want to get anyone into trouble." "Now, what exactly do you mean by that, Annie?

The girl hesitated for a long time before she answered. "I would rather not say if it is all right by you madam."

"Oh no! It is not all right by me young lady. You *will* tell me, Annie. Has someone here been bothering you in some way, because if they have, I need to know?"

Annie's study of the floor became intense. Her face flushed and turned scarlet to the roots of her hair. A single fat tear began to make its way from the corner of her right eye down her scarlet cheek.

Sarah's heart filled with pity for the poor wee thing – "come on now lass" she said gently, "let me share your problem."

Annie let go with a great sob -

"It was the quarry manager, madam, he was bothering me." "How exactly do you mean *bothering* you?"

"I was outside one night and passing the big barn when he came out and pulled me into the barn. He tried to take my clothes off, but I managed to get away from him and ran back to the house. He shouted after me that he would get me one of these days. I think he had been drinking, madam."

"How long ago was this and why did you not tell someone?"

"I was frightened of him and I thought he would say I was lying and I would get fired."

"If anyone gets fired here it will not be you Annie, so never fear. I will get the master to deal with this. That is all; just go back to your duties."

Sarah was furious and had no doubts whatever that Annie was telling the truth. She had heard John and his father discussing the Quarry Master before and knew the man was not at all liked. Later, she spoke to John about it. His first question was if she was sure that Annie was telling the truth.

"Absolutely, John, I have no doubts that she was, and I am sure Cook would back me in that. Annie is a good girl, I cannot see any reason why she would come up with a story like that. I would believe her before I would believe that man."

"Fine! Leave it with me and I will deal with it." said John grim-faced, adding; "He will probably deny that he touched the girl."

John carefully thought about what he had been told, and how he would handle the problem.

He decided not to tell his father, because Grandpa Murdoch would probably lose his temper and want to hit the man.

Without doubt, Neil McLachlan would deny Annie's story; even that such a thing had ever taken place. It really was the man's word against that of the girl.

However, Sarah was adamant that Annie was telling the truth and John would not be surprised if she were. He would have to tread carefully and not rashly accuse McLachlan of molesting the young girl. He therefore made his way to the quarry, feeling nothing but smoldering anger. He found McLachlan talking to the men.

"I want to talk to you in private up at your office." said John, not waiting for a reply, but turning and marching off in that direction. McLachlan had no option but to follow on behind.

Entering the tiny office, John turned to face the man.

"Shut the door behind you." he ordered brusquely, then got straight to the point.

"I have heard that you molested our young serving girl, Annie, a few nights ago.'

"Lies, all lies, I never touched the girl. Prove it." blustered the man. John pressed on;

"She says you pulled her into the barn and tried to undress her.

Fortunately for her, she escaped from you. What do you have to say about that?"

"She is a lying little tramp and is just asking for a man to get her; flaunting herself the way she does. Are you surprised I took a fancy to her?"

This last answer from Mclachlan was more or less an admission of guilt. John was furious with him. He continued.

"That is exactly what I expected you to say; but Annie is no liar and I would take her word before I would take yours.

There is no way I will tolerate such behaviour from any member of staff - particularly a senior member. You are dismissed! Collect any belongings you have here then come to the house and I will pay you the wages you are due."

Having dealt with the Quarry Manager, John then headed back for the house and looked at the books to see how much pay was due to McLachlan. By the time the man arrived, he would have the exact amount ready to be paid to him.

Before this, he had gone into the kitchen and told Annie to stay there and not to come out until he said so. Cook, witnessing all the goings-on, thought... *All very mysterious. What is happening here?* But she too cautioned Annie to stay put. So to keep the girl occupied, she gave her some extra dishes to wash.

When McLachlan finally arrived at the house carrying his worldly possessions, John paid the money due to him and told him to clear off. He took great satisfaction in telling the man:

"Get out of here and do not come back!"

Once he knew the man was well clear of the house. John went into the kitchen and told Annie all was now well and that she need have no more fears... McLachlan had gone!

Naturally, Cook was filled with curiosity and asked Annie what it was all about. The latter, being so relieved that the man had gone and that she need have no more fears concerning him; then told her the whole story

Later on that day, when Annie saw Sarah, she thanked her for believing her.

Sarah liked the girl. She reminded her of the days when *she* was in the same position with no relatives near at hand.

Annie's mother, father and two brothers worked in the coal mines, but her mother had been adamant! She wanted something better for her girl Annabella. The girl was the only daughter she had left...the only girl who had survived all the childhood ailments. Annabella was not going to be allowed to follow in her mother's footsteps. The coal mines were an horrendous way to earn a living - so filthy, and such hard work.

Fortunately, when her daughter was ready to go to work, the woman had heard that Mr. Edward Munro of *Westcroft* was looking for a girl to work in the Big House. So she got Annabella dressed up as best she could and sent her off with one of her brothers to see Mr. Munro. Luckily the girl was hired on the spot - her mother was ever so thankful!

Annie, as she preferred to be called, was a very good worker. Though quiet, shy and rather naïve; she was a well mannered efficient, very polite and respectful girl. Above all, she loved children and was at her happiest when the mistress asked her and Cook to look after the wee ones for a little while.

She was very good with children and in turn, the children thought Annie was wonderful. To them, when she played with them, she wasn't really an adult.

Annie really did enjoy being in this house, and would have been devastated if the mistress had not believed her story about the Quarry Manager and asked her to go. What would she have done? Her only alternative would have been to go back to her parents and probably get a job at the coal face. It didn't bear thinking about.

Following the Quarry master's sudden departure, John went to see his father and give him the good news.

Grandpa Murdoch was delighted. Now he could do his "thing" and run the quarry himself... the way he wanted to.

When Janet heard the news, she too, was delighted. Now her husband might stop moaning about that Quarry Manager and do what he had wanted to do all along. He really could be quite trying at times... so impatient and quite a temper to go with it. Maybe now he would be happy!

It followed, that as planned, Grandpa Murdoch promoted Dugald to farm manager and hired another hand on a permanent basis to take his youngest son's place. Things were working out nicely.

Sarah was pregnant yet again! At the same time, word came from Murdoch that Agnes was also pregnant.

Four years had passed since Agnes had miscarried. At that time, they had thought she would never conceive again. This time; Murdoch hoped she would keep well throughout the pregnancy and birth.

When Agnes told him she was pregnant, he was pleased; he would love to have more children. On the other hand, if it meant her being ill again, would it be worth it?

However, when Murdoch heard his brother's news about Sarah's latest pregnancy, he thought to himself; *Sarah has already produced four children without complications now she is pregnant again! It is not fair! If only Agnes would be well this time... then maybe we will have more children. Wait and see and say a little prayer!*

Meanwhile; Sarah was delighted to be having another baby. She loved her children and delighted in every moment she spent with them.

Little Murdoch now had a tutor and was doing very well. He was a clever boy with a very enquiring mind and took a great interest in his lessons. His wee bother John would sometimes come into the room during a lesson and want to know what they were doing.

Although very young, wee John was beginning to take an interest in what his big brother was up to. John and Sarah noticed this and decided that he too should start learning ... but they would not force him into it. He would only be allowed to join in the lessons if he really wanted to.

As for mummy Sarah and her reading and writing lessons; these had completely fallen by the wayside. There never seemed to be enough time. She would occasionally practice her letters and words, but had no real interest in the subject. She had thought she might join in the class with little Murdoch and learn along with him, but changed her mind. It would be rather demeaning on her part.

On the other hand, the time would soon come when her little son would know more than she did. She didn't like the idea of such a thing therefore she was spurred on to take up her lessons once again and asked John to help her. He had been too busy to notice that Sarah had abandoned her lessons and felt guilty at neglecting her. When she raised the question again, he admired her for wanting to make the effort.

And so it was that they closeted themselves in the drawing room every evening after dinner and Sarah resumed her lessons with great determination. She worked very hard and learned quickly. Her goal was to steal a march on her little son. Her aim was to be able to answer questions he might have concerning specific words in any book he was reading. So she thought; *get the head down Sarah and learn quickly.*

Chapter 21

 urdoch had found quite a number of outlets for the sale of grindstones, and was making extra money from his new enterprise. He had employed a good Farm Manager, thus allowing him more time to spare for this extra activity.

As a bonus, the arrangement gave him more time to spend with Agnes.

She had kept reasonably well during her pregnancy, so that too was a positive development. However, he remained very apprehensive about the forthcoming birth...constantly assured his wife that: *things will be fine since you are in much better health than the previous time.* Inwardly, he hoped that would be the case.

Sarah eventually gave birth to *her* next baby. The birth was just as quick and as easy as all the previous ones.

The new arrival was another fine baby daughter... to be named *Susanna*.

The parents had argued about a choice of name. Sarah wanted to name the little girl after *her* mother... protesting that it wasn't fair that all her children, except little Sarah, had Munro family Christian names. She wanted to break from this by naming this latest girl child Susan. Since John did not like the name Susan; they compromised and called the little mite Susanna. That kept everyone happy.

Murdoch's wife Agnes finally gave birth to her third child and produced a fine healthy baby boy.

Unlike Sarah she did not have an easy time. Her baby was born after a great deal of effort and ordeal. Consequently, she was not too well after it. Nevertheless, she was glad when it was all over. It took time for her to recover, but was mighty pleased with her new baby.

They decided to name the baby *John,* after her father.

Agnes quietly wished her father had survived to see this new little boy who bore his name.

As for her other children: little Agnes, who was now six years old, was thrilled with her tiny new little brother and simply adored him. Her older brother Murdoch was not the least bit interested in this latest addition to the family. *It was just a baby - so what?*

The Scottish farming industry was now at its best - better than it had been for many-a-year.

As with Glasgow; the population in the area around the Munro farms was growing. Therefore demand for food was growing accordingly. All spare ground was turned over and utilised for growing. Things were moving along very nicely.

Sarah was delighted that she now had extra money to buy most things that she wanted. She had nice dresses - the children were well dressed and shod - *everything in the garden was lovely.*

As for her actual gardens: they bloomed all summer; producing lots of sweet scented, colourful flowers.

She was a very contented woman.

John's brother, Murdoch, visited him and his parents quite often, but only once or twice did Agnes accompany him.

Once in a while, John, Sarah, Janet and Grandpa Murdoch along with the children, were invited over to *Eastfield* for afternoon tea.

During these short visits, the children of both families would play together.

Unfortunately, Agnes's son Murdoch was a horrid boy who looked down his nose at Sarah's boys...making all sorts of nasty comments to them. He was sly though, and careful to make such comments out of the earshot of his parents...otherwise he would have been severely chastised for being impolite.

On one particular occasion, one of his nasty remarks led to him being punched on the nose. With the result, he ran to his mother, wailing that *Cousin Murdoch had punched him.*

Agnes was outraged. To her, this kind of behaviour was just not acceptable.

Her husband tried to make light of it, saying in a jocular manner: "Boys will disagree about things and settle it in their own way. I remember John and I doing much the same thing when we were young." It didn't work! Agnes would not be convinced,

"It is not correct protocol to behave in this manner when you are a guest in someone's house."

John made no comment, but inwardly thought - *Oh Agnes! Relax a bit! They are just children! My dear wife really can be quite prim and stuffy at times!*

Sarah, of course, was hardly able to hide her anger. Her Murdoch should not have done that *but then...*she thought - *his cousin Murdoch probably deserved it, the little horror! This is the last time I will bring my children here!* Another thought came to mind. *Agnes's children will be old before their time. Seems to me, they are not being allowed to be children.*

After they had left for home, Sarah got hold of her son Murdoch and shook him.

"What did you think you were doing hitting cousin Murdoch like that?" she demanded.

"He pushed me down and I bumped my head and it is sore. I hate him, he is horrid."

"Well, it is very bad manners to fight when you are a visitor in somebody's house. Do not let it happen again"

"It won't, mama, it won't; because I do not want to go back there again. I do not like that place."

Sarah gave him a sharp slap on the wrist and told him not to be disrespectful. It was his uncle's house and he would go back there if he was told to!

Later that evening, when she was alone with John, she decided that brother or not, she could not keep her opinions to herself.

"Agnes is such a high and mighty person. Protocol and good manners are all very well but she puts these first in her life. Her children are like little adults, so polite and mannerly, sitting there like dolls. As for their son Murdoch; I have to say it; he is a horrible sneaky little boy and I would smack his bottom if he was mine!"

John just laughed at her and gave her a kiss and continued in a consolatory tone.

"My, my, we are all annoyed about this, are we not? Forget it my dear, it is what children do. At least my brother tried to make light of it. I think Agnes was just a bit annoyed. You know what she is like, that is her way. So be it! Let us not worry about it." With that, the subject was closed.Dugald finally announced that he and his young lady were going to be wed.

On hearing this; Sarah would love to have planned something really grand for her young brother-in-law, but it was not up to her - that was the privilege of the girl's parents.

However, Sarah's thoughts about wedding plans were shattered by Dugald's next statement.

"We do not want a big fuss so we are going to Monklands to be married there. Nell has a sister who will be happy to be her witness, and I would like you, John, to be *my* witness."

The family had already met Nell and found her to be a very likeable young girl, who they thought would make a good wife for Dugald.

John was delighted!

"Of course! I would be pleased to do that for you" Will anyone else be going to Monklands besides the four of us?" He asked this, knowing full well that Sarah would want to poke her nose in and be there too.

"No, just the four of us!" confirmed Dugald. "Afterward, we will go to Nell's house and have a small celebration there.

Of course; Sarah, mother and father will be invited." adding reluctantly; "and I suppose I will have to invite Murdoch and Agnes as well."

John knew Dugald's feeling concerning his sister-in-law. On the other hand; he was very fond of Sarah. But then - she was completely different from Agnes. However, he advised his young brother:

"Well, I think our brother would be rather insulted if you didn't invite him to your wedding, do not you?"

"I expect so." agreed Dugald reluctantly. Then... "I will let you know the arrangements as soon as I know what they will be."

The wedding between Dugald and Nell eventually took place. It was a very nice simple affair. Even Agnes - contrary to everyone's expectations - seemed to enjoy herself. Outwardly, she was polite to Nell's parents and chatted quite a lot with them. What was in her mind was anyone's guess!

After the wedding, Dugald and his bride came to live in the farmhouse with Grandpa Murdoch and Janet. They all seemed to get along together quite nicely until one day Dugald announced that he and Nell were leaving.

"I am sorry, mother and father, but we have decided to go to Glasgow. Maybe I will get some work in the new shipyards there. I have always hated farming and have only stayed here till things were going well for you both. Now that I am married and have responsibilities, I want to go and find something else to do.

Nell is in total agreement with me about this. She has never been out of this area and would like to see a bit more of the world."

Predictably, Grandpa Murdoch acted exactly as Dugald had imagined he would... the same way he had reacted to his other sons John and Murdoch when *they* told him *they* were leaving home many years previously.

"So, who's going to run the farm then? I cannot do that and run the quarry as well. I was not expecting this to happen."

"I am sorry father, you will just have to employ a Farm Manager to run it for you."

Janet stepped in at this point.

"Dugald has every right to go and find other work, Murdoch." she protested. "If he hated farming so much yet hid it, he has done well by us." Turning to her youngest son she continued....

"If things do not work out for you in Glasgow, son, you know you can always come back here."

"Will I be welcome if I did?" asked Dugald, rather tetchily.

"Of course you will lad! Never be stuck or run out of money to live. We could not stand by and see you wanting."

Dugald inwardly felt the burden of worry rising from his shoulder.

"Thank you mother" he exclaimed with obvious relief. "But father do you give us your blessing?"

His father had been listening and now felt a little ashamed of his initial reaction to the news.

"Of course I do, son! I was just rather taken aback with what you said. I never realised you hated the farming so much."

Dugald's world suddenly was a much brighter place!

Before Dugald and Nell left *Oatlands*, Sarah threw a family farewell party for them. The whole Munro family attended; Grandma and Grandpa Murdoch, Murdoch and Agnes and their children, John and Sarah and their children. Nell's parents and sister were there as well.

Between them, they had collected a sum of money which they gave the young couple to get them started.

Dugald protested that although the gift was very much appreciated; they did not need it since they had money of their own which they had saved.

Sarah brushed his protest aside

"There is nothing worse than being without money. We all know about that, so take what is offered to you and keep it safe for a time when you may need it. And furthermore; Glasgow is not so far away, so come back and see us sometime."

That was that! A few days later they left to start their new life in the big city.

Grandpa Murdoch had been lucky enough to have a good labourer permanently on the farm, therefore, he promoted him to take Dugald's place as Farm Manager

In turn - the young man in question was delighted to be promoted and proved his worth... rewarding Grandpa Murdoch's faith in him by running the place extremely well.

The following winter, Janet caught a bad cold, but refused advice to go to bed till she got better.

"I have had colds before and kept going. I will just work it off as usual, so do not pamper me please. It will go away by itself."

However, the cold did not *go* away and Janet was forced to go to bed and keep warm.

Sarah and John were worried about her, but Grandpa Murdoch told them as Janet had done: that she had had colds before and they eventually cleared up. However this time was different and the cold did not *clear up* but steadily got worse.

Days later, John was visiting his mother and noted a change in her. As he was at the door, about to take his leave, his father confessed to him.

"I do not like the look of your mother, John; I think we should get the doctor to have a look at her. She seems to be getting worse and is quite fevered. She doesn't want to eat and that is not a good sign. She is not as young as she used to be and things just do not *go away* as easily at her age."

"I think you are right father. I do not like the way she is either. I will go right now to the village and see if I can find him and ask him to come as soon as he can."

The doctor arrived later in the day. After examining Janet, he told John that he was of the opinion that his mother had developed pneumonia, and that such an ailment was very serious at her age.

"I will give her medicine and you must try to get her to eat a little and particularly to drink fluid. I will come back in two day's time to see how she is doing."

When the doctor returned, he could easily see that the medicine was not working and Janet was much worse. In fact, he knew she would not survive. Reluctantly he informed Grandpa Murdoch of his prognosis. Grandpa Murdoch was devastated, and when he gave the news to John and Sarah, they too were shocked to the core. This, they had not expected! John was first to gather his thoughts.

"I must go and get Murdoch to come immediately while mother is still conscious, so that he can speak to her. I will leave right now."

When John arrived back with Murdoch, the latter was appalled to see the condition of his mother. His immediate reaction was "We have to get in touch with Dugald. He turned to John.

"You have his address in Glasgow do you not?"

"Yes, I do," his brother replied, "but I do not know where it is in Glasgow. I am afraid to leave in case mother gets worse and I am not here." "I see your dilemma" said Murdoch. "Is there someone we could get to go and find Dugald, do you think?"

"I cannot think clearly of anything at this moment," replied John Murdoch had another idea…

"Perhaps there is some postal way we could get a message delivered to him. I will try and find out if there is, but it would need to be urgent. Better too, that someone goes and brings Dugald back here."

Murdoch stayed for a while, then left to try and think of someone he could ask to go to Glasgow and get his brother.

He eventually discovered that one of his farm hands knew Glasgow well. The man agreed that as long as he did not lose any wages, he would go there and fetch Dugald. Murdoch assured him he would not be out of pocket in any way… that he would pay for any expenses and that he would reward him with extra money over and above his wages. All he asked in return was that the man left immediately on the quest to find Dugald.

As luck would have it, there was a train leaving for Glasgow in about two hours. Murdoch gave the man Dugald's address and some money for his fares and off the man went.

Agnes was sad to hear of her Mother-in-Law's illness. She liked this kind, gentle woman and knew what her Murdoch was going through at the thought of losing his mother. She did not remember her own mother, who had died when Agnes was very young, but she knew only too well how she had felt when her father had died.

Murdoch was going back to see his mother that afternoon and Agnes decided to accompany him.

When they arrived, Murdoch carried on to visit his parents. Agnes did not go with him but went straight to John's house. She found Sarah at home.

"This is dreadful news about Grandma Munro' she began. Before she could continue, Sarah interrupted.

"Would you like to go over and see her?"

"No!" This said almost too quickly. "I do not think so. It would bring back too many memories for me."

In truth, Agnes did not like to see ill people and was afraid of catching whatever they had.

However, Sarah was made of sterner stuff. She had been taking it in turns with Kate and Annie to nurse Grandma Janet. Kate in particular, was very good with her frail patient, giving her sips of water and thin broth, as well as mopping her brow from time to time. She would sit and talk to her for a little while until she fell asleep, then afterward, just sit there quietly and think of happier times.

She was really sad to see this lovely lady so ill and fervently wished she would recover. Many a tear she had shed just sitting there in that quiet room.

On several occasions, Grandpa Murdoch would come out and in to see his wife. He just could not concentrate on anything else. His reliable Farm Manager kept the farm going, but Grandpa Murdoch hadn't been near the quarry since Janet became ill.

The chief Stone Cutter had told him not to concern himself with the work of the quarry. It would be kept running smoothly there until things at home got sorted out. Old Murdoch was satisfied. He knew that the man had been at the quarry for many years and knew his job well.

Meanwhile, Murdoch's farm hand had found his way to Dugald's Glasgow address fairly quickly, but no one was at home. He asked a neighbour if he knew where Dugald worked, but the woman could not help him. The only answer was for him to wait it out until someone appeared.

Fortunately, it wasn't too long before Nell came home from work. At first she was afraid; seeing a stranger standing at her door, but the farm hand assured her he came from the Munro farm.

The man then told her that her husband's mother was very ill and that he had been sent to fetch him back immediately.

Nell told him that Dugald would be home soon, but they would first need to find out if there was a suitable train running from Glasgow to Lenzie at night.

The man advised her that he had already made enquiries when he arrived at Glasgow earlier... he too had to get back to Kirkintilloch that night! The last train left Glasgow at 7 pm so they would have to be on it.

Nell was alarmed at the news. She knew Dugald would want to rush off immediately so she decided to go back on the train with him... arrangements for this would need to be made! However she had a guest and was neglecting him.

"You must be hungry and thirsty after your journey" she said "I have some bread, cheese and milk."

"Och do not put yourself to any trouble on my part Mrs. Munro, the master gave me some extra money for that very purpose. I have it here." "Nonsense!" exclaimed Nell. "Just put that money away in your pocket man. Sit down there, she ordered. "and I will bring you something."

When Dugald eventually arrived home, Nell told him the story, adding that she had packed a few things for both of them in a bag She also had a light meal ready for him knowing he would be hungry after the long day at work.

As soon as Dugald had eaten, the three of them immediately set-off for the station arriving there in time to catch the train to Lenzie.

On arrival at Lenzie they were surprised to see Murdoch was already at the station. He had gone there earlier and discovered there was a train arriving that night from Glasgow so had taken the chance that Dugald might be on it. He was therefore thankful to see that his brother had indeed managed to catch this last train. He was also pleased that young Nell had come with her husband.

From the station, he took them straight to his father's farm at *Oatlands*. They were shocked to see how Janet had deteriorated from the happy, healthy person they had last seen. Now they saw lying there on the bed before them; a poor, weak, helpless, frail old looking person. Janet was literally gasping for breath. She knew she was dying, but had been determined to hang on until her *baby* arrived.

And so the family sat by her bedside that night until, in the early hours of the following morning, Grandma Janet passed peacefully away.

A million tears flowed that morning. Cook, Annie, James and Kate were all so very sad to hear the news.

James took the pony and trap and fetched the doctor to verify the death and write the certificate.

Sarah was beside herself with grief. She had loved this woman who had been like a friend and mother to her. She would miss her so very badly.

Poor Grandpa Murdoch was so grief stricken and bewildered. He did not know what to do. His sweetheart, wife, mother of his children and best friend Janet was no longer there to advise him -listen to him, and look after him as she had done all those years.

Murdoch and John arranged their mother's funeral. It took place a few days later and as with all funerals... or so it seems... it was a bitterly cold day. Just to emphasise the misery of the occasion; as the mourners stood round the grave side, there were frequent flurries of snow.

Sarah tried to explain to the older children about their grandmother, but it was very difficult for such young minds to grasp it all.

A few weeks passed - Grandpa Murdoch was suffering from severe melancholy – just barely getting by without his dear Janet. He knew in himself that sooner or later he would need to set aside his grief but could not focus on the everyday things going on around him. The family was sympathetic but worried he might drift into a deeper melancholy from which he might never re-surface.

The very first signs of spring were just showing. John was visiting his father which he now did at least twice a week. He and Sarah had decided that Grandpa Munro needed to be reminded of the life he still had to live. Looking around and seeing the way things in the house were rapidly deteriorating, he decided to take the bull by the horns.... he also knew that was what Grandpa Murdoch would respond to.

"Father, you really do have to get on with life. I know it will be hard without mother, but you have responsibilities. People depend on you. You have a farm and a quarry to run and the house is being neglected. Mother would not want her lovely house to get in such a mess. You have to look at it this way; the last few years of her life were wonderful for her. Having this lovely house, some money to spend and her family round her. She was very happy here."

After a short silence and a sigh of resignation, as John knew he would; his father responded.

"I know son, I know that. It was nice we were left this place and she could have the last few years in reasonable comfort. She worked hard all the earlier years with little or no reward, except with her family. She was a good wife, and mother to you lot, and seldom complained. I am glad she was happy here. I know I have to move-on now for all the reasons you say but I cannot look after the house and all the other things I have to do.

John had a flash of inspiration...

"You say the Farm Manager you have is really good and has kept the place going well these last few weeks. Where is he living?"

"He lives in the village, but he is always here early in the morning and leaves late at night except in the winter. He tells me he is getting married soon."

John immediately pounced on this bit of intelligence.

"Now here is a perfect solution then! If he weds, he could move into the spare bedroom here at *Oatlands* and maybe his wife would like the job of running the house and doing the cooking?

With Kate coming in her usual two days to do the laundry and help with the cleaning, it would take one worry off your mind. What do you think of that idea?"

Old Murdoch raised a barrier of indignation... "You mean she would take your mother's place. I do not think so."

"For goodness sake, father!" exclaimed John with exasperation. "Of course she wouldn't take mother's place, no one could do that. The woman would merely be looking after the house and making sure you had decent meals, that is all."

Abruptly changing the subject, the older man responded with:

"I will think about that, but in the meantime, I suppose I will have to go and see what is happening with the quarry."

Later that night, when he was sitting alone, Grandpa Murdoch thought about what his son had said and suggested. He grudgingly had to admit to himself, the house really was a bit of a mess. He was no great cook.... that was woman's work! He wouldn't even allow Sarah or Kate to come and help.

He knew full well that Sarah was getting annoyed with him always refusing her help. She had frequently prepared a tempting meal for him in her own kitchen and brought it down to him at the farm, but he had refused to eat it; telling her he didn't want it and to "just take it away." Knowing his daughter-in law, he knew full well that this could not go on...one of those days she would lose her temper with him and give him a talking to.

Inwardly, he was relieved that the problem had come to the surface. However; to outwardly admit there was one was an entirely different kettle of fish!

Grandpa Murdoch took his time about considering John's plan, then, having made up his mind, asked his Farm Manager what *he* thought of the idea.

Secretly, Tom Jamieson, the young man in question, thought it was a brilliant idea. Barely able to hide his excitement, he thanked his employer profusely and said he would speak to his intended and let him know as soon as possible.

Tom's mind was racing ahead. It was only two weeks until the wedding. What a wonderful start they would have to their marriage! They would have a nice place to live free of charge and have paid jobs in the same place. What more could they ask for?

However, as well as being good at what he did, Tom was a sensible young man and knew things did not always pan out so perfectly. There would be problems. He thought of one right away: *They would be staying in the same house as the boss. Was that a good idea?*

Later Tom met with Mary, his bride-to-be, and told her of his meeting with his employer.

Mary carefully considered what was on offer before giving her opinion.

"It certainly *would* be a good situation, Tom, but I really do not think I would like to stay in the same house as Mr. Munro. We would be sleeping next door to him and spending our evenings in his company... we would have no privacy! If there had been a farm cottage available, it would be fine. Do you see my point?"

Tom felt a little deflated. He knew Mary was right, there was a lot more to be considered.

"Yes, of course, Mary; I have to say you are right. I had thought it would be a good thing for us to be working in the same place. However, I admit that I too, thought that living in the house was not such a good idea but I couldn't accept or refuse Mr. Munro's offer without first discussing it with you. Maybe we can think of something else." Inwardly he thought; *How am I going to put this diplomatically to Mr. Munro? He has been very good in promoting me to farm manager. I wonder how he 'll take our refusal? It is a good wage and I do not want to lose the job. On the other hand, Mr. Munro is a very down-to-earth man who calls a spade a spade...maybe I should just say what I think?*

Next day Tom approached Grandpa Munro and more or less told him what he and Mary were thinking. He was surprised but delighted to hear his employer's response.

"I had given this some thought myself, Tom, and I also wondered if it was a good idea. However, I would hope that this does not cause you problems, as I would hate to lose you as my manager. Perhaps we could come to some agreement?

I would be delighted to have your new wife to do the cooking and some cleaning for me on a daily basis and for you to stay on as Farm Manager. There is another lady who worked two days a week for my wife, and she helped with the cleaning and did the laundry. Perhaps she would be willing to come back under the same arrangements. She has not been back here since my wife died, so the house is not in good order the way my wife liked it." Then; changing the subject:

"Now, as to the problem concerning where you and your wife can stay: I thought I might have a cottage built near the house. This would of course take some time but until it was ready you would be welcome to stay in my house. Would that solve the problem?"

Tom was astonished with this last suggestion but was only too willing to go along with the idea.

"I am sure Mary would be very happy with that solution, Mr. Munro."

Grandpa Munro wasn't finished with the surprises:

"We have a small load of stone lying at the quarry. It was ordered and paid for some time ago, but it seems the customer who ordered it went out of business and the stone was never collected. I think there would be enough there to build your cottage. On the basis that your Mary is happy with the; arrangements: and since there is not much to do now on the farm till sowing starts in the fields I would set some of the men to work on the building your cottage right away. you might want to help out in your spare time."

"Thank you - thank you very much, Mr. Munro; that would be splendid. I will be more than willing to help with the building work" answered Tom. He could hardly wait until he could see Mary again and share this wonderful news. His heart soared! *A free place to live, two wages coming in and the two of them working on the same property. They would be off to a good start.*

Chapter 22

With all the work going on, time passed quickly. John was kept very busy, keeping his eye on what was happening on the farm as well as seeing how things were going at the quarry. His father spent most of his time there and was quite happy to let his manager run the farm.

Tom was very conscientious and worked hard. His wife, Mary, proved to be diligent in keeping the house in good order and making tasty nourishing meals for Grandpa Murdoch.

Kate was pleased to get her old job back; doing the laundry as well as helping Mary in the house.

After Dugald left, John had to take over the job of keeping his father's books. All-in-all, he had a lot to do. He liked being busy!

Sarah was pregnant yet again - she thought it was time to have another boy. Since the previous three had been girls - a boy would be nice! She was also kept busy all year round. With the children, household matters, and in the spring and summer; with her little gardens.

Murdoch would come over to see them from time to time - to find out how they were all getting on, and how his father was faring. During these visits, the brothers discussed their father... both agreed that they saw quite a difference in him of late. He had aged somewhat since their mother's death but at least he had plenty to keep him occupied and take his mind off that tragic event...which was a good thing!

Eventually, Sarah gave birth. Not the son she had hoped for but yet another daughter! As with the previous births, she was well during and after the event. Also, as before; this latest arrival was fine and healthy. She was a pretty little baby whom the smaller children thought was wonderful.

The older boys were far too busy to pay much attention to a baby. Their days were filled with learning things and running about with Ben, the dog, who still followed young Murdoch everywhere.

The Tutor was a lady from the village. Every school morning, James went to fetch her and afterward, when lessons ended at four o'clock; took her home again.

As they did not have a proper school room, the children were taught in the dining room. It did not matter to Sarah where they were taught as long as they were properly taught.

During lessons, Ben the dog would lie outside the dining room door patiently waiting for Murdoch to come out. The two of them were inseparable. Without his parent's approval, Murdoch would sneak Ben into his bedroom some nights and let the dog lie at the bottom of the bed. In the morning, before anyone found out, he would get him out of there and back down to the kitchen. No doubt - one day he would get caught and have to face his mother's wrath, but until then, he would take the chance!

Co- conspirators, Cook and Annie kept his secret!

The new baby had to have a name, but they were not sure what to call her. Sarah had a favourite Aunt in Ireland called Joan, so they decided to call the baby after her.

By this time, Sarah was beginning to think she had a large enough family, but how could she avoid having more? There was certainly one way, but obviously that was out of the question! However, there was now a three year gap between little baby Joan and Susanna, so things were slowing down! *Thank goodness,* she thought.

Agnes on the other hand, had managed to keep clear of any more babies. Perhaps she was not as fertile as Sarah? However, when baby Joan was a year old, Murdoch arrived with the news that Agnes was pregnant again.

Seemingly, she was not a bit pleased. She was feeling ill again and moaning that she did not want this baby. On hearing this news, Sarah felt a little sorry for her sister-in-law. If *she* had suffered during childbirth as had Agnes, then she too would not want another one.

The existing children of Murdoch's family were growing up. Her first born boy Murdoch Junior was now fourteen years old and much to his disgust...still being tutored.

He was a bright boy, but hated discipline, and got up to all kinds of tricks. His father tried to control him more than his mother did.

Young Murdoch was his mother's darling boy who, as far as she was concerned, could do no wrong. However, the time was fast approaching when Agnes and Murdoch would have to think about where their son was going in life. His father knew that whatever course was suggested to him, he would go against it. The boy was extremely stubborn and would make up his own mind... doing exactly what he wanted to do.

As for daughter Agnes; like her mother, she was a prim little miss... just a nice young girl of twelve who obeyed the rules and was happy with her life. Six year old John, the youngest child, had yet to shape up.

The birthing time for Agnes finally arrived. Once more, she had a very bad experience.

Eventually after many hours of exhausting and painful labour, she gave birth to a daughter. The baby was fine and healthy, but once again: Agnes was a wreck and it took quite some time for her to recover. She made up her mind that after that birth that Murdoch could go and sleep somewhere else. There was no way she was risking going through this again, not ever.

Poor Murdoch! It was not his fault that Agnes had to suffer at these times. She was not an old woman and still had a few child bearing years left to her, so her decision would make sure there would be no more children. She was lucky she had not conceived every year as some other women did!

They decided to name this new little daughter after Murdoch's mother. However, Agnes didn't like the name Janet, so they compromised... they named her Jessie.

Back then, children were not given fanciful names but were normally named after a close relative. This was the case with the Munros. Readers will have notice that up to that time: there were five Murdochs and three Johns in the Muneo family. However, in Scotland, to avoid confusion, it was common to use substitute or shorten names. The substitute name for Janet was Jessie!

Thinking ahead, Sarah approached John and asked him what he thought of her idea about asking Murdoch and Agnes and the family to dine with them around Christmas time.

"I thought you asked them before and they made excuses not to come. Are you willing to accept another rebuff?"

"I know I have asked them twice in the past and they made excuses not to come. I thought that just this one more time I would make the effort. If I am refused, I won't ask them again.

I was thinking; just for once and before your father gets any older; it would be nice for all the family to get together, I think he would enjoy seeing his other four grandchildren for a change as well as our lot. I do not know when he last saw them...they never come *here*."

John sighed in resignation.

"Well, if that is what you want to do, go ahead and ask them. They can only say no, or make some excuse. When exactly were you thinking of asking them over?"

"Perhaps the day after Christmas Day, or the day after that.

Last year was such a quiet, miserable Christmas. Only your father was with us and it was so soon after your mother's death. No one was in the mood for festivities. Your father seems to be a lot better now, that is why I thought of this plan. It would be really nice to have all the young ones together and the five adults; it would make quite a party."

"It *is* a nice idea, Sarah." said John with a trace of doubt. "There is not much to do now on the farm till sowing starts in the fields.... so I hope for your sake that they'll accept your offer."

The next time Murdoch came to see them, Sara put the idea to him. She tried to be as diplomatic as possible.

"I was just thinking Murdoch; your father is sixty-eight and getting on a bit; He seems to be much better now...but since your Mother passed away, he must get very lonely at times. I thought it would be nice for him to see all his grandchildren together around Christmas and have everyone over here for dinner. I would really like to do this, so what do you think of the idea?"

"It is a very nice idea, Sarah; I will consult with Agnes and see what she thinks. I will let you know as soon as possible, so that you can make your arrangements."

John and Sarah were going into the village a few days later, so decided to drop in on Agnes and find out if she was accepting their invitation or not.

Agnes was quite surprised to see them and welcomed them into the house. After all the usual pleasantries and protocol which Agnes seemed to have to go through, they got down to the question of whether they would be able to accept Sarah and John's invitation.

"It is a very nice invitation, and Murdoch and myself would be happy to accept. Will the day after Christmas suit you? That would be a nice time for us all to get together, do you not think?"

Sarah nearly fell off her seat. She was absolutely sure she would be refused, so this came as quite a surprise to her. Regaining her composure, she responded.

"The day after Christmas would be ideal and I am sure Grandpa Munro would be so pleased to see you all. He leads quite a lonely life now without Mrs. Munro. He occasionally accepts an invitation to dine with us but doesn't do so very often.

So that is settled then! We will look forward to seeing you all on the day in question around midday, if that suits you?"

"Yes." confirmed Agnes. "That will be fine, thank you again for asking us Sarah."

Soon after, Sarah and John continued their journey to the village. "What a surprise!" exclaimed Sarah. "I think Murdoch must have said something to Agnes that made her accept our offer, do not you think?" "I really do not care who said what to who; the fact remains that they are coming on the day you wanted them to come and everyone will have a pleasant time, that is what really matters."

John did not want to get into a discussion with Sarah about what might have been said. That was it! Subject closed!

There was a huge flurry of activity in the household. Sarah spent some time with Cook discussing menus for their own Christmas dinner and for the day after, for all the family, then she went about getting small presents for the children to lay on the table.

Cook, Annie and Kate were all kept busy with the planning of the meals. They had to remember that quite a number of the dinner guests would be children and include good things for young appetites.

James wanted to help and make himself useful, so he offered to clean the silver and any other task which needed to be done. He was so glad to have been able to stay here and was very happy. This Munro family who employed him were nice and did not make him feel a burden.

Sarah was wound up for a week before Christmas - wanting to make sure everything was perfect for the following day.

She planned to place John at the head of the table with their son Murdoch on his left. She would sit at the other end of the table with John's brother Murdoch on *her* left and his son Murdoch next to him. She knew the young Murdoch cousins did not get on very well. Keeping the two of them well apart next to their fathers would ensure harmony... at least during the meal. What happened later would remain to be seen. They were both getting a bit older, so maybe they would behave themselves.

Christmas day finally arrived, and turned-out to be as intended: as it should be... a lovely family day which included Grandpa Murdoch.

There was no rush...everything progressing nicely. However, Sarah could not relax and enjoy it for thinking about the following day. She could not stop talking about it and wondering out loud if everything had been properly prepared.

"For goodness sake, Sarah, can we not just enjoy Christmas day without you going on and on about tomorrow? Everything will be fine. I am sure Cook has it all under control. You have made sure that everything else is ready. Relax for a little while...please!"

At first, she was a bit huffed with John's words but then realised she *had* been going on about it all day. Thereafter she concentrated on enjoying her Christmas Day with the family.

The following morning, she was up and about early - THE big day arrived! She wanted to be absolutely sure that things would be ready for midday and not be rushing about at the last minute. However her worries in that direction were foundless. When she went to the dining room, she was surprised and delighted to find the dining room table was already set with all the *good* crockery, cutlery, silver and glassware. How nice it all looked. She would add some little decorations to it later...along with the presents and the names where everyone was to sit.

It transpired that Cook, Annie and James had also been up early and had got to work doing all this. They realised Sarah had been very worried about the arrangements...this was the first time she had entertained the *Other Munros* and it was so important to her that everything was just right.

They too wanted it to be a success for her sake.

She and Mr. Munro were really kind employers. Normally they did not entertain, which meant that the staff did not have to work late at night. This was indeed a special occasion to make an extra effort.

Back in the time of Mr. Edward, it had been a different story – he had frequently entertained his friends with lavish dinner parties so they- the staff - had plenty of practice!

Thus, all was in order when Murdoch, Agnes and the family arrived just after midday.

As soon as greetings had been exchanged and James had gathered heavy winter coats and hats, the family guests headed for the drawing room where an aperitif was served and pleasantries were exchanged.

The women chatted about this Christmas and Christmas times gone by, while the men, as usual, discussed work. The two young Murdochs eyed each other up like cockerels in the yard, but did not speak at all!

Agnes had brought a present for each of Sarah and John's children, who, after thanking their aunt, immediately opened them. Sarah, likewise, gave gifts to Agnes's children.

While the adults made small talk, the girls played together, with young Agnes acting the roll of governess. She was now thirteen years old and enjoyed - in her mind - her superior place as the oldest girl child.

Later in the afternoon when everyone was relaxed James announced that dinner would now be served.

By this time everyone was feeling the first pangs of hunger. The delicious aroma of food helped to ensure there were no dragging feet as they all headed for the dining room.

There were gasps and exclamations of delight when they saw the way everything had been laid out. Cook had lit candles at each end of the table and the flames from these glinted warmly from the glittering crystal and gleaming silver. The children's attention was immediately taken by the mysterious little parcels in front of each table setting.

Sarah's moment had arrived! Out of the corner of her eye she could see her sister-in-law. To her delight and gratification, she saw a look of sheer pleasure on the woman's face – truly a rare sight but a sure certain sign that all the effort put into this moment had been well worth while. Sarah made her awaited announcement.

"Now then everyone, please find your place. This is where you children can show us how well you have learned your reading lessons. Each of you has a little card with your name on it – let us see if you can find where you are supposed to sit.

With little squeals of delight, the younger ones scrambled round until they found a card with their name on it. Sarah laughed, adding; "I am sure the Mothers and Fathers will be able to find their own names, if not, one of our young scholars might like to help them!" This brought a chuckle from the adults.

In no time at all everyone was settled in their place and the meal was about to be served. Before this though, John gently struck the empty glass in front of him with his soup spoon.

"Before we enjoy the efforts of Cook and her staff, may I have everyone's attention just for a moment?"

Then, addressing Grandpa Munro, he asked: "Father, would you please do us the honour of saying Grace?"

Old Murdoch was caught unawares and responded with "I thank you son, but this is your house and your table, that honour should fall to you."

"Under normal circumstances father, that would be the case, however, this is a very special occasion. Not only is it Christmas time but it is Christmas time with all the family gathered together – just the family - and you are head of this part of the Clan Munro. Please do us, your children, and Grandchildren the honour."

Grandpa Munro was about to respond in his usual stubborn way when his second son Murdoch lent aid to his brother's plea.

"Yes father, please! We would all be honoured."

Grandpa Munro felt a great flush of pleasure as everyone tapped the table adding force to Murdoch's plea.

"Then let us pray together."

They all sat, adults and children with heads bowed, as Grandpa Murdoch said grace:

"Dear Lord, we thank you for the food we are about to share at this table. As we enjoy Thy bounty, may we be ever thankful, and forever remember those who cannot be with us at this happy time. Amen!"

The adults noted a slight tremor in the old man's voice at the last sentence. Obviously he was remembering his beloved Janet. They all repeated "Amen", with the voices of the smallest children faithfully echoing the example of their parents.

The word "amen" was the signal for cook and her staff to bring the laden plates and serve everyone.

It was a delicious meal and everyone tucked in...eating far more than they would have done normally; and since Cook had made some very special things for young tastes and appetites; even the children ate well and excelled themselves.

Throughout the meal, the young ones could hardly contain their curiosity and excitement over the mysterious little parcels in front of them and were desperate to finish eating so that they could find out what they contained.

After the meal, everyone moved back to the drawing room and chatted for a while. The children were finally able to open their presents.

"Oh it is not much" said Sarah apologetically, " just a wee extra minding!"

"Nonsense!" exclaimed Agnes. "It was very thoughtful and kind of you. I am sure the children are delighted."

"We are...we are!" they all shouted and everyone laughed.

Eventually Agnes said it was time for them to go. Her son Murdoch sighed with relief, he was bored to death - too old to be with the rest of the children, yet too young to join in the adult conversation. He was at that awkward age of being neither a child nor an adult.

James brought the overcoats and hats. As he helped Agnes into her coat, she turned to Sarah and John.

"Thank you both for having us; we have had a wonderful time. And thank you for the gifts. It was kind and thoughtful of you." Then turning to James:

"Thank you James and please pass our thanks and Christmas greetings to cook and the rest of the staff for all their hard work. They did us all proud."

John secretly thought he had never heard his sister-in-law uttering the word *thanks* so often in such a short space of time.

After everyone had left and they were alone, John turned to his wife. "Well, that seemed to be a success, do not you think? They all seemed to enjoy themselves and even the two Murdochs behaved."

Sarah was secretly very pleased with herself but hid behind modesty. In a worried tone she replied.

"Do you really think so? You do not think I overdid things a bit do you?

"Nonsense my dear! Congratulations, Sarah, you did really well. Quite the hostess indeed!

We should also be delighted with our staff. Cook, Annie and Kate certainly made a fine dinner, and served it up very nicely. As for James: he just put the finishing touches to it all. He really is so much the gentleman's gentleman!"

"Oh I know." sighed Sarah happily." It really was a very grand day indeed." She stifled a yawn and sighed again.

"You must be exhausted." John said laughing. "Did you sleep at all last night? Just as well we do not do this very often or you would be a wreck."

"I really enjoyed it, John, and yes, the staff did very well indeed. I must thank them for their efforts to make this a success. And yes, I *am* exhausted. No, I didn't sleep very well, if at all, last night. I am getting the children to bed right now, then I think I shall be following them very soon after."

Once all the children had been bedded down for the night, Sarah went to the kitchen and thanked the staff for their wonderful dinner and service. She told them she was well pleased and felt things had gone very nicely.

The staff were, in turn, delighted that she had come to thank them. It made all their work worthwhile.

Returning to the drawing room, she collapsed wearily into a fireside chair, and removed her formal shoes...her feet were killing her!

John poured them both a glass of wine and they sat for a little while, not saying much, just relaxing and unwinding. Sarah's mind wandered through the events of the day, relishing in the highlights, then tiredness won them both over and they headed upstairs for some much needed sleep.

Chapter 23

Time marched on, as time does; with many changes in the world taking place.

The farming industry had improved with new machines being developed over the years. Some years had been very profitable with good growing weather therefore crops and vegetables were in abundance. Other years however were not so good with little sunshine and a lot of rain, ruining some crops just before harvesting, but the good years made up for the bad ones.

John and Sarah were very lucky in that they still retained all the same staff from when they had first taken over the farm. Unlike many such workers, none of them had moved on. Everyone worked so well together and seemed to be happy enough with their lot. John valued the staff, therefore, as a mark of appreciation for this stable state of affairs, he would from time to time, favour them with some little extra reward.

Two years had passed since THE family Christmas dinner. At *Eastfield,* and Sunday dinner was over. The staff were clearing away the dishes when young Murdoch made an announcement. He told his parents that he had been considering his future and had decided that he wanted to go to University and study Law.

This was a huge surprise to them since he had never given any indication that he was remotely interested in the subject... or any other subject for that matter.

After the initial surprise had died down, Murdoch and Agnes expressed their absolute delight at their eldest son's news. His father was the first to speak.

"A very noble career indeed, my boy, and one that we are sure you will make a great success of. My - just think - a lawyer in our family!"

Agnes agreed wholeheartedly and gave young Murdoch a huge hug and announced...

"Tomorrow we will find out how this may be brought about."

During the next few days there was a flurry of comings and goings. The family lawyer was consulted for advice on the matter. He was able to direct them to the right people and the proper channels and in no time at all, it was arranged that a place would be available for young Murdoch at Glasgow University... the second University in Scotland and famous throughout the world.. And so, the budding lawyer set off!

Shortly after young Murdoch left for University, Agnes noticed that John, her nine year old son, was looking flushed. He had also developed a cough and was complaining of a sore throat. She felt his forehead and he was burning-up with fever. *Oh dear,* she thought, *another doze of cold!* The germ had been going the rounds of the village children and she was not really surprised that John had finally got his share of it.

"Bed and a hot drink for you young man", she ordered, and the lad was packed off to bed with a hot water bottle and given a drink of fresh hot lemon juice sweetened with two large spoonfuls of sugar. He could barely sip the drink and his mother noticed that the back of his throat was red and swollen.

The next day John was no better; in fact he seemed to be getting worse. Agnes's instincts told her this was no ordinary cold and she started to feel a deep foreboding. The doctor was sent for immediately.

"Well then Mrs. Munro, where's our little patient?"

"Upstairs in bed doctor, I thought it best to keep him warm and away from the other children."

"Very wise of you. However there are a lot of colds around. I will have a look at him and see what we can do to get him back to normal." Without waiting, the he thumped his way up the stairs to John's room - adding: "Do not bother coming up Mrs. Munro, I know the way and I will be back in a moment."

He was gone longer than Agnes had expected. Slowly her anxiety began to grow. Ten minutes later, the Doctor came down the stairs quickly.

"I will wash my hands first if I may. Is Mr. Munro about?" Now the alarm bells were ringing very loudly for Agnes.

"Yes, as a matter of fact, I see him in the yard. Why? what is the matter doctor? Why?"

"I think we should have a word about the wee lad" interrupted the doctor, "please call your husband."

When Murdoch and Agnes were seated, the doctor gave them his diagnosis. He told them that their young son had contracted Diphtheria. Both parents knew how very serious this illness was in young people at that time.

"Oh my God!" moaned Agnes. Murdoch's normally ruddy features turned grey.

"What are his chances doctor?" he asked.

"I must be honest with you both, Mr. and Mrs Munro, the boy is desperately ill. I have seen a few cases recently but these were in older children. I am afraid the outlook is not good. I am so very sorry. I will do the best I can with what I have but I have to be brutal, I do not think he will last the week."

At these last words, Agnes completely broke down and sobbed uncontrollably.

"My poor wee boy."

Murdoch was equally devastated by the doctor's report but showed no outward signs of it.

After the doctor had gone, Agnes went up to be with her son. A little later Murdoch set off for *Westcroft* to give John and Sarah the news

At Murdoch's request John and Sarah made arrangements for their own children to be looked after. Thereafter, they returned to

Eastfield with Murdoch to see how they could be of help... particularly in supporting Agnes.

Sadly, the doctor's prognosis proved only too correct; a few days later young John passed away.

It turned out to be a blessing in disguise. The lad ' s last hours were spent in agony, gasping for breath, as his throat slowly but surely closed with the swelling.

The entire Munro clan was saddened to the core by the death of one so young. Death was no stranger to them but that such a young life had been taken seemed completely unfair.

Sadly; young John would not be alone in the next world - many other children in the village had died from this same terrible disease. Agnes and many village mothers wept gallons of salt tears over the loss of these little ones.

Arrangements were made for the funeral – a day everyone thought of with empty dread. When it arrived, Agnes was understandably inconsolable. Her husband Murdoch did not show any grief. He would keep that to himself for a more appropriate time. Perhaps a premonition of what was to come?

Sarah was lucky; all her children seemed to keep healthy, but she was not complacent about this. She knew full well that disease could strike at any time, and she worried continuously about all her young ones. However, her worries were about to increase. Much to her dismay, she found that she had conceived yet again. When she was absolutely sure of it, her mind turned to the practicalities. *Oh well!* She thought, *not much I can do about it. This one had better be a boy. I have plenty of girls already.*

As with the others, Sarah's pregnancy went the full term without a hitch. In the fullness of time, this latest Munro infant was brought into the light of day and Sarah's wishes were fulfilled... this one *was* a boy! She - and particularly John - were delighted to have another son.

The problem of what to call this latest arrival taxed their minds once again. They had not given much thought about a name before the birth there was too much else to think about then. Now the moment was upon them. Sarah had had her own idea for a name but decided to pass the responsibility on to her husband.

"Now, what do we call this one, John? She asked.

"How about Dugald or Angus after my brothers?" "Yes" agreed Sarah," nice family names but which one?

She was quiet for a moment then…

"I had another thought. I was thinking it might be nice to call him Edward, after your father's cousin Edward. After all: if it hadn't been for him we wouldn't be here. How on earth would we have managed if we were still in the little cottage on the Lennox farm? Where would we have put all the children we now have? It doesn't bear thinking about."

John hardly gave time for thought and replied immediately and enthusiastically.

"You are right, as usual, my dear, we will call this little fellow Edward after our benefactor. What a good idea!"

And so, the new baby boy was named Edward… the first break in a long tradition of naming boy children in the Munro family.

Several weeks after the birth of wee Edward, James came to Sarah and asked if he might speak to her privately.

"Of course, James, you know you can speak to me any time at all. Come into the drawing room."

She sat down and asked James to sit also. When they were settled, Sarah opened the conversation

"What would you like to discuss, James?"

The manservant shifted awkwardly in his chair, gathering his thoughts, then, placing his hands in his lap, he spoke:

"As you know, madam; I have no relatives at all. I have saved quite a tidy sum of money over the years but regretfully, have no living relative to leave it to. I was thinking it would be nice if this money was split evenly among Cook, Annie and Kate.

As well as being my friends; they have been my only family for some time now. Therefore when the time comes for me to depart this world,

I would dearly wish to see them gain a little extra. Would you see that this is done on my behalf?"

Sarah remained silent for a few moments after James had spoken. Inwardly she thought; *what a thoroughly decent, nice man.* It also occurred to her that she had received the highest accolade from the man sitting in front of her in that he trusted her implicitly with his life savings and to carry out his last wishes

"Of course, James! I would be honoured and only too pleased to be of assistance in this way. I would like, though, to make a suggestion to you...I take it your savings are in a bank?

"Yes madam, in fact in the same bank used by Mr. Munro and the rest of the family."

"Splendid! exclaimed Sarah. "Obviously I will help you in every way, but I suggest you make an appointment with the manager and discuss your plans with him. He will doubtless advise you. Have you made a will containing your wishes?

"I had thought about it" admitted James. "Would *you* advise me to make one madam?"

Sarah replied instantly in level warning tones while moving her head from side to side by way of emphasis.

"Oh most certainly James! And I am sure the Bank manager will advise the same thing.

He can assist you with that. He would then retain the completed document in the Bank for safe-keeping. What is your opinion of that?"

James thought for a moment.

"You are probably correct, madam, that would seem to be the sensible thing for me to do. I will go to the bank as soon as possible and get things put in order. Thank you madam for listening to me and for your help and suggestions. I hope I have not wasted your time"

Sarah smiled broadly.

"Nonsense James! As I said at the beginning of our conversation; anytime you wish to discuss private things, I will be pleased to listen. I would also add; our conversation here today and anything else you tell me in confidence will remain private between us."

James thanked her profusely once again and went away a happy, contented man. To have had this little discussion with the Mistress had lifted a burden from his thoughts.

John's father had not been feeling very well for some time. Although he had kept it hidden from the family, he had been neglecting things and not attending to the quarry as he usually did. However, John had noticed the change in his father and questioned him about it.

Wishing to avoid sympathy, the older man told his son:

"I am getting too old for this now, so I am going to retire from being the quarry master and I would like you to take over that job. Would you do that for an old man?"

"Of course I will father! But what are you going to do with yourself all day?" John asked.

"Och! I can occupy my time very well thank you. For example, it would be nice to just while away the day - have a stroll in the countryside. Maybe go over to see Sarah and my grandchildren. Dear me! The last time I asked about your young Murdoch, he was nearly seventeen years old! I have been so busy and time has flown past. What is the boy going to do with his life?"

"To be truthful father, I have no idea, and neither does he for that matter. I do not think he has any ambition, but he may change. However your other Murdoch grandson is doing well at University and who would have ever thought *he* would have settled down and do something like learning the law? So there is hope for *our* Murdoch yet!"

"So the matter of running the quarry is settled then!" said Grandpa Murdoch, returning to the main point of the conversation. "The sooner you take over the better. I will inform the men and make everything ready for you in the Quarry office."

During the weeks and months that followed; Sarah complained that she hardly ever saw John. He was snowed-under with work! What with the quarry, the farm, and doing all the accounts for all the businesses: he didn't have a spare minute. To add to it all... people were coming to see him in increasing numbers with a view to buying grindstone. It was becoming a great profit-maker. Many of the local businesses were now ordering grindstones from the Munro Quarry for the purpose of sharpening tools...giving the Munros their business, rather than ordering from quarries further away.

The two great advantages the Munros had were - quickly filled orders and prompt delivery. These in turn gave local industries the competitive edge over their rivals. Thus, there was little or no time for a social life. Not that it mattered too much since the families seldom saw each other.

Murdoch and Agnes never asked John and Sarah to call on them or to dine with them. Sarah said not a word about this. As she had often remarked on a previous occasion... *Oh well, that is the way they are, we are not of Agnes's class and will never be invited to join their social group.* How right she had been!

Grandpa Murdoch's health continued to fail. He had lived for seventy-two years which was a remarkable achievement for the times. Anyone surviving *that* long was considered to be *ancient*.

On one occasion when visiting John, old Murdoch complained of being breathless and being tired even after a good night's sleep.

"I think all the blood in my body is gathering round my ankles." he moaned. "Just have a look at these will you." he said, raising his trouser legs.

John could hardly believe his eyes. His father's normally skinny ankles looked as if they had been stuffed full of plum pudding. The skin was purple and stretched so tight; it looked as if it might burst at any moment. John was vaguely reminded of a haggis! He called Sarah to have a look. She too was aghast at the sight.

"Dear me Grandpa Munro!" she exclaimed. "This will not do, you must go and see the doctor. No; better still," turning to her husband she continued, "John, you just get yourself down to the doctor's surgery right now and bring him back here."

In due course, the doctor arrived and despite protests from Grandpa Murdoch, insisted on examining him. Afterward he met with John.

"I am afraid it is your father's heart. At his age, it just cannot keep up with life. All the little things he is experiencing tell me that his heart is failing. I cannot cure him but rest will help. You must see that he gets plenty of it."

After the doctor had gone, John approached his father.

"I have had a word with the doctor father. He advises that you start taking things a bit easier. Rest a bit more...lie in bed a little longer in the mornings. You know...those sorts of things."

Heknew his father only too well... knew he was wasting his breath. It was all too easy to suggest such things to him but would Grandpa Murdoch take such advice? - Absolutely not! Hardly had he finished speaking when his father completely rubbished any such ideas.

"Nonsense! There is nothing much wrong with me. I am just getting to be an old worn-out man."

John thought to himself *Aye! And a stubborn old bugger at that! I will see if Sarah can work her magic on him. He usually listens to her.*

And so it was left to Sarah to see if she could persuade her father- in law to see sense.

As usual, Sarah came up with a solution. She suggested that he come and stays with them and rest in their house. That way, she could keep an eye on him. But the old boy was too crafty; he saw right through the ploy and was not having any of that. And so, he went back to the familiar surroundings of his own home. However, if he thought that would keep his relatives at bay, he was to be disappointed. Much to his annoyance, Sarah and Kate were in and out all the time. He did not hide his feelings concerning their visits and could be very bad tempered on such occasions.

One morning, a few weeks later, Sarah arrived early as usual, just to check on him and to see how her father-in-law was. She noticed immediately that he was not, as he usually was, sitting in his chair in the kitchen and that the fire had not been lit. She thought it was very strange indeed because despite warnings and the pleading of his family, he had continued to get up just after dawn. She had a look round the yard and shouted his name but got no response. She then decided to go upstairs.

On the top landing, she called out his name again, still no response. Approaching his bedroom door she knocked loudly.

"Good morning Mr. Munro – It is just me – Sarah. How are you this fine morning?" Still no response. Now alarm bells began to ring in her head. Wasting no more time she entered the room and found him; seemingly sound asleep in bed. She thought it odd he was still in bed.

"Mr Munro" she said louder this time, "*Mr. Munro.*"

Looking closer, she could not hear a sound from him, nor could she see the slightest movement. Suddenly it dawned on her. She drew her breath in a gasp of sudden panic - *He is gone – he is dead – Oh my dear Lord!* Turning, she ran from the room and almost tumbled down the stairs and out into the yard.

Leaving the front door open in her wild panic, she continued to run as fast as she could back to her own house to tell John. Even before she arrived at the door, she was shouting her husband's name – "John! – John!"

John came rushing out of the house, a look of fear and alarm on his face.

"What is the matter? What has happened to you?"

By this time, the tears were steaming down Sarah's face. She sobbed...

"Oh John! It is your father, I think he is dead." She went on, her words almost running together, "I went over this morning as usual and"

"Stop a minute" said John in a quiet voice. "Calm yourself down and tell me again, slowly this time." Sarah related what she had found.

A wave of sadness tinged with hope was John's first reaction.

Then practicality kicked-in. "Are you sure he is dead?" he asked his wife. "I am almost certain" replied Sarah.

The two of them returned to *Oatlands*.

On arrival, John told his wife to stay downstairs and he went alone up to his father's bedroom. He found the old man as Sarah had described. Then, having verified that his father had indeed passed away, he stood there for a moment looking at the mortal remains of the man he had known all his life and thought, as the tears welled up and a lump rose his throat, *How peaceful he looks.*

Back downstairs, he confirmed the sad news to Sarah. She of course, could not stop crying. Being an emotional person, she was very easily moved to tears.

On returning to *Westcroft*, they sent James for the doctor, and afterward to inform Murdoch.

After the doctor had left, John sadly remarked "Ah well Sarah! The one consolation is that he obviously died in his sleep while in his own bed." Adding "and it seemed to have been a peaceful end. He seems not to have suffered any pain. I suppose he was, after all, quite an old man. Still, he had a good life here. He is away now to join his beloved Janet." This last and final observation, of course, brought fresh floods of tears from Sarah.

On the way back from the doctor's, James had called on Murdoch and given him the sad news.

Having dropped everything he was doing, Murdoch arrived at *Westcroft* shortly after James,

John met his brother at the door. Murdoch's face was crumpled with a mixture of sorrow and disbelief. As he shrugged out of his overcoat he asked "Where is father? What happened?"

"He is still in bed over at *Oatlands*." replied John.

"Are you sure he is dead? Sometimes mistakes can be made", this last sentence said with a tinge of hope.

"We left him as we found him. I am absolutely sure Murdoch. He has no breath and is cold as marble. However, I have sent for the doctor. He should be here any time now. No doubt he will be able to tell us what happened after his examination."

The brothers consoled each other for a few minutes then pulled themselves together and turned to practicalities. Murdoch was first to think of the other members of the family.

"We better send a message to Dugald and Nell to let them know what has happened."

"Yes, of course but we should wait until the doctor has been and seen father before we do anything else. Father has to be officially examined and the cause of his death registered. We cannot make any arrangements for a funeral or anything else until this is done and a certificate issued."

"You are right!" exclaimed Murdoch. "However, one of us should eventually attend to funeral arrangements, will you attend to these, or do you want me to perform that task?"

"As I am the oldest member of the family, I think it is my duty to do so. I must say, it is not a task I view with any joy, however it must be done, but it would be a great assistance to me if you would take on this task. Ah! I see the doctor has arrived."

The brothers accompanied the doctor over to their father's farm at *Oatlands* and waited while the official examination was made. This took but a few minutes then the doctor returned.

"I am very sorry for your loss gentlemen." he told them." Your father passed away very peacefully as far as I can tell. He did not suffer," adding; "I knew this would happen sooner or later. It was his heart." He then sat down at the kitchen table - took an official looking printed sheet from his bag and began writing.

When he was finished, he stood and handed the sheet to John.

"That is a copy of the official record of my finding Mr. Munro. It will be entered into the Register for Births Deaths and Marriages for this Parish. In the meantime, you can use this to commence arrangements for the funeral. May I say once again: please accept my sincere condolences for your loss."

With that, he closed his bag and departed - leaving the brothers standing there.

After the doctor had gone, Murdoch broke the silence. His voice held a tone of decisive finality.

"Right then! I will get off now and start making arrangements for the funeral. Once I have the details, I will come back here and we can send word to brother Dugald in Glasgow. At the same time we can contact all fathers' friends and give them the news."

"Right" echoed John. "While you do that, Sarah and I will make a list of those we must contact. We will have to write to Angus and our sister Catherine in Inverness right away and let them know."

Eventually all the arrangements were made and the day of Grandpa Murdoch Munro's funeral arrived.

The brothers had discovered that their father had no close friends outside the immediate family, their house servants and other employees; consequently, very few people attended the grave-side. Just the immediate family: John, Sarah with their two oldest children, Murdoch and Agnes with their two oldest.

Dugald and Nell from Glasgow also managed to attend, as did Kate who wished to pay her last respects. She had nursed Janet and helped to look after Grandpa Murdoch.

Also in attendance was the old man's farm manager, Tom Jamieson, along with some of the senior members from the building trade.

While the adults and older children attended the graveside ceremony, Cook and Annie looked after the younger children and prepared food, tea and drinks for the return of the mourners.

The burial itself was a quiet, sad affair. Despite the sadness, everyone was glad when it was over.

Some days later - following a respectable time of mourning - Murdoch came by to speak to John about their father's farm.

"I think we need to go to the bank and see the manager there. It might be a good idea to get his opinion as to what we should do with the farm, whether to sell or rent it out."

"Yes" answered John. "We do not even know what father's wishes would have been. He never spoke of it to me. He thought he would live forever."

The next morning the brothers went to the bank and had a meeting with the manager.

After the formalities, they got down to business.

They were astounded when the Bank Manager informed them that their father had made a will. He had been quite specific as to what should happen to his property after his death.

The farmlands and house were to be sold to a farmer who would work the land. The proceeds of the sale were to be divided equally between his sons Angus, and Dugald and his daughter Catherine.

"Well, well!" exclaimed John, with not a little admiration in his voice." The sly old fox! He had it all cut and dried and never said a word to either of us. He might have been stubborn and a bit bad tempered but he was neither naive nor was he stupid, that is for certain."

"Never thought he was" said Murdoch, "but what about the quarry?"

"Oh yes!" confirmed the Bank Manager." The Quarry is also mentioned in his will. It has to remain as it is...equal shares between yourselves...his other two sons, Murdoch Munro and John Munro. May I take this opportunity to congratulate you on your good fortune?"

"Well now!" said Murdoch; it all seems very satisfactory. At least we now know exactly what to do."

John; whose mind was already directed in a practical direction, continued by asking the Bank Manger;

"Can you handle the sale of this property?"

"Certainly, if that is what you both wish. I can get things moving right away. Farmland around here is very valuable, as there is a scarcity of it."

"I presume the money in the account will be added to the money from the sale and divided among our brothers and sister?" asked Murdoch. The manager glanced through the document in front of him.

"Ah yes! Here it is. Yes, that will be the case after expenses have been deducted. I will see to it that all outstanding monies owed will be paid from the current account of your father's farm.

Since you are a beneficiary, you - Mr. John - will not now have access to it. I will therefore require you to deposit all account books with me here at the bank. We will take over and make sure everything is in order before any sale is finalised."

"Of course," agreed John "I will hand-in the books to you tomorrow morning."

The business having been concluded; the brothers left the bank.

Outside on the pavement John expressed amazement at what they had learned about their late father's affairs.

"I cannot believe he was so forward thinking. Quite a surprise, do not you think?"

His brother agreed.

"Indeed it was! Who would ever have thought he would have done all this and never said a word?"

Since the old man's house would be going on the market, a lot needed to be done to make it ready.

First, John and Sarah cleared Grandpa Murdoch's personal belongings out of the house. Afterward, with Kate and Mary's help, Sarah set to work cleaning it from top to bottom. If people were coming to see the house, with a view to purchasing, she wanted it to be nice and clean. The old man was gone but she did not want any gossip about how he left the place... people did talk!

A few months later, the Bank Manager contacted John and Murdoch and told them he had received three offers for the property. Two were from builders who wanted to build houses on the land, and the third from a man who was at present a Farm Manager but wanted a farm of his own. The potential house builders had put in generous offers which exceeded the offer of the Farm Manager but it had been Grandpa Murdoch's wish that a farmer should buy his land

While the wishes of their father came first, the brothers did not want houses built on the land between their respective holdings. Consequently, they instructed the Bank manager to accept the Farmer manager's offer.

The man was delighted with his good fortune. He and his family soon moved in and were pleased with their purchase. As John welcomed them to their new home and showed them round the house, he could see they were ecstatic about it and all its belongings. It reminded him of how he and Sarah had felt when they came to this place at first. As a bonus, the new owner was also happy to keep Tom Jamieson on as Farm Manager and wife Mary to assist in the house as before.

Chapter 24

*L*ife went on as usual at *Westcroft* Farm with the family quarry continuing to make good profits. The children were all growing fast. Daily life was good for the Munros. However, once again, they were to be reminded of the passage of time.

Everyone in the household had noticed that Ben, the dog, had slowed down somewhat over the previous year... particularly in recent months. He wasn't so keen to go out and would only take a short walk round the farm with young Murdoch. He preferred to stay in his bed in his little corner of the kitchen and sleep. To tempt him, Cook would make tasty little meals for him, but he wasn't eating much.

Young Murdoch was worried about him and asked his father what he thought was wrong with the dog.

John explained; "You must remember that he is a very old dog now son. He was here about three years or so before we came, so that makes him about sixteen years old or even more. He is just very, very old now."

A few mornings later, the boy came down early to see how Ben was keeping.

"Oh young master Murdoch, I am so sorry." Cook said gently. "I am afraid old Ben just slept quietly away in his bed during the night."

Murdoch knelt down beside the dog and stroked him for a while, then hurried out the door and ran round the back of the farm buildings out of sight. Once there, he cried like a baby. He had loved that dog... even more than people. He had taken care of him; brushing his lovely silky black and white coat every day until it gleamed - oh how he was going to miss him!

When Sarah and John came down, Cook told them what had happened. Sarah, her face filled with concern immediately thought of her son. upset."

"I must go and find Murdoch and console him. He will be so

"No," said John, "leave him be with his grief for the moment. He will come back to the house when he is ready."

The other children were already in the dining room and asked where Murdoch was.

"He has just gone out for a while" explained their father.

After breakfast was over, Sarah told the other children what had happened. Young John just sat and said nothing. He felt very sad, but he was fifteen now and was not going to shed tears in front of the girls. The girls of course, all cried.

"What do you suggest we do with Ben?" Sarah asked her husband, when the children had left the dining room.

John thought for a moment... "When Murdoch appears we will suggest that Ben be buried in a little corner of the nearest field. I think that would be best."

About an hour later Murdoch appeared. He was quite calm and had composed himself, so they told him what they thought should be done with Ben. The boy approved of the idea then he and his father went to the field beside the house.

After Murdoch had selected a spot, his father dug a deep hole to receive the body of old Ben. They wrapped him in his bed blankets and then laid him to rest.

His father had returned to the house but young Murdoch stayed and gazed sightlessly at his old friend's grave. He stood there for a while before turning away and returning to his room and did not reappear until the middle of the day.

Every day, for the following week, he would go and sit at the dog's grave for a little while. Soon after, his visits became less frequent until he only went there occasionally.

Time being the ultimate healer, as it moved on... memories of Ben receded from Murdoch's mind and the minds of the rest of the household.

John and Sarah's oldest boys were growing up quickly. Number one son Murdoch was fast becoming the bane of his parent's existence. He would just not settle down. His idea of a career was to get a horse and cart and become a Contractor or Carrier. He reckoned there was money to be made at it - moving people's goods from place to place, or taking mail and things to Glasgow.

John and Sarah tried to talk him out of the idea on several occasions... thinking; *what a waste of a clever brain!* The boy was intelligent and an ardent reader, his nose was forever in a book. He had learned very many things about numerous subjects but he was adamant – this was what he wanted to do!

Eventually his parents gave up trying to change Murdoch's mind. *It was just a fad and would pass when he got fed up being so fanatical about it!* They carefully avoided the subject when in his company. If they even hinted at anything at all to do with it, he got really tetchy. Often they thought; *why on earth cannot he be like his cousin and name-sake who is studying law and who's not nearly as intelligent?*

As for their second son John; he had made up his mind that in a few months time, when he became sixteen, he would go to Glasgow and learn to build ships, like his Uncle Dugald. The River Clyde was becoming a very busy place, ship yards were being set up all along It is broad banks and many ships were being built. The industry was booming and he wanted to be part of it.

His parents were pleased to see that the boy had ambition and obviously had a feel for the future. Therefore his father did not dissuade him in any way, but suggested he might like to stay with his uncle Dugald and auntie Nell.

Grandpa Murdoch's legacy of a third of the sale of his farm had been a delightful surprise to Dugald. It had allowed him and his family to move to a much bigger house. Although they had two children, they still had plenty of extra room. Consequently, John promised he would talk to uncle Dugald and see what could be arranged. Perhaps young John could stay with them and pay them for his keep?

Daughter Sarah was now fourteen and declared that when she was old enough she wanted to be a nurse and help sick people to get better.

Fortunately; there was time enough to worry about the career choices of the rest of the children. Their childhood would end soon enough.

Murdoch and Agnes's son was doing extremely well at University. He was very interested in the law, had studied hard and passed every exam with flying colours. He was now in his final year and looking forward to graduating.

At the beginning of that the year, he had developed a bad cough. Probably a cold, he thought. David McCulloch, a fellow student with whom he shared rooms, advised him to go and see a doctor about the cough, but he refused point blank; saying it was just a cold and that the cough would clear up when the summer came.

At the time, he was studying well into the night for his final exams and was often missing-out meals.

When eventually *did* go to sleep, he would waken his room mate with his coughing.

However, despite all this; when he eventually sat his final exams; much to the delight of his parents; he passed them with flying colours. They were very proud of him.

After the exams, young Murdoch went home for a break.

While there, his mother heard him coughing and told him to go to their doctor.

As with David his room mate; he fobbed her off saying that it was just the remnants of a bad cold and that it would soon clear up.

Young Murdoch eventually acquired a position with a prestigious firm of lawyers in Glasgow. Again he felt he had to prove his worth and sat up half the night reading law books. The cough was still with him.

The increasingly frequent bouts of dreadful coughing, lack of sleep and decent meals were taking their toll.

David continued to plead with him to see a doctor, but he just would not be convinced that he was ill and in need of help.

Things continued like this for a while, during which, Murdoch did not go home very much. This was because he knew he would be badgered by his mother about seeing a doctor. Truth be known; he was afraid of what a doctor might tell him.

And so, he carried on with his usual routine, working hard and getting thinner and paler by the day. He was always exhausted.

Eventually, David could no longer stand idle and see his friend decline in this way... he decided something must be done about it. Unbeknown to his friend, he wrote to Murdoch's parents, telling them of his fears for their son's health.

When John and Sarahthey received David's letter, they were filled with alarm and immediately set off for Glasgow to find out what David was so worried about...what exactly had prompted him to write such a letter.

On arrival at young Murdoch's address, they were not exactly impressed by the surroundings. They knocked on the door.

Their knock was answered by a nice looking, pleasant young man who introduced himself as David McCulloch. He invited them in... telling them that Murdoch had not yet come home from work and that he was always very late in doing so.

When they were seated, Agnes and Murdoch asked this young man what he thought about their son's health.

"If you wish me to be honest with you, sir, I would say your son Murdoch is not a well person."

Murdoch thought this young man was being very guarded in his reply, so he asked him for the truth.

"The truth, Mr. Munro, is that I think Murdoch is really quite ill and will not see a doctor. His cough has worsened over this last year or more and I know...although Murdoch does not know that I know it... he has also been coughing up blood." The young man finished with; "I hope I was right in telling you about this." adding; "Murdoch would be very angry if he knew I had written to you, but I did not know what else to do."

"Do not you worry about that now! You were perfectly correct in doing so', exclaimed Agnes. "We needed to know what was going on and he was obviously not going to tell us. You did the right thing and we are both grateful that you did."

They chatted for a while and David made them some tea.

Looking round her, Agnes noted that it was a rather miserable place with little heating and smelled of dampness. When she thought of the comfortable home Murdoch came from it made her a bit sad that her son should be ill in a place like this. After what David had told her she had a feeling of deep foreboding!

About an hour later Murdoch appeared. They were shocked when they saw him ...one look at him made them realise that they had not worried needlessly - their son was very ill indeed!

Young Murdoch was taken aback when he saw them both sitting there, but he quickly recovered.

"Well now, this is a pleasant surprise indeed. What brings you both here, may I ask?"

His mother did not waste time with pleasantries. "Murdoch!" she began, in a tone that he knew full well brooked no interruption, "Your father and I want you to come home with us right now. Anyone with an eye in their head can see that you are ill and very much in need of medical attention."

"I am fine", the young man protested. "Except for a bit of a cough, I am perfectly well. Besides, I am very busy at the moment. I have employment that I just cannot leave because you want to take me home like a runaway child. I will not come with you. I can take care of myself perfectly well."

He had got quite worked up about this and it made him start coughing. He could not control it this time, and was coughing up quite a lot of blood. His mother got the fright of her life. His father was also dismayed, more so at seeing his fine son in this state. Secretly, he had his suspicions as to what was wrong with him, but did not want to alarm anyone by voicing these suspicions. He made up his mind.

"You are coming with us tonight, my boy, whether you like it or not. Get a few things together and we will go to the station and get the train home. There is one in about an hour's time and you will be on it with us!" He was not taking no for an answer. He knew if he left his son in this miserable place, he would die and that was not going to happen if he could prevent it.

Murdoch was so weak from his bouts of coughing...he was just too tired to argue. He got a few things together and prepared to leave with his parents. At the door, as they were leaving, David asked his friend:

"Will I inform your place of employment that you are unwell and will be away from work for a little time? Is that what you would want me to say to them?"

"Yes." agreed Murdoch junior, "That would be good of you, thank you David", adding... "I will be back as soon as this silly cough has cleared up."

Inwardly, David had his suspicions that this would possibly be the last time he would ever see his friend alive.

Agnes again expressed her gratitude to David. She also promised to keep him advised as to how Murdoch was progressing.

On the way home, the train journey took its toll on young Murdoch. By the time they reached the station at Lenzie, he was absolutely exhausted. His father sent for a young boy who lived nearby and asked him if he would go to *Eastfield* and get someone to come to the station with the pony and trap. Then the three of them waited at the station for it to arrive.

After what seemed to be forever; the trap, driven by Murdoch's manservant, arrived with the boy on board. Murdoch thanked the lad profusely and rewarded him for his efforts. By the expression on the boy's face when he looked in his hand, the reward was generous.

By this time young Murdoch was helpless. His father and the manservant helped him into the trap and after everyone was settled on board, they headed back for home.

Although it was late when they arrived, some of the staff were still around. When they saw the state the young master was in, they were totally shocked and when young Agnes saw her brother, she almost fainted. She could hardly believe how ill he looked.

Agnes told one of the servants to prepare Murdoch's bed and to heat it. Meanwhile, they all went into the drawing room where a bright fire was burning. Agnes sent for tea and some food. When it arrived, young Murdoch refused to eat at all, but said he would drink the tea. His mother didn't push him into eating. She was worried and angry with her son but decided not to lecture him. Instead; they all just sat quietly in the warmth of the room and waited until the servant eventually arrived to tell them that Master Murdoch's bed was ready. Then he and his father went upstairs where Murdoch Senior helped his son undress and get into bed. Murdoch felt like weeping – he instinctively knew his oldest son was extremely ill and suspected the dreaded tuberculosis. The doctor would be sent for first thing in the morning. Meantime, better to let the boy sleep tonight in warmth and comfort.

As for Young Murdoch, he felt so tired, but was glad to be in his own bed at home. It was such a comfortable feeling. Soon he drifted off into a deep sleep.

After leaving the bedroom, his father went downstairs and back into the drawing room and found his wife and daughter weeping. Murdoch put his arms round them both and quietly shed a few tears himself. His wife expressed the nightmare she was experiencing.

"He is very ill, is he not, Murdoch, I fear he may be dying." Murdoch tried to allay her fears.

"Of course not my dear, he is just ill and we will get the doctor in the morning who will give him medicine to clear up this dreadful cough he has. You will see; then he will be fine again."

"Murdoch, I am not stupid, you know. I am thinking he has the dreaded consumption, and if that is the case, he will die from it Perhaps if he had not been so stubborn and sought the advice of a doctor when he started coughing, they may have been able to do something for him, but I fear it is too late now and the disease has gone too far."

Her husband continued to try and lighten the situation:

"We will wait and see what the doctor says tomorrow and not jump to conclusions tonight. It has been a long day and is very late. I think we should all go to bed and try to get some sleep, so that we can get up early in the morning and fetch the doctor."

Neither of them slept much that night.

Even through the thick walls, they could hear their son having bouts of coughing.

The night seemed never-ending but eventually morning dawned.

Murdoch immediately dressed and went to fetch the doctor.

On arrival at the doctor's house, he found the man was still in bed. But on hearing the description of the patient, the doctor realised the urgency of the case and quickly donned his clothes and got his medical bag. In the shortest time possible, the two men were on their way back.

When the doctor examined young Murdoch, he knew without a doubt that the lad had Consumption (Tuberculosis). Tragically, he also recognised that the untreated disease had advanced rapidly and was now in its terminal stage. The young man was not going live for very much longer. He left the sick room and went downstairs to give the parents the result of his examination.

On receiving the doctor's prognosis, Agnes collapsed into a chair and sobbed hysterically.

She had already lost her nine year old son John, and it seemed now she was to lose her first born boy who was the apple of her eye – *he had been doing so well - why did this have to happen to him? It was so unfair!*

Her husband's instinct was to cry-out in anguish and share her sorrow, but he resisted the urge... he had to keep control of his feelings at this moment for the sake of his wife.

Their daughter Agnes heard the commotion and came down to find out what was going on. When she saw her parents, her first thought was that her brother was dead.

"What is happening here?" she asked - anxiety, concern and fear chasing each other across her features. "Is my brother dead?" Not waiting for an answer, she went on: "I could hear him coughing during the night and it sounded dreadful."

Her father answered her.

"No, he is not dead, but I am not going to lie to you Agnes, your brother is a very sick young man. I am afraid he is not going to recover from this. As your mother and I suspected, he has Consumption and it has progressed so much that it is now too far advanced for the doctor to stop it."

At her father's news, Agnes, like her mother, dissolved into tears. She collapsed beside her mother and the two of them hugged each other, desperately trying to obtain mutual comfort.

The doctor - who had been standing to one side - then came forward and announced he would take his leave. Murdoch accompanied him to the front door.

As the doctor left, he gave Murdoch a small, square bottle made from brown ribbed glass.

"Here is a little medicine Mr. Munro. It may ease the boy's cough somewhat, but unfortunately there is little else I can do for the lad. I will be back again tomorrow. Meantime, just keep him in bed resting and perhaps you could persuade him to take a little nourishing liquid food."

What a desperate day that was. They were in and out of the sick room continuously, trying to assist young Murdoch when he had his coughing bouts, but there wasn't much else they could do for him. He slept quite a lot, which gave him a little peace for a while.

Murdoch had sent his manservant with the pony and trap over to his brother John's farm to give him the news. John and Sarah were shocked to receive it. With dismay and great concern, their first thoughts were for the sick boy's parents. Surely Murdoch and Agnes were not going to lose another son?

Life had being so terribly cruel to them in those past few years.

Then they thought of Murdoch and Agnes's other children.

Daughter Agnes was old enough to understand the situation, but what about wee Jessie? She was only seven years old. Poor child, she would not understand all the grief in that house and would be very confused. *What could they do* they wondered? Probably not very much except give some comfort to the distraught parents and family.

John and Sarah waited until the following afternoon before going across to *Eastfield*.

When they saw Agnes, she had aged overnight. She was pale and drawn and had no life about her. Lack of sleep was also taking its toll. They did not waste time but went up stairs to see their nephew Murdoch.

At first sight they were inwardly horrified to see the extent of the havoc wreaked by the disease on his poor young frame. The boy had the unmistakable death -look. However, he was awake, so they put on a bright face and made all the right noises concerning things getting better, etc. They didn't stay long though; the conversation was obviously tiring for the lad since he almost fell asleep several times as they talked.

When they left the room, Sarah burst into tears, it was so sad to see this fine looking young man reduced to this.

John attempted to console her.

"There is obviously nothing we can do to help here except give comfort to Murdoch and Agnes. Maybe they would prefer just to be on their own with the two girls. I do not think we should stay too long."

"You are right my dear" she sniffed," but it is so sad to see yet another of their sons dying." adding... "Because I am sure that is what is happening. It doesn't bear thinking about. We better go downstairs and put a face on it. But wait till I dry my tears."

On entering the drawing room, they found the family sitting there silently in an absolutely devastated state. Murdoch broke the silence.

"I am forgetting my manners. Would you like some tea or a drink or something?"

"No thank you, brother." answered John: adding: "Would you prefer us to leave now, or would you like some company for a little while?"

As if he hadn't heard; Murdoch continued:

"Was young Murdoch asleep when you left him?"

"Yes, he fell asleep" confirmed John. "So we decided to leave him in peace. He will need his rest."

There was an awkward silence for a few moments then, almost absently; Murdoch answered his brother's first question.

"I think it best if we were on our own at this moment. I am afraid we are not very good company."

Silently, everyone hugged and thereafter John and Sarah left. Words at times like these seemed totally inadequate. It was to be the last time that they saw their nephew Murdoch Munro alive. A few days later, the boy breathed his last... yet another young Munro life snuffed out like a candle!

The funeral took place a few days later.... for everyone, another; dreadful affair, especially the parents Murdoch and Agnes.

As well as the older members of the Munro clan employees from the Quarry, both farms, and young David, who had shared digs with Murdoch, plus a few work colleagues, attended that sorrowful graveside.

When it was thankfully all over and everyone had returned to their respective homes, John and Sarah reflected upon this latest tragic event to strike their clan. Both hoped that this would be the last family funeral for some time to come.

As for poor Agnes and Murdoch: as well as the latter's mother and father: In a short space of time they had attended three more such heartbreaking affairs in their immediate family. Surely there would now be some respite now from all this sadness?

Not so! Life had to move on. People grew old and died; that was as it always had been, but the death of young people at the threshold of life was not anything anyone could get used to or accept without great sadness.

John, Sarah and *their* family all seemed fit and well. Long might that situation remain!

Their son Murdoch had eventually set up and was still working away at his Carrier business. In fact, it was actually doing quite well.

Sarah had thought he would have tired of it quickly and given up. He seemed quite contented with what he was doing. *Aye! for the time being anyway* -Sarah thought wryly! However she was pleased that he was making some money and still living at home - a situation which suited her perfectly well. He was where she could keep an eye on him!

It would have been an entirely different matter if he had taken up with a specific young lady and decided to wed. In that event, he would have found it necessary to get a home together, and then perhaps he would have been forced to do something better with his life than what she termed *carrying.*

In fact; young Murdoch preferred the grander name of ' Contracting'. It had an important ring to it and sounded much better!

The golden age of farming was at its height. More crops were being grown on every available space of farmland.... vegetables were now an important earner.

More and more people were moving into the city of Glasgow, thus creating a great demand for fresh fruit and vegetables.

The summers continued to be perfect for growing all kinds of things, and huge profits were being made.

John and Sarah were very wise indeed. They did not spend, spend, spend on frivolities as did some of the other farmers. Not them! John was quite happy to spend their money investing in the latest farming machinery, which made ploughing, sowing, threshing and harvesting, much easier. This, in turn, reduced the need for so many labourers.... cutting the costs of growing and harvesting.

Because of the wet climate of the area, investment in drainage pipes was also a huge benefit since by installing them; the ground was kept from being waterlogged in winter, thus making ploughing so much easier after the New Year.

Sarah was also careful about what she spent; she did not go rushing off spending lots of money on useless fripperies. If a thing was needed, then it would be bought. She thought that having extra money was no reason to be rash and stupid with it.

Furthermore; they both agreed that if things were not as good in the future, they would have money to fall back on. This proved in hindsight to be a very wise decision. For many farmers, the future turned out to be a bit of a disaster and they subsequently went bankrupt.

Chapter 25

As with many families of the times, tragedy was never far from the doorstep. Soon it would visit the other Munros yet again.

On one of his visits to his brother, Murdoch mentioned that his young daughter Agnes had a bad cough.

"She had a nasty cold a while ago." he explained. "and of course, she developed a cough. It being so soon after poor young Murdoch's passing, it is no wonder that the alarm bells rang loudly in her mother's ears. She was terrified of a repetition of the last time.

So, to lay her fears to rest, we called the doctor. He examined Agnes and said as far as he was concerned; it was just the result of her cold and not to worry. This was a few weeks ago, but her cough has got worse. I told Agnes that the doctor had said not to worry; that this cough will probably take its time to clear up."

John inwardly felt his stomach churn. *Not again he thought!* He responded.

"I can well imagine Agnes being very worried about your daughter: I wouldn't blame her. After what happened to young Murdoch, every family cough will naturally be interpreted as something more sinister than it really is. I wouldn't worry about it too much."... *Easier said than done!* came into his mind.

The brothers carried on discussing various subjects including of course, the farming industry.

Murdoch was making good profits on his farm. These, plus the money from the rented farm, and half the profits of the quarry were providing a substantial income. He too, like his brother, was wisely keeping his money and building up his capital for a rainy day. *Joint wisdom!*

Living for John's family had become easy and very pleasant. His eldest daughter Sarah had realised her life's ambition and done as she had always wanted to do when she was a young girl and she had become a nurse.

She loved her work and was good at what she did which was helped by a huge personality which she shared with her mother.

Her patients adored her, as did her mother, who was immensely proud of her first born daughter.

Janet, the next daughter, had become a school teacher. She too was good at her work.

She taught infant classes and loved the little children in her care. They responded to her since she encouraged them to learn, and that included the ones who did not want to do so.

The youngest members of the family were not sure about what they would like to do when they grew-up.

Susanna would have preferred just to stay at home and do nothing much, but help around the place, and the two youngest were still being tutored.

As for young John... he seemed to be doing well at the shipyards in Glasgow. He loved all the noise and activity of the place - the sound of riveting hammers and of the yard machinery - sharing this love with his uncle.

Dugald played *his* part by making sure that his nephew John stayed on the right road, and didn't get involved with some of the older men who liked to drink overmuch alcohol after their shift.

Unfortunately, like all idyllic times, they came to an end.

As always with the Munros, the end manifested itself in the form of bad news. John received it from his brother Murdoch when visiting him on quarry business.

Murdoch told him that his daughter Agnes's cough had dramatically worsened. They had called in the doctor who, after examining her, declared that she too had developed the Consumption. He had told the parents that it could be infectious, particularly from close contact with someone who had the disease that since young Agnes had sat for long periods of time with her brother when he was ill; this was more than likely the source of her illness.

"Oh my God!" exclaimed John in dismay. "Brother, I am so deeply sorrowful for you. How is Agnes coping with this?"

"Not well at all. It is to be expected... she was almost hysterical when the doctor announced this latest horror story."

John went on... "Surely something can be done for her? After all, it cannot be nearly as far advanced as it was when young Murdoch was diagnosed with it?"

Murdoch, face grey and drawn with anxiety, sighed in resignation. "Unfortunately the doctor said there was no real cure at this time. However if she rests and takes nourishing food and gets some fresh air on good dry days, it could prolong her life for some time. He also told us that patients could live quite a long time with this disease, so, with proper care and attention, there is hope that our daughter will be with us for a number of years to come.

John inwardly wept for his brother. What had Murdoch done to deserve this? He was a good man... conscientious, hard working... a loving husband and father who looked after his wife and family well - giving them everything life had to offer. He thought; *The rest of we Munros thought Murdoch was the brother who had landed on his feet when he got the job at the Mitchell farm. Then he married Agnes, the farmer's daughter..."* Now he was the unlucky one, the one whose path in recent life had been repeatedly dogged by tragedy.

When John returned home and told Sarah the news, she could not believe what she was hearing. He repeated the news for her benefit.

"Oh dear Lord, dear Lord! I cannot believe this is happening to them again. The tears welled up and flowed down her cheeks..." Dear Lord, what have they done to deserve this?

Your poor, poor brother and his wife; how tragic for them. Surely they are not going to lose *another* child? How must they feel? They must be distraught to think that this might just happen again and they might lose another bairn. I feel so sorry for them. Dear me! I will never complain about anything again in my life."

With that, she turned on her heel, left the room and ran upstairs, yet again weeping in sorrow for her poor relatives.

One day, young Murdoch announced to his parents that he had decided to give up the *contracting* business. They were totally taken aback by this news. However, that was not all he had to tell them. He was not now unemployed but had got a job as railway porter at the station in Lenzie.

Sarah was mystified but delighted. At last he had a *proper job*.

Murdoch was not finished with his news! Casually he added: "I met a very nice girl in the village the other day."

"Oh really?" said his mother in a tone which was the fore-runner to the obvious question; "and what is her name?"

"Mary Wilkie"

"And does Mary Wilkie work for the Railway too?"

"No mother" said Murdoch in a scornful tone..." She works as a serving girl in one of the big houses in Lenzie. She originally comes from Campsie." With these few words, the information dried-up!

Sarah's curiosity was now fully switched-on. *Did Murdoch decide to get a proper job because of Mary Wilkie or perhaps because he was bored with his carrier business? Very curious! Well, he wasn't going to disclose any more for the time being. No doubt all would be revealed in due course.*

John and Sarah were pleased about this new turn in their son's fortunes and had hopes that if he stuck this railway job for a while, he might even make Station Master - a rather important position.

They knew that the present Station Master was getting close to retiring age and might be giving up the job in the not too distant future. Who knows? Perhaps their Murdoch might just step into his shoes?

To their minds; things were looking up for their eldest son. They were happy - employment-wise; both their sons and first two daughters had found suitable work.

As for Susanna... although her first choice would have been to lounge about looking languid and interesting; she had finally realised she was not going to be allowed to hang around the house doing nothing, so she had a bright idea! She told her parents she would like to learn bookkeeping and help her father with the farm books when he was busy with the quarry. To her mind, this was the nearest excuse she could come up with, which would allow her to stay at home and not have to do too much!

Young Sarah had a boyfriend - a very nice young man from one of the larger houses in Kirkintilloch.

After a year of them *walking out* together she announced to her parents that she wished to get married. Her mother was delighted. This was something she could revel in. Her mind immediately started working overtime, planning the perfect wedding and reception to follow.

Shortly after this announcement, the bride-to-be's parents were invited to the young man's home to meet with their daughter's future in- laws.

Sarah was excited about this! When the day came, she took great care with how she dressed... wanting to make the best impression for her daughter's sake and in particular - to indicate that she was prosperous and suitable soon to be mother-in-law.

And so, everyone had a very pleasant evening with the young man's family...all seemed to go smoothly and both families were satisfied with the choice of their respective offspring.

Subsequently, the wedding arrangements were made and the momentous event took place one bright sunny summer day shortly after

The wedding ceremony took place at the local Parish Church. Afterward, the guests were transported back to *Westcroft* for the wedding reception.

The spread Cook, Kate and Annie came up with would have suited royalty. James, of course, added a touch of class, pouring wine for everyone and being the perfect gentleman's gentleman. Although he was now well into his seventies, he did not look or act his age. Most important, he still had a very steady hand for pouring the wine!

The extensive guest list included Murdoch who came along with young Jessie, but Agnes stayed at home with their sick daughter. She could not leave the poor girl at home alone. Additionally; she could not allow her to be among a crowd of people with that dreadful cough which might, perhaps, even spread the disease! In any case, she didn't think her daughter would be welcome since most of the people in the area, without doubt, knew of her illness. Servants talked!

As it was; young Agnes had told her mother she did not feel up to it anyway... nor did her mother for that matter!

The wedding itself was a beautiful affair. The bride looked radiant. As for her new husband, he was a rather plain looking, uninteresting young man. However, he had one redeeming quality; he seemed to have such a pleasant personality. Sarah and John were well pleased with their daughter's choice of a husband.

After young Sarah's wedding, things settled down again into the usual everyday routine... this was not to last!

Six months after the wedding, Janet...daughter number two... announced she had fallen desperately in love with a fellow teacher and she too wanted to get married. Joy, oh joy, Sarah could plan yet another wedding! Young Sarah's wedding must have been infectious... putting her sister in the mood to be wed.

And so plans were made for Janet to be wed...similar plans to those made for her big sister's wedding.

Although happy for his second daughter... John thanked the powers that be that his finances were able to withstand the shock of two weddings in such a short interval!

Within a year of her sister Sarah's wedding, Janet and her young man were married in the same church and had their wedding reception back at *Westcroft*. It was a late spring wedding, but the sun shone on the day and the weather was kind to them. Everyone had a lovely time and the young newly-weds got a great send-off.

Now, with two daughters married and gone to live elsewhere, Sarah and John had a little more room at home and less to concern them. But not for long!

Not long after Janet's wedding, young Murdoch made a most unexpected and devastating announcement. His Mary Wilkie had given birth to a son, and he was now a father.

Sarah was speechless - she could have slapped him. When she regained her composure and her power of speech, she took her eldest son to task.

"For goodness sake Murdoch," she began "Why did you allow this to happen? You surely have known all this time, yet you have not married this girl. Why not? It is most un-gentlemanly and unfair of you to treat the girl in this way." She went on:

"What is to be happening to her and this baby? Who is looking out for them? I think, Murdoch, the proper and right thing to do is to marry this girl and do your duty. Do you love the lass or were you just dallying with her? You have known her for some time now and given her the impression, no doubt, that you cared for her. I am not pleased with you at all. Your father will no doubt have something to say to you when he hears about this."

Murdoch waited until the tirade was over and his mother had run out of breath. Then, in a calm almost accusing manner he replied:

"Well now mother! If you just let me explain.

How could we marry? We have nowhere to live and Mary does not want us to be married without a proper home for the baby. Her mother is looking after the baby meantime.

The Station Master was talking the other day about retiring. If he does, we will get his railway cottage, so *then* we will wed."

"Talking about going to retire?" asked his mother..." talking about it? It had better be soon. In any case, when are we going to meet this girl? Your father and I have never even seen her! How old is she?"

So far, Sarah had not in the least been pacified by her son's replies. Despite this, Murdoch detected a slight easing of his mother's disapproval. He wisely took the opportunity to answer her questions. It was a subject on which he was the expert.

Mary ' s twenty years old. Her people come from Ireland, but Mary was born in Campsie, so she is really Scottish. Her father and his parents came to Scotland when he was very young."

Sarah had calmed down by this time and was listening carefully. At this latest bit of intelligence, and since she herself was born in County Antrim in Ireland, her curiosity was really aroused.

"Ireland you say? Where about in Ireland do her people come from then."

Now Murdoch knew he really had his mother's undivided attention, and hit home with:

"They are from a place named Kilskerry, in County Tyrone, so your daughter-in-law to be comes from Irish descendants... same as do you."

Then it suddenly struck Sarah - she and John were grandparents! She had been so upset and concerned about Murdoch, she had quite forgotten; the most important fact was that there was now another Munro infant. Her maternal instinct kicked – in.

"Well! If You are going to marry the girl, do not you think It is about time to bring the young woman home so that your father and I can meet herAdding... "Oh and the baby of course!"

At this last remark, Murdoch truly knew he had won over his mother.

Sarah on the other hand was apprehensive as to how her husband would receive this momentous news. She need not have worried.

When he heard Murdoch's news, he was not the least bit indignant about it. In true male fashion, his response was:

"If the boy wants to marry this girl, well and good, but it is up to the two of them to decide what to do.

Sarah; this sort of things happens all the time when young girls get themselves pregnant and the man responsible has no wish to marry. It is very unfortunate for the poor girl but that is the way of things. It will come right in the end – you will see!"

News from the other Munros was not good. Their daughter Agnes was in a very bad way and was now confined to bed. The girl was wasting away... exhausted with coughing and bringing up blood. Evidently, her illness was in the terminal stages. The doctor had told her parents she wouldn't last much longer and to prepare themselves for the inevitable.

On receiving the news, John and Sarah dropped everything and went to visit their niece.

Entering the sick room; they were immediately struck with the similarity between the girl's condition and what they had witnessed two years earlier, when visiting her older brother Murdoch.

She was deathly pale, her skin alabaster-white...almost transparent, yet she managed a wan smile when they drew close to the bedside. It was pathetic in one so young. Her Uncle and Aunt were overcome with a deep sadness... she looked so gravely ill.

Her mother, on the other hand, appeared cold and calm about it all. Inwardly, she was experiencing a deep empty feeling of despair. She had gone through this already - just over two years previously when she had lost her eldest son - there now seemed little emotion left in her. Without doubt the flood gates would open when the inevitable happened and her daughter Agnes finally died. But for the time being... in a strange, detached, matter-of -fact way...her thoughts stayed firmly with the healthy, living members of her shrinking family. It occurred to her that when young Agnes finally died; out of their four children; she and husband Murdoch would have but one daughter left...young Jessie who was ten years old. Then came the macabre thought: *wouldn't it be a tragedy if Jessie also succumbed to the Consumption?* She gave herself a mental shake! Jessie seemed immune so far... that might auger well for her.

Again, her thoughts took over...became alarming and more personal: *What if I catch it? Och no! of course not. Obviously I have some immunity... after all; I have nursed two of my children through this and have not contracted it long may it continue!*

Had she looked into a mirror at that moment, she would not have gained any comfort! She was looking as bad as her sick daughter...thin, gaunt and careworn. The long days and nights nursing young Agnes, aided and abetted by lack of sleep and eating very little had taken their toll.

On many an occasion, her husband tried to get her to go to bed... to get some rest and eat a proper meal, but she would have none of it. He had even asked the doctor to give her something to make her sleep, but Agnes wouldn't take it. There were times when in despair, Murdoch wished it would all end and his poor daughter could be laid to rest with her brother. He wasn't being callous; he loved his daughter, but just hated to see her suffering in this way.

Sadly but inevitably, a week later, Murdoch's wish was granted. At the threshold of her young adult life, Agnes finally died. Another chapter in the Munro story had come to a sad end.

Young Agnes was laid to rest beside her brother Murdoch. It was over! Everyone hoped and prayed to God that this would be the final chapter... an end to the premature deaths on that side of the Munro family.

Following the funeral, Agnes retreated into herself...going about zombie- like... mind a blank...unable to find interest in even the smallest every day happenings.

However, time the healer did its work and after a few months; to a certain degree, she started to pick up her life again. But the joy had gone, never to return. There was no more socialising, she and Murdoch simply ran the farm and got on with their daily lives. Everything had changed.

Chapter 26

Mary Wilkie finally made an appearance at the farm with Murdoch. She was a strong, pleasant looking girl, polite and well mannered but with an air of capability about her.

Although respectful, Mary was not subservient.... Sarah liked this and quite took to her!

During the first formal introductions, Mary seemed a little aloof. Sarah put it down to the circumstances... *maybe the girl felt awkward and strange*? She decided that it would be silly to ignore the situation.

After she had arranged for tea and biscuits to be served and the three of them were settled in their chairs, Sarah - knowing that new mothers loved to talk about their first child - opened the conversation with reference to the new arrival.

"Well then Mary!... our Murdoch tells us you are to be congratulated - that you and he now have a baby son. I was hoping you might bring him over today to let me see him."

Mary, blushing, but head held high, replied... almost defensively...

"I thank you Mrs. Munro. Yes, we have a fine, sturdy boy." Sarah noticed the slight accent on the word *"we."*

Mary continued.... "I did not bring him because when I left him, he was sleeping over at my mother's house and I did not wish to disturb him. He did not have a good night last night." she added: "As Mr. Munro is not present it is perhaps just as well; since if I had done, he would not have been here to see the little one."

"Perhaps you were wise to do so." agreed Sarah. "Have you a name for the child?"

"Oh yes!" exclaimed Mary. "That was easy." "What have you called him?" asked Sarah.

"We named him John after Mr. Munro - Murdoch's father." Sarah was inwardly pleased at this reply.

"That is very nice, Mr. Munro will be honoured I am sure."

There was a minute ' s awkward silence then Sarah continued the conversation, deciding to give the girl the opportunity to talk about her own family.

"What of your family Mary?"

"My family are all farming people. My father - Charles Wilkie farms over at Campsie. My mother's maiden name was Elizabeth Young and her people farmed over at East Kilbride."

"Well now!" retorted Sarah, permitting herself a little smile – "we are all farming people together so it seems. That is nice!"

The chat continued for a bit longer in the same stilted manner until Murdoch thought Mary had been grilled enough.

"Well now mother" he exclaimed, "It is getting late and I will need to get Mary back to her mother's house. The wee lad will be needing fed and we do not want to put too much a burden on Mrs Wilkie."

Sarah was well aware of the tension and felt she had pried enough.

"Of course! What am I thinking about? Never mind, away the two of you go now. It was nice to meet you Mary. Perhaps the next time you come to see us, you will bring the baby along so we can see him?"

"Yes. Of course Mrs Munro. He is a fine boy. I am sure you and Mr. Munro will be well pleased with him.

"I look forward to that…"…*Sarah really meant it*!

Mary ended the conversation with "I thank you for the tea and for our little chat. We will be going now…good day to you Mrs. Munro!" With that, she rose and left with young Murdoch.

Sarah got the distinct impression that once outside the door; the girl would be heaving a sigh of relief!

Later that night when Murdoch came home, Sarah discussed Mary's visit with her son.

"Your Mary seemed a bit shy of conversation and only answered questions. I felt I was asking for her background as if I was going to employ her."

"She was very embarrassed mother, because she didn't know what you would think of her having a baby and us not married."

Sarah well understood, but in saying so, could not resist another dig at him.

"She might well be, but the girl is not to take all the blame as I have told you. Let us hope the situation is resolved quickly for the sake of the child if for nothing else."

A few weeks later, fate played Murdoch and Mary a fortunate hand. The Station Master retired and his cottage became vacant. As expected, Murdoch was offered the job of Station Master.

Therefore, as soon as it could be arranged, he and Mary went to Monklands and were wed.

It was a very quiet affair – just the Bride and Groom and two witnesses. Afterward, the newly weds went back to the railway cottage and immediately began to set it in order.

Sarah had offered to give them some sort of wedding reception or even just a dinner with the family, but they didn't want anything... they just wanted to get on with their lives.

After a suitable time had passed, Sarah and John went to see Murdoch and Mary in their new home. Little baby John was still being looked after by Mary's mother at the time.

As soon as she entered the cottage, it was obvious to Sarah that the young couple didn't have very much by way of furnishings. The place was very bare.

Knowing how independent and proud they were, she carefully avoided making any direct comment but as she and John were leaving, she told her son and his wife that she would send down some bits and pieces to help them get started.

A few days later, Mary collected her baby from her mother's house and took him over to *Westcroft*.

It was the first time John and Sarah had set eyes on their first grandchild. Sarah was thrilled to see the lovely strong healthy baby boy. As for Grandpa John... he was quite overawed by the little chap, but felt very proud that this was his very own grandson. The baby reminded him of when he and Sarah had started out and when Murdoch was born. So many years had passed since then.

A couple of weeks after seeing her first grandchild, Murdoch told his mother that Mary was pregnant once more! All going well, this baby would be born when baby John was just eleven months old.

"For goodness sake, Murdoch, the two of you are not wasting any time, are you? At least I had two years between each of my first four children. I do not envy Mary."

She would have been very surprised had she known that in the future Mary and Murdoch would end up with fourteen children!

Sarah's daughter Susanna had met the love of her life and was *walking out* with him on a very regular basis. It transpired that the young man was one of the grandsons of Thomas McLeod the builder... the man who had befriended and supported the Quarry many years earlier.

Old Mr. McLeod had long since retired and his two sons were now running the business.

The romance blossomed until eventually Susanna announced she wished to marry young McLeod. Yet another Munro wedding was on the horizon! However this latest event would cause problems for the bride ' s parents. It would not be a modest affair. The McLeods were a prominent local family and had many friends and associates who would need to be invited as guests.

Fortunately for John and Sarah, a solution was quickly found. The couple decided that the reception would be held at the groom's home. His was a very large house and would be more than capable of accommodating the entire planned guest list.

Initially, Sarah had not been too pleased with the decision; protesting that it was traditional for the bride's parents to make such arrangements. However, John pointed out to her that there was not enough room in their house for all those people.

Reluctantly, Sarah accepted the fact and went along with the original decision. This done, she set about compiling a family guest list. Inevitably it was a lengthy one!

Their branch of the Clan Munro was growing! It occurred to Sarah as she wrote the invitations - *Heavens! All these and there is another two on the way - her daughter Sarah was pregnant again and expected to give birth soon. Mary, young Murdoch's wife was also pregnant yet again!*

Finally the list was complete and the invitations sent out. Of those sent out to the immediate family, everyone... except Agnes, promised to attend. She declined on the grounds that she had a bad cold and a cough.

The wedding day finally arrived. It was a magnificent affair and Susanna was a radiant bride. She was a very beautiful girl, and by far the prettiest of John and Sarah's four daughters. Everyone enjoyed the whole thing immensely and had a wonderful time at the reception.

When it was all over and the bride's parents had time to relax, Sarah thought: *Daughter number three married and away from home now. Only Joan and Edward left.* Then it occurred to her... Goodness! *Joan's nearly eighteen. No doubt it will be her turn soon. So far she has no great interest in any specific lad.*

Joan was working at the bank, but the staff there, were all much older than she was. There would not be any prospects in that direction. It just had to be relied on that she would find the perfect man in due course.

Chapter 27

*A*gnes was now feeling very ill. The doctor had finally concluded that she too had contracted the deadly Consumption.

Murdoch was aghast! *Was there something wrong with this house that all his family were dying around him with this disease? Surely this just could not be true?*

In his heart, he knew it was so... the evidence was there... it was a repetition of his two children who had died of this very same disease. He could not bring himself to tell thirteen years old Jessie that her mother was dying so decided that a white lie might prolong the time when the brutal truth would be all too apparent to the child. Therefore when his daughter asked about her mother, he told her that she was suffering from a very bad cold and cough, and it was making her very weak and unwell.

"You will see that with good food, rest, care and attention, she will no doubt recover and be back looking after us in no time at all."

Jessie accepted this story... why should she doubt her father?

However, she insisted on entering the bedroom to visit her mother.

Fearing the danger of infection, Murdoch was reluctant to allow this but how could he stop her?

Then again; Agnes had been coughing badly for a long time... long before she had been confined to bed. If the disease had been passed on to Jessie, it was already too late and the damage had already been done. However, it occurred to him that he had managed to escape this disease so far. *Did he have some kind of immunity to it - surely he must have? That being so... perhaps Jessie had the same immunity?*

Hopefully this state of affairs would continue. He wanted to see this daughter grow up and perhaps get married. However - to be on the safe side - he decided to put the girl off from entering the bedroom.

"I think it best that you keep clear of mother for the time being my dear. She is resting just now and the doctor has told me her cough may yet be infectious. We do not want you to be coming down with it now, do we?"

This excuse put Jessie off... for the time being anyway!

Eventually, Murdoch felt he had to go over to his brother's house and give them the news about Agnes.

As soon as they saw him at the door, John and Sarah knew something was very wrong. When they were seated, Murdoch confirmed this.

"I am the bringer of very bad news yet again. Agnes has the Consumption and is rather ill.

John and Sarah sat there dumbfounded. Murdoch continued:

"As you know, she has had a cough for quite some time now, but wasn't feeling ill with it – it was just annoying! But a few weeks ago, it suddenly developed further and she started feeling ill. I asked the doctor to call and examine her, and he said he had his suspicions as to what was wrong. He couldn't confirm it for sure but would wait and see what developed."

At this point, Murdoch's voice became thin and strained.

"A couple of weeks after that, she started bringing up blood, I recognised the signs having seen them before – knew it was definitely the Consumption and he doctor confirmed my worst fears a few days ago. It seems to have progressed very rapidly with her." Murdoch was close to tears at this point.

Sarah and John had sat in silence throughout. When Murdoch finished his story, the three of them continued to sit in abysmal silence. Such was the effect of this terrible news. Finally, Sarah put her arms round Murdoch and hugged him tightly. She could not find any words of consolation. She didn't want to shed tears in front of her brother-in-law for fear of upsetting him further. Having done so, she excused herself and, head down, left the room and went upstairs.

After she had gone, John and Murdoch left the sitting room and adjourned to the study. When the door closed behind them, John allowed his emotions to get the better of him. He felt so very sad and sorry for his younger brother. Facing Murdoch and placing a hand on each of his elbows, he looked at him with tear filled eyes...

"Oh brother! My little brother! What can I say that will help me share your pain?"

Murdoch visibly crumpled at these words. Raw emotion took over and the brothers hugged each other, as they had not done since they were children. Both wept silently.

When Murdoch left, Sarah came downstairs; her eyes were red with weeping.

"Oh, John," she said, almost crying again. "This is dreadful news. This is just not fair. Poor Murdoch does not deserve this. He is a good man and has looked after his family and wife very well. How I grieve for him. I am sorry" she continued; "I just could not find words of consolation to say to him when he was here."

By this time, John had pulled himself together.

"I understand my dear and I know Murdoch understood as well. I must say, I too was quite overcome with emotion. It is, as you say, not fair.

"I suppose we should go and see Agnes soon. Did Murdoch say anything about that?" asked Sarah.

"No, he didn't, but we will go in a few days time just to show we care and hopefully neither of us will catch this dreadful illness. It must be infectious for so many of his family to have caught it. We will go for a short time and see her, for Murdoch's sake. Maybe, of course, Agnes won't want to have visitors."

A few days later John and Sarah went to *Eastfield*.

On arrival, Murdoch said that Agnes didn't want to see them or anyone that day, so they contented themselves by asking how she was and were told that she was rather poorly and had had a bad night coughing and was very tired and staying in bed.

Having stayed for a short time, they left, promising to drop in again some day soon to see how Agnes was feeling.

Over the following months, they called at *Eastfield* on several occasions, but each time Agnes was in bed and did not want to see them.

They never saw Agnes alive again! She died six months to the day after Murdoch had first come to *Westcroft* with the news.

And so yet another desperately sad, heartbreaking, family funeral took place. After that - of that branch of the Munros - only Murdoch and Jessie remained living at *Eastfield*. Murdoch now fervently prayed that he would be spared from a premature death – at least long enough to see his last daughter safely married with someone to care for her.

The first few months following the death of Agnes were very bad. The house was now so strange and empty. However, as before when such tragedies had struck; time eventually passed; healing as it did so, until Murdoch and his last remaining child finally picked themselves up and got on with life.

Fortunately, Agnes had taught Jessie about the running of the farm and how to keep the books and accounts, so at least she was able to take over from her mother in that respect.

As for Murdoch - he had little choice but to get on with the daily routines...seeing to the farm and also the grindstone business. Thankfully, his duties kept him occupied. During the day, his mind was fully occupied with the work in hand and kept clear of his personal worries. It was the lonely silent evenings he dreaded most.

One evening, after Jessie had gone bed, as Murdoch sat there, alone in the large sitting room staring into the flames of the fire, he cast his thoughts back in time. *How similar things were turning out!*

Agnes and *her* father had been left on their own, with *her* father running a farm and she doing the books and accounts. Now, history was repeating itself; he and Jessie were in exactly the same situation; another generation, doing exactly the same thing!

It seemed to him, in his desolate frame of mind, that this house of his seemed to have been cursed. *Maybe a change of house might alter his fortunes?*

Perhaps so, but he couldn't just "up sticks" and leave the farm; he had to earn a living and make a home for Jessie. He supposed he would just have to grit his teeth for her sake and get on with it! His father-in-law, John Mitchell had had to do it when his wife died. However Mr Mitchell had only one child...Agnes. He at least had been spared the suffering, distress and deep sorrow that the loss of three children had brought to this house!

Sarah and John visited Murdoch on many occasions after the death of Agnes. On each occasion, they invited him and Jessie to come and dine with them. At first Murdoch had refused, but then eventually he accepted. Jessie was the motivation for doing so.

He thought it wasn't fair... her to be so young and to be cooped up on the farm every day with no other youngsters... she needed to be out in the real world.

His first outing after the death of Agnes surprised Murdoch... he actually quite enjoyed himself!

As for young Jessie: she felt like a released prisoner and immensely enjoyed the company of her cousins who she had not seen for a considerable time.

The success f the first outing prompted Murdoch to invite his brother and his remaining family back to his house at *Eastfield*. Thus, it became a fairly frequent event.

On one of their afternoon visits, Sarah broached the question of the house to Murdoch.

"Why do not you take Jessie away from this house of death? Sell this farm, buy another nice place nearby? With all the suffering and illness that has occurred here, both of you can have nothing but horrible memories"

Murdoch was silent for a moment; then...

"I know what you mean Sarah and the thought has already crossed my mind. It wasn't always such a bad place; we had many happy days here as well. But you are right! The sorrow and sadness of recent years has completely rubbed the happy ones away like the chaff from the corn. But Sarah," he pleaded," what would I do for a living - more to the point - what would Jessie do? This, after all, is her home too!"

Sarah lowered her eyes to her lap - shaking her head from side to side to emphasise her next words.

"This house is cursed, Murdoch, and if I was in your shoes, I would take my daughter away from here. After all is said and done, you would still have your rented farm, half the share of the quarry and the grindstone business to occupy you and bring in money. Jessie could still do the books for them. She is already very accomplished at the work. As an added asset, when she gets a bit older, she might even get extra work doing some other company's books. She already has a lot of knowledge in that department."

Murdoch gave serious thought to what Sarah had suggested. Giving a heavy sigh by way of resolve, he replied.

"I will think about what you has said Sarah."

Throughout all of this conversation, John had not said a single word. He hadn't known Sarah was going to broach such a delicate subject. Inwardly he thought that she shouldn't have said any of this to Murdoch; after all, it was none of her business. However, he had remained silent, deciding to keep his counsel and say nothing to his wife. He knew she meant well; just maybe she was right He would let things take their course.

Chapter 28

*J*ohn and Sarah - the Senior Munros - took great pleasure from their ever increasing number of grandchildren.

Sarah was particularly pleased when Mary and Murdoch decided to name their second daughter '*Sarah Hendrie Munro*'.

There was but fourteen months between this latest arrival and their first girl; *Elizabeth Young Munro* and only eleven months between her and little John Munro, their first child.

With so many grandchildren, the question of naming all the little ones was beginning to create a problem. Mary and young Murdoch had broken with tradition; with the exception of John, their first born, they gave their children middle or second Christian names. Now- Mary was once more with child.

All of John and Sarah's girls were producing babies. Grandmother Sarah and Grandfather John took great pleasure in visiting them all on a regular basis. The Munros were a very close knit family!

Their youngest - Edward - had decided that he wanted to be an engineer. He had it all planned out and had already written to his older brother John to ask if he might stay with him.

John, who had lodged with Uncle Dugald and Aunt Nell in Glasgow to begin with, now had a good job with reasonably well paid wages. He had since moved into a place of his own and had an extra room. Consequently, he was quite willing to have his little brother come to Glasgow and stay with him. *What was family for anyway?*

So, it was all arranged; Edward would go to Glasgow and stay with John. The latter agreed to speak to his employer and find out if Edward might be taken on as an apprentice. Failing this, John would ask around the shipyards to see if his wee brother could get an apprenticeship with one of them. *Exciting times in a young man's life!*

Time moved onward relentlessly and with it, once again, things started going amiss.

The following summers were diabolical; nothing but rain accompanied by low temperatures. So for many, the crops were ruined.

However for some farmers, the worst effects of these unkind acts of nature were avoided. A lot of them had diversified.

Instead of growing so much barley and oats, they were now growing more potatoes and vegetables, for which there still remained great demand.

Fortunately, the Munro brothers had followed the example of those who had diversified into those other crops and so, helped to keep some money coming in.

Murdoch had opted to ignore Sarah's suggestion to sell and decided to stay at *Eastfield*. He kept a large herd of dairy cattle and these became more valuable.

Imports of beef cattle and other farm produce from other countries were now flooding the British market, thus making locally produced beef and certain other products, too expensive. However, vegetables and dairy products were the exception so Murdoch still had a ready market for his farm produce.

The fall in demand for beef, in turn, affected the hay market. It was still grown in quite large quantities, as it was used mainly for feeding the horses and as bedding for the cattle in winter but there was no money in it!

The sale of hay was falling off rapidly as the demand for home grown beef collapsed. Most of the beef producing farmers had been forced to sell off their cattle at ridiculous prices just to get rid of them.

Sheep farmers were in no better a state. Over the years they had overgrazed the land, making it poor and almost non productive.

Adding to all the other woes - the unprecedented amount of rain had caused cases of foot rot to break out in the herds.

To top it all; cheap wool was being brought in from other countries and the local producers could not compete.

Thus; the Scottish farming industry was plunged into a deep depression.

The Munro Clan were lucky because in addition to their farming assets, they had the quarry. Lots of houses were still being built; there was still a buoyant market for stone. This allowed them to hang on for longer than most but inevitably, the depression made itself felt.

The first farm to fail was Murdoch's other farm; the one he had inherited as his share of Edward's legacy to him. The people renting it gave up and left.

Not long after that, the next to give up and leave was the man who had purchased Grandpa Murdoch's old farm, *Oatlands*. The poor man was bankrupt and just could not carry on.

One night after dinner, John and Sarah sat down and talked the whole thing through. Gesturing round him with arms outstretched as to encompass the house and the land surrounding it and shaking his head John exclaimed...

"We just cannot go on like this, Sarah; we are going to have to sell; that is if we can! The problem is; who's going to buy our land?" He went on, not waiting for an answer.

"Things are not all bad though. If we do manage to sell it, we will at least have the quarry and the grindstone business remaining. These will give us an income. Besides that, we have put by quite a bit of money during the good years. Our savings, together with what we get for this property will enable us to buy a nice house. Oh I know, of course, It will be much smaller than this one but adequate for our needs. What is your opinion of the situation?"

Sarah thought deeply for a moment then gave a great sigh of resignation.

"I suppose we do not have much choice, do we? Now that Edward has gone to Glasgow to become an engineer in the shipyards, there is only Joan left at home. I will be terribly sad to leave this lovely house, it has been such a happy place for us, hasn't it?" she smiled gently.

"Yes, it has" agreed John echoing his wife's sigh of regret.

"I too will be very sad to part with it, but we must think of the future. If we stay here, we will use up all our savings just to keep the place going. Eventually, we will have nothing left but worthless land and a house that nobody wants. But before we rush into anything, we should think this over for a wee while. After all, we will have to try and find out if the land is saleable in the first place. Besides which; it will give us time to think of where we might like to move to."

Sarah nodded in agreement. Then, extending the subject to include her brother- in-law;

"I wonder if Murdoch will do the same, now that things are taking a turn for the worse? As I have said before; time he and Jessie were out of that place anyway."

A few days later, they decided to go to *Eastfield* and see what Murdoch was planning to do in light of the current situation.

They had more or less made their minds up that they would try and sell *Westcroft*. They knew about the market only too well, having talked to the man who had bought *Oatlands*.

He had told them that he had abandoned the place in desperation. He had tried to sell his farm right up until the last moment but never did find a buyer and finally had to give up and leave. The place was still on the market.

This was an added problem because if they put their farm on the market, there would be two such properties on the same Estate!

As always, Murdoch was glad to see them and have their company for a little while. Once they were settled with a cup of tea and a few biscuits, John broached the subject of the farms.

He told his brother of his decision to sell his own farm property then sat back and let the news sink in. It produced a mixture of worry, regret and indecision in the younger man's face, so John decided to grasp the opportunity, take the bull by the horns, and put the idea of selling into his brother's head.

"I was thinking, Murdoch...perhaps if you were willing to sell your other farm, we might perhaps sell the whole estate as one big lot, rather than try and sell three separate farms. Mr. Sinclair, the man who bought father's farm, has gone and his property remains unsold.

Murdoch was astounded.

"Sinclair's gone?...gone you say?"

"I am afraid so." confirmed John. "Right up until the last day he tried without success to sell. It is still on the market. He left us an address where we could reach him just in case anything came up and there was an interest." Then as if he had been suddenly inspired: "Now here is a thought - if we *were* lucky and *could* sell all three farms and the attached land as a single lot, Sinclair would get his share of the sale for his farm. I am sure he would be delighted with that. What do you think?"

Murdoch's face lit up; for a moment there was a glimpse of his old self.

"That certainly sounds a great idea John. I would certainly be willing to sell that other farm as part of the whole Estate." Then his expression changed back to a look of doubt. "But who would want to buy all that useless farming property given the state of farming as it is? I think it would be a long time before we could be rid of it without giving it away and I am certainly not for that." Then as an afterthought... " What about the quarry? What do we do with that?"

John did not hesitate.

"We keep the quarry; most definitely... we keep it! It will be our only real means of getting an income.

Sarah and I thought that maybe some of the builders might be interested in the land. It is not really what I would want to see, but if they offered us a good price for it, I do not think we could turn up our noses." He continued:

"You will remember; a few years ago, two builders offered us a good price for father's farm and we turned it down because of father's will that it was to be sold to a working farmer. There is still a lot of building going on and I think builders just might be interested in what we have to offer. After all, our Susanna is married into the McLeod building family, so maybe that would make a difference, who knows? What do you think of the idea?"

Murdoch had been listening to his brother intently.

"I like the whole idea. But as you do; I think it would be a shame to see building work ruining such lovely farm land." This, accompanied by a deep sigh of regret. Then his expression changed to one of worry.

"They *are* builders; would they not want the quarry as well?"
"Probably" John said, "but they are not getting it, and that is for sure. We need to keep it! If you agree, we can approach the McLeods and find out if they might be interested."

To his brother's surprise, Murdoch made his mind up there and then. soon."

"Yes, we could do that. We will go together and speak to them

The brothers continued discussing the finer details of the plan for some time. Finally, before John and Sarah left for home, the both agreed they would approach the McLeods within two days.

John and Murdoch had their meeting with the two older McLeod brothers in their office. The proposal to sell the Estate and three farms was put on the table.

"Did you have a figure in mind for the property?" asked the older of the two.

"Not really," replied John. "It is early days yet and we have just recently decided to put the place on the market.

Because of our family association, and the length of time we have done business together, we thought it only fair to offer your company first refusal. If you are not interested, we will of course approach other similar companies with the offer to sell."

The Mcleods looked at each other, giving nothing away.

"As you know, Builders are always on the lookout for good building land. But as you also know, the decline in the farming industry has resulted in a lot of good land becoming available. I admit we are needing more land but our interest in what you have to offer would depend on two things: your asking price and whether the Quarry is included in the sale."

Without hesitation, John replied "The quarry is not included in the sale. We want to keep it."

"In that case" retorted the younger McLeod brother. "we can not come to any agreement. The quarry would need to be included in the sale." "Absolutely not!" Murdoch answered emphatically, "The quarry stays in our possession and we would sell you the stone for building" There was a moment's silence then:

"I do not think we could agree to that, but we will think about your proposition and let you know our decision soon.

In the meantime, we may wish to come and take a look at the property. Would that be all right with you?"

"Yes, of course" said John, "feel free to come whenever you wish. We will be there most of the time. If not, the farm manager will be there to help you."

The Munro brothers did not keep their *"eggs in one basket"* but decided to go and see other builders with the same proposition. They received a similar reception from each one and a promise that the offer to sell would be considered but again that a visit to the property would be necessary before any decision could be made. Things were, therefore, left hanging there.

In the meantime, John and Sarah started looking around the Lenzie and Kirkintilloch area for somewhere to live. For a time there was nothing that appealed to them, and then one day Sarah saw the perfect house.

It stood on It is own at the end of a lane - had two stories - and ample accommodation for the three of them, as well as a spare bedroom for visitors.

There was nice front garden loaded with flowers and shrubs at the front. The rear sported an ample area of grass plus a large garden with vegetable plots. Sarah thought to herself; *oh the fun I could have with this garden!* It was perfect! The owners were selling through the local bank, so off she went to find out the selling price.

It turned out that the asking price was a bit more than they had planned to spend; however, Sarah was sure she could persuade John to put up the extra money needed to buy it.

First of all though; they would need to sell their own farm to raise the capital needed. After all, they didn't want to buy a house with their savings then find out they could not sell their existing property. Full of excitement, she hurried home to tell John all about her find.

When Sarah finally managed to speak to her husband about I the house, her excitement and enthusiasm got the better of her; she started off talking ten to the dozen.

"Oh, John", she enthused, eyes shining as she warmed to the subject; "it seems to be just what we are looking for."

Then, hardly pausing, launched into a minute description of every detail before finishing with; "but it is a little more expensive than be were willing to spend. I think it is perfect for our needs and would be worth putting the extra money into it."

John did not need convincing that this was a house Sarah would be happy to live in. She was so excited about it all.

"All right, Sarah," he said with a broad smile, "we will both go to the bank tomorrow and ask if we can view this dream house of yours. Then we can work out if we can afford it."

"Thank you, my wonderful husband, you are so good to me." she answered; giving him a big hug and kiss.

"I know!" agreed John." You will notice I always give in to your wishes." This said with laughter in his voice.

It seemed to take forever for the builders to make up their minds about the purchase of the farmlands and of course there was a great deal of haggling over the quarry.

Eventually the McLeods put in an acceptable offer and agreed to leave the quarry out of the sale. In due course, the bank would work out what proportion of the sale money each farm was entitled to.

The minute Sarah knew the farm had definitely been sold, she went rushing off to see the agent for the people who were selling the lovely house she so wanted, and made an offer for the property. Shortly after - she was jumping for joy the offer had been accepted.

In no time at all, a date of entry was settled upon.

Except for Annie; the staff remaining at *Westcroft* were all of retirement age; some of them were even past it and were not too unhappy about the place being sold.

James had passed away many years previously so the only house servant left who needed to work on was Annie. Fortunately, she had managed to get another position as housekeeper in one of the larger houses in Lenzie. She had lots of experience and was totally trustworthy so had obtained employment without any trouble. The farm hands - not that there were many of them - were all paid off.

There were no staff problems at the other two farms since everyone had been paid off when the occupants had left.

Chapter 29

Jessie had a secret, which she wanted to keep at all costs from her father. She had a bad cough! However, she managed to suppress it most of the time.

When they were sitting together in the evening, she would excuse herself and go upstairs to cough.

During the night, she would cough into the bedclothes so as to muffle the sound.

After what had happened to the rest of the family, she knew her father would be horribly worried if he suspected anything was wrong with her. She also knew he was under a terrible strain trying to keep the farm and house running with minimum staff and field hands. She could see from the books that money was tight. It would therefore have been a very bad idea to let him know she had a cough.

She was also a little worried herself that this cough might be the start of the dreaded Consumption, but comforted herself with the thought that it could just be due to a cold that she had picked up somewhere.

As for her father; he had noticed these frequent sudden departures upstairs. His curiosity eventually got the better of him.

On one such occasion, when she disappeared from the room, he decided to go upstairs and see what she was doing.

As he got nearer to his daughter's room, he could see the door was closed but the noise of violent coughing and choking coming from behind it was so loud that the door may as well have been left open.

Murdoch was aghast to hear his daughter coughing so badly. *How long had this been going on?* He tried to think back. *Had she been hiding this from him for some time?*

When Jessie eventually stopped coughing, he knocked on her bedroom door and asked if she was all right.

"I am fine, father! I just have a bit of a cough, that's all." she replied from behind the closed door.

Murdoch went back downstairs and waited for her to join him.

When she entered the room, he could see she was distressed.

"How long has this cough been going on, Jessie - and I want the truth, please."

Jessie lowered her eyes and replied in almost a whisper, "Quite a few months now father."

"For goodness sake girl! Why did you not tell me before this? You must see the doctor right away, tomorrow in fact." Jessie looked up with tears in her eyes:

"I didn't want to worry you father, knowing how you would react I thought it would just eventually go away."

Murdoch's eyes softened, he spoke to his daughter, in pleading tones... "You are the only one I have left now, dearest Jessie...we must get this cough treated right away. Oh I wish you had told me sooner."

"I would have done "explained Jessie," but you have had so much worry with the farm and everything, I didn't want you to have an added worry."

Murdoch wrapped his daughter in his arms: "Oh my dear! Your health is far more important to me than any damned farm or quarry. You should know that."

Next morning the doctor examined Jessie. Afterward, he told Murdoch that her cough was deep seated and far down in her chest. He did not share with him his suspicions as to what it might be... it could just be an ordinary chest infection. He left a bottle of mixture for her to take to ease her coughing. As he was leaving he advised Murdoch.

"I wouldn't worry too much about the girl, Mr. Munro; it could very well clear up soon. Sometimes when people get a bad chest infection, it takes quite a long time to shift. See that she stays indoors when it is wet or cold. If this cough doesn't clear up within the next two or three weeks, let me know and I will come back to examine her again."

During the following weeks, Murdoch fretted over Jessie constantly. Eventually, he had to admit to himself that his daughter's cough was most definitely getting worse. The doctor was called in once more. After examining Jessie, his worst fears were confirmed... the girl had contracted the Consumption.

As he had done so on previous occasions in this very same house, the doctor closed the girl's bedroom door and went downstairs to give her father the result of the examination.

He found Murdoch waiting for him in the drawing room... a pathetic look of hope mixed with anxiety on his face.

"I am afraid to tell you Mr. Munro that in my opinion your daughter has contracted Consumption." He went on ....

"This, I know, must be a terrible blow to you considering the past members of your family. You have my sincere sympathy. I am so sorry to give you this dreadful news."

Murdoch could not take-in the appalling news he had just received. He visibly shrunk and crumpled all at the same time. Sitting down heavily, he openly wept. His mind was in a turmoil of despair...asking himself questions that did not seem to have an answer: *What have I done to deserve all this? I am a good man. I have never, never harmed a living soul... have never done anything bad in my entire life that I am aware of.* Then suddenly! *Maybe I should have listened to Sarah a few years ago when she said to take Jessie and get out of this house. She was right! This house was truly cursed. So many deaths and now....*

When John and Sarah heard the news, they too were appalled. To be happening again was almost unbelievable. How could one man suffer so many losses in his family?

When Jessie died, his whole family would have been wiped out in just a few years.

Sarah again wept oceans of tears. Through them she vehemently declared to her husband...

"That house is determined to kill off the whole family. When Jessie is no longer with him, Murdoch must get out of there before it gets him too."

Secretly John was inclined to have the same opinion but being of a less dramatic nature he simply replied...

"Do not be ridiculous, Sarah, It is only a house made of stone. It doesn't have a mind of It is own. I have never heard you say anything so silly. There will be a perfectly sound reason for all of this. Who knows?

Perhaps the germ of Consumption is there in the house, maybe that is possible? But rest assured; the house itself is not killing people. Utter nonsense! Where are your wits, woman?"

Sarah would not be dissuaded... not by reason or in any other way.

"I am telling you, John Munro, the devil is in that house and I do not care what you say!"

The day for moving to the new house came all too soon.

For some time before it, Sarah had been going through all the belongings they had collected in the years previously...discarding things she didn't need or want and selecting what she would take with her to the new home. It was totally remarkable how many useless bits and pieces, odds and sods that they had accumulated as a family over all the long years they had been living at *Westcroft*. Reluctantly she parted with more than she would have wanted to, but needs must!

Eventually the carriers arrived and started loading their belongings onto three large wagons drawn by massive Clydesdale work horses. Before this; John had gone on ahead to the new house and would be waiting for them to arrive to unload their cargo. Sarah had given him specific instructions as to what was to go where in each room. Heaven help him if he got it wrong!

Finally, all the Munro family worldly goods had been loaded on the wagons and the load was secured. When this was done, the three of them trundled off down the farm road for the new abode.

After they had gone, Sarah sat in the hall of the now empty house - she was thinking of the past. Remembering when they had first come here ...how they had both felt.

She had given birth to five children in this house, and what a happy house it had been for all of them. She could almost hear the rooms ringing with cries of delight and laughter of young children. Now all was silent...even the loud "ticking" of the Grandfather clock that until moments previously, had held pride of place in the hall was no longer there.

She shed gentle tears as she thought of all these happy times... of the good, faithful staff they had once had. Just then - at that moment, she felt so dreadfully reluctant to leave.

Ah well! she thought. *All good things must come to an end.*

Circumstances had made it so and there was nothing she could do about it.

She hated the very idea of this lovely place which had brought so much joy and happiness becoming a building site. How wrong that seemed to her.

However; reluctantly she knew she must think positively... think of what she and John still had. They had been -and still were - so lucky compared to her poor brother- in-law Murdoch.

Life had given him a raw deal and continued to do so. His daughter, Jessie, was still alive, but in pretty poor shape. Sarah was sure that it would not be long until the time came for Jessie to depart from the world. She was equally sure that when this did happen, Murdoch would sell as fast as he could and get out of there. That house was home to far too many horrible memories.

Thus, she closed her mental book of memories with one last thought: *Thank your lucky stars, Sarah Munro, you have not had the tragedies Murdoch has had. Give grateful thanks for what you have!* With that, she stood up and walked out the front door, closing it behind her...closing it on that part of her life for the very last time.

Turning away; she squared her shoulders and started off down the driveway toward the front gate - .Off to the new house and a new and different style of life!

Chapter 30

The change of residence and fortunes was an exciting time for John and Sarah. Life was certainly different! They had no servants so Sarah had to do all the housework. Daughter Joan helped when she had time off.

Sarah's passion was her garden. However; because the house had lain empty for some time...the gardens of the new house were overgrown and neglected.... a lot of work was needed to bring them back to their former glory. This was a task she did not object to. She tackled the front garden first.

When she had finished the work at the front to her satisfaction, she started on the garden at the rear of the house. *It* was a different kettle of fish. It was massively overgrown... the grass was waist high. What had once seemed to have been vegetable plots looked like a field which had lain fallow for ten years!

It took Sarah a lot of time and effort to clear the area, but over a number of weeks, she eventually had it cleared to her satisfaction. Then she got John to dig over some patches and plant vegetables.

Sarah also enjoyed cooking. She had learned a lot from the Cook at *Kirkland* and from her own Cook at *Westcroft* ... now she could put what she had learned into practice! It was not a difficult job... there was now only the three people to feed.

A few weeks after they were settled-in, Joan announced she had decided to take a holiday from work and go to Glasgow. She thought she would stay for a week or maybe longer with Uncle Dugald and Aunt Nell, if they would have her.

"What brought this on then?" asked Sarah.

"Nothing really mother. I have never had a real holiday and I just thought it might be a good idea. I will write a letter to Aunt Nell and ask if this will be all right with them."

Actually, the idea had been fermenting in her head for quite a time. In truth, her plan was to see how she liked Glasgow and if she did, perhaps she might look for a job in a bank in that city, and stay with her relatives.

However, until she had been to the place and found out if there would be employment for her, she would keep her ideas to herself. In truth; Kirkintilloch and Lenzie bored her to death.

There were no presentable young men there who were not already spoken for, and there was nothing to do. It was so dull! She wanted to experience a bit more excitement, just as Edward, her brother, had done.

Edward and her other brother John enjoyed being in Glasgow with all the bustle and noise, so it wasn't as if she didn't know anyone there. She had them *and* an Aunt and Uncle to turn to if she got into difficulties.

Murdoch ' s daughter Jessie ' s illness had progressed... she had become quite ill. Nevertheless, she put on a brave face and, as near to normal as was possible, kept on going... doing the books and paying wages.

Business was rather quiet; there wasn't all that much to do. The only books with any activity in them were the ones concerning the quarry and grindstone business. If it hadn't been for these, she and her father would have had very little income at all - not even enough to live on.

Jessie knew she was going to die in just the same tortuous way as her mother, brother and sister had done. At eighteen years of age, it was a horrible thought! She was afraid of dying. But she was a brave, thoughtful, considerate girl who loved her father dearly, therefore, she did not share her fears with him; he, poor man, had enough to worry about.

Although it was plain to her that her ill health was tormenting him, there was absolutely nothing she could do about it.

She felt so sorry and helpless - she was causing him so much grief. She in turn, did not realise just *how much* suffering and anxiety her illness was affecting her father. Simply because Murdoch tried his best to hide his feelings from her in every ways he could... it was so difficult. It wrenched at his heart strings to see her wasting away while trying to put a brave face on it and keep going as if nothing was wrong. How he loved this child of his and wished with all his heart and soul that this had never happened to her, but there was no cure and her death was inevitable.

Every day he tried his utmost to make things as nice, normal and cheery for her as possible. Deep down, he knew that soon, the dreadful day would come when she could no longer cope with normal day-to-day life. Then, this evil disease would dictate her capabilities and she would have to be confined to her bed... soon thereafter, to gasp away her last tormented moments on earth... in the same way as her mother and siblings had done before her.

He wondered in deep despair, if he could actually stand by and watch this cruel thing happening to his beloved daughter. Many a tear he shed in private. When the time arrived for her to go, he knew he would be inconsolable. Meantime, he would try not to think about it and get on with what he had to do. While work on the farm and quarry was a necessity... under the circumstances, it had no real meaning - it was just something to do.

John and Sarah visited quite often. Each and every time they returned home, they were plunged deeper into gloom filled sadness at the prospect of what was to come.

Sarah cried many tears over the state of affairs at Murdoch's home.

Jessie was such a lovely girl who should be looking forward to a life of happiness instead of what lay ahead for her. It was criminal that this should be happening to her.

After their latest visit, John, who had kept his feelings to himself, could do so no longer and expressed them to his wife.

"I am so sorry for my wee brother, Sarah, and for young Jessie. Today was agony! I have seen the lass wasting away a little more every time we go there...and her trying to be so brave about it. Murdoch is losing weight, getting thinner and ageing by the minute. This is taking its toll of him. He is become an old man in front of our eyes. Now - except for looking after Jessie - life means nothing to him. I hate to think what he'll be like when she leaves us all."

"Oh I know! I know," exclaimed Sarah. "It is dreadful!" John continued:

"I am beginning to get quite worried about him. When the lass goes, he won't care if he lives or dies. We'll have to watch out for him!"

Sarah agreed.

"We' ll certainly look after him, that' s for sure and give him all our support. Anything that we can do to make his life better, we will most certainly do." She continued...

"We have been so lucky that none of this has happened to us. We should be thanking God for that.

Your brother Murdoch will have no family left... no prospect of ever having grandchildren. That will end with Jessie.

He would have been looking forward to her eventually getting married and producing more Munro babies and he would have given her and her family everything. It is so sad."

As she finished speaking; the tears once again rolled uncontrollably down her cheeks. Being such an emotional person; she really felt the grief of others - treating it almost as her own. But as her mother had once told her *do not let it worry you girl; there is nothing wrong with sharing the grief of others.*

A few months later Jessie died.

In one way, Murdoch was glad that her suffering was over, but the event of her passing wrenched at the core of his very being.

As Sarah had predicted... he was totally and completely devastated. *Oh dear God! How he was going to miss this lovely child of his... his very last real treasure!*

Many attended Jessie's funeral to pay their respects and condolences to her grieving father. Murdoch, went through the motions expected of him, but was wishing everyone would go away so that he might be left alone with his grief.

Eventually - except for John and Sarah - all the mourners left. Then the three of them sat for a while; each wrapped in an individual blanket of grief. Eventually John spoke:

"If you want us to go as well, Murdoch we will do so. We appreciate you might want to be by yourself at this time so we won't be offended if you do. We just hate to leave you here on your own, but if you prefer it that way, that's all right with us." He finished with "We wish you would come home and stay with us for a few days, would you consider that?"

Murdoch was not too deep in sorrow that he was unable to recognise his brother's anxiety.

"I much appreciate your kind offer, John, but I know you will not be offended if I decline for the moment. I just want to be by myself."

"We understand, and we'll come the day after tomorrow and see how you are. Would that be all right?"

"Yes, that would be fine. And by the way, do not worry; I won't do anything stupid you know."

"Good, we'll leave now and see you in two days" time."

For a while after they had gone, Murdoch sat in a trance. Then one by one, big wet salty tears welled up in his eyes and followed each other in ever increasing numbers down his cheeks until he was weeping uncontrollably for his lost daughter.

Eventually, Murdoch was all cried out. After he regained his composure, he had a few drinks before climbing the stairs to his bed. As he made his unsteady way upward, the despairing thought hit him like a ton of bricks. *How was he going to live the rest of his life alone? Oh God! How he hated this damned house.* He made his mind up there and then: as soon as he got over Jessie' s death, he would sell the whole lot if he could and go somewhere else – anywhere, as long as it was away from the place.

Bitterly, it came home to him... he should have done that a long time ago. He was left with one miserable consolation; at least he had a plan, which would keep him going for a while.

Chapter 31

*J*oan wrote to her Uncle Dugald and asked him if she could stay with them for a week's holiday. The answer came back fairly quickly saying he and her Aunt Nell would be delighted to see her. The same day she received the reply, she arranged with her employer to have time off for ten days and that night, her letter to Uncle Dugald was in the post; advising him she would arrive in Glasgow the following Friday evening. Not a minute to waste!

And so, when Friday arrived - decked out in her finest and carrying her clothes in a carpet bag - Joan left the house and headed for the station.

At exactly 6pm; filled with hope and excitement, she boarded the train for Glasgow.

When she arrived at Glasgow' s Queen Street station, Joan was met by her brother Edward who, as always, was pleased to see her.

After he had retrieved her luggage from the cavernous luggage van at the rear of the train, the two of them headed out of the station and hired one of the many carriages standing there, and gave the driver the directions to take them to their uncle's house.

They arrived at their destination and Joan was warmly welcomed with a big hug from her aunt and uncle, then shown up to a very bright spacious room.

"Make yourself at home Joan dear." invited Aunt Nell. "When you have unpacked and had a wash, come downstairs and have something to eat. Poor dear! You must be starved." With that, she left; closing the door behind her.

Joan was thrilled with her surroundings - she instantly liked where she was. This would be perfect if they would have her as a permanent guest. However, she would need to find work first - then broach the subject to her Aunt and Uncle.

A week's stay was one thing but...

After she had settled in for a few days, Joan thought it was time to put the next part of her plan into action – she would now go out and look for employment.

As it turned out, she did not have very far to look. One of the bigger banks in the city was looking for extra staff with at least a little experience of the banking system. She obviously impressed them because after they had interviewed her, they immediately offered her a job. Young Joan was thrilled to bits and rushed back to tell Aunt Nell.

As soon as Nell saw Joan's face, she knew the girl was bursting to give her some momentous news.

"Well now lass" she began "You are back early. I thought you'd be away for the day. Just as well you caught me in the house. I was just about to go off to the shops to get something for your uncle's tea."

Joan could hardly contain herself, her news and request burst forth in one long breathless sentence.

"Oh Auntie Nell! I have had the most wonderful bit of good luck. I was down in the town and I went into a bank and asked for a job and they gave me a job right away. So now I need somewhere to live and I thought..."

"Calm yourself girl." interrupted Nell. "Slow down a bit.".…"Joan continued as if she had never heard that advice...

"I thought I would ask you and uncle Dugald if you would have me as a lodger. What do you think?" she finished; her voice conveying the utmost anxiety while her eyes were wide with hope.

Her aunt's face beamed in delight.

"Of course we would be delighted to have you stay with us dear Joan. We've got plenty of room and it would be nice to have a young lady in the house."

"Oh thank you, thank you" Joan gushed as only a young girl in such a situation could do. "I am so happy!"

Eventually Joan' s initial jaunt to the big city came to an end. She bade farewell to her relatives and caught the train back home to Lenzie. Immediately she arrived at the house and before she had even removed her coat, she blurted out her momentous news to her mother.

"Well, Miss Secretive", Sarah began." Why didn't you at least give us a clue as to what you were thinking of doing? Did you think we would try and stop you?" Answering her own question, she continued. "We would not have done so out of hand but the big city is not a place for a young girl on her own - especially one who has had a sheltered upbringing in the countryside. Your father and I would most certainly have tried to discourage you. However, the fact that you have your uncle Dugald and Nell to go to makes me a little easier in my mind.

Your father and I will miss you terribly but if that ' s what you want to do, and you have made up your mind, then we will not stand in your way." She went on "It all seems to have worked out beautifully. You certainly must have impressed the bank people no end, for them to have offered you a job there and then. Good for you! But young lady; before you go away, you and I *will* most certainly need to be having a little talk about all the things NOT to do, and to beware of, during this great adventure of yours.

Never mind; it is a comfort to know your Aunt Nell will be keeping an eye on you and whom you associate with. You'll also have two big strong brothers to look after you!"

Joan was desperate to get a word in, but as usual, her mother seemed to go on and on. *The impatience of youth!*

Eventually - when her mother finally stopped to take a breather - her chance to speak came.

"What do you think father will say when he comes home?"

"More or less the same as what I have said" answered her mother.

Later that evening, when John came home, Joan repeated her news to him.

After he had listened to her, he was silent for a moment. Then, as her mother had predicted, replied along much the same lines as she had done. He put his thoughts to her in a slightly different way by adding:

"I have no objections to you leaving, Joan, if that ' s what you want. You are a big girl now, not a silly romantic wee lass. I expect you to have some common sense about the dangers of the city and the people you get involved with...particularly men. No doubt your mother will advise you on that."

"Yes, father," Joan sighed. "She has already said we will have a talk together before I go away.

"So what is your next move then?" asked her mother.

"Well; I will need to let the bank here know that I am leaving. I may have to work on there for a bit before I can leave so I will need to find this out first. I told the people in the bank in Glasgow that I would write to them and let them know when I could begin working with them."

John then brought this momentous family meeting to an end. Stretching his arms wide and giving a loud yawn he remarked...

"Well young lady, you have had a busy time and by the looks of things, you are going to be busier. Time for supper and bed for all of us I think!"

The following day Joan returned to her workplace and informed the manger of her plans.

The man in question was very disappointed to be losing her but had secretly guessed that someone as bright and clever would one day wish to spread her wings. He reluctantly let her go with his blessing, adding that she would only have to work one more week.

Joan was relieved that there had been no hitches and when she returned home, she immediately sat down and wrote to her future employers in Glasgow; advising them she would be able to start work there in two weeks time.

As she wrote, she suddenly had misgivings and for a moment, felt very vulnerable and a little frightened. But it was only a moment; perhaps even half of one...then her enthusiasm and youth kicked-in and all misgivings were swept out of her mind.

Meantime, Sarah had decided to have a send-off party for Joan before she left.

To this end, she invited all the close family that were left in the area. It would take place the day before Joan was due to leave for Glasgow.

On the morning of the send-off party, Sarah and Joan had the promised cautionary discussion. Afterward, Sarah disclosed her party plans.

It came as a complete surprise to Joan. Her mother had kept the secret well; although Joan *should* have known her mother's "thing" was planning parties, and would therefore have arranged something to mark the event.

Nevertheless, she was thrilled and immediately unpacked something to wear for the event.

The party itself was a sad-happy affair enjoyed by everyone.

The following day Joan' s time to leave the nest arrived. Before she left the house there were, of course, the inevitable tears and last minute bits of caution mixed with advice.

At the station, besides her mother and father... Susanna, Janet and Sarah turned up to see her off and wish her well. Again more tears. *What a tearful family they were!*

As the train finally pulled out of the station, they all waved to the diminishing figure waving frantically out of the carriage window. Soon the train chuffed its busy way out of sight leaving everyone on the platform to go home their separate ways.

Back home; Sarah and John suddenly realised they were back to where they started all those long years before. It seemed strangely quiet... no awareness of another presence.... only the two of them in the house. They remembered that they had only been on their own for one year until first son Murdoch was born. There had always seemed to be so many people around them. Now it was all so quiet and Sarah wasn't sure if she liked it very much; it was alien to her. No job - no family - no servant… nothing but the two of them. Well, at least they still had each other. That was a bonus.

As promised at Jessie ' s funeral; John and Sarah visited John's brother Murdoch. They were pleased to find that he seemed to have come to terms with his situation. He looked well and assured them that he was looking after himself and the businesses, but the books were his main problem.

John, who only had the Quarry accounts to attend to, jumped at the opportunity to help.

"Och now Murdoch! I think I can be of assistance to you in that direction. I have got too much spare time on my hands now since things have got so quiet. I will take on that task for you if you'll let me? Actually I am quite the dab-hand at such work!"

Secretly, Murdoch was delighted at this offer.

"Not at all brother" he protested. Then, after a respectable pause and with doubt in his voice… "Well, if you think it would be all right?"

John did not give him time to change his mind. "Right then! That's settled!"

Thus, the two brothers were once again together after all the long years since they had left the North, albeit for short periods!

And so, the world continued on its daily trip round the sun. Day inevitably followed its older siblings as it had done since the beginning of time itself.

On one of the days, when John was working on Murdoch's accounts, the latter, without preamble suddenly announced:

"I'm selling the farm, John, and will look for a small house just to suit myself."

John was quick to comment.

"I think that would be a good idea. Do you think you ' ll find a buyer?"

His brother did not answer that question at first but in a reminiscent tone came back with:

"You know, as a young lad over forty years ago I came here to *Eastfield* on my own. Now, as an old man on my own, I will be leaving it! A lot has happened in-between times - some good years, but a lot of very, very bad ones. I will be glad to get away from here, I can tell you."

Then, remembering John's question:

"I have already spoken to a man who seems interested and wants to see the books. If you would be so kind as to get them up to date for me, I can then let this man see them and hopefully he' ll buy the property." He added… "It is still quite a reasonable venture with the dairy cattle and the fruit and vegetables, so someone could probably make a living out of it if they also had some capital to fall back on."

John digested this news. He could see that his brother was looking for approval.

"That would be good if this man bought *Eastfield*. It would allow you to get on with your life. Buy a smaller house as you have planned, though I doubt you'll be able to sell at the price the place is actually worth. You'll maybe have to take a lower price than you would wish."

"Oh doubtless!" Murdoch sighed; adding; "I do not care too much about the price he offers as long as it is a reasonable one. I just need enough money to buy another, smaller house. I have quite a bit of money saved from the good years we had in farming. That'll keep me going for as long as I am going to live."

"Right enough!" said John. "And do not forget; If we keep the quarry for a few years yet, we ' ll get some kind of income out of that as well." we are both getting on a bit, you know." he added laughing; "and besides, it would also give us both something to do for a while."

"Indeed we are not getting any younger" agreed his brother, "It doesn't seem that all those years have passed since we tramped down that long road together from the North looking for work…young lads in their prime with high hopes, ready to set the world alight. Now does it?"

"No Murdoch, it does not. At least we're both still together after all the good and bad days. Unfortunately, it seems you got the unfair share of bad days, but believe me, I shared those days with you as did Sarah."

"I know, John and I was grateful to both of you for your concern and that you were both always there to help me and Agnes during the darkest days"

This conversation set the two grey-heads into reminiscing. They sat there swapping memories like two old sea-dogs; talking over their young days on the ocean, until John realised the time and took his leave and returned home to Sarah.

A few months later, Murdoch had sold *Eastfield*. As expected, he was forced to accept a price well below what the property was worth. The buyer really got a huge bargain. Murdoch didn't care, he just wanted rid of it.

When the deal was sealed, he thought to himself: *John Mitchell would turn in his grave if he knew what his old farm had sold for. Just as well he never lived to survive his daughter and all his grandchildren. If he had done so, he would have been like me - a very sad old man.* He gave himself a mental shake. It was time for him to move on.

While waiting for the sale to go through, he had found a suitable house for himself in Boghead Road; a quiet location literally in the suburbs of Kirkintilloch. It was a fairly new and substantially built sandstone structure – one of a row of similar houses. When he first saw it, it occurred to him that in all probability, the sandstone used to build it came from his very own quarry!

As soon as the deeds were signed for the sale of the farm and those for the purchase of his new house, Murdoch lost no time and moved in to his new abode. A few days after that, John and Sarah came to see him settled in and to see if there was anything he needed.

Murdoch was delighted to see them and took great pleasure in showing them round.

Sarah was immediately taken with the place.

After the guided tour, the three of them returned to the small, neat parlour and had a cup of tea. As usual; Sarah opened the conversation.

"Murdoch, this is a delightful house, just splendid! and exactly made for you. You have made an excellent choice."

Her brother-in-law received this with a broad smile.

"Thank you Sarah" ... continuing enthusiastically... "I have already met some of my neighbours.... quite a mixture of ages. Some of them are actually just youngsters."

"Now that's a good thing." interjected John with a laugh - "Remember what I told you about how old you are getting! At least you'll have nearby help in your dotage."

All three of them laughed at this, but secretly, John and Sarah were relieved. They could see welcome improvements in Murdoch.

After that first visit, the brothers visited each other regularly and dined together quite often. They still went to the quarry... not every day, but at least twice a week.

The grindstone business was as good as ever, but they knew this situation could not last and that one day the quarry would run out of stone. In the meantime, until they wanted to retire properly, they would keep it going. It was a good source of income for them all.

By the time John reached the age of sixty-five, he decided he had had enough! He was fed up trudging to the quarry. It was all right in the summer on a nice day, but when it was wet and the winter set in, he really did not want to venture all that way out there and back. He preferred to sit by the fire...especially on a cold, dark, wet and windy winter ' s day. However, since Murdoch had said that he personally didn't mind keeping things as they were - John kept going to work for a couple of more years ... until Murdoch also got fed up and tired of it. It didn't bother John too much and besides, the income from the quarry was more important to Murdoch.

And so, at the end of the two years, the day arrived. They finally sold the quarry to the builders who had been eager to get their hands on it in the first place. Fortunately, they managed to get a good price which satisfied them both and they split the proceeds between them.

Chapter 32

When all their business interests had been sold off, the three of them - John, Murdoch and Sarah - met for dinner at Murdoch's house.

After Sarah had cleared away the dishes from the table, they sat sipping a glass of Madeira...the two men breaking tradition and lighting up fine cigars without adjourning. Sarah, the only lady present also broke with tradition and stayed with the men while they smoked. Thus, well fed, warm and comfortable in each other's company, the three of them looked back over the years gone by.

The unanimous agreement was that the world was changing at a rapid pace. Comparing now with then, caused them to find it difficult to comprehend some of the changes. Listing the principal ones that they had witnessed in the last fifty years, they all three agreed that they were privileged to have been present during so many momentous changes.

In their time, many laws had been passed giving workers rights. And, aiming at certain employers...banning many dreadful working practices. However; they agreed that there remained a great deal to be done.

Murdoch, who had above all of them experienced the ravages of illness and death, remarked that disease itself, which had curtailed and regulated life expectancy, was being brought under control.

Everything was getting better. They were all well read and had studied all the latest reports in the newspapers concerning the provision of clean drinking water, drainage and sewage disposal. Even the streets were getting cleaned up a bit better! Who would have thought of such a thing a mere ten years previously?

And so, the after dinner conversation reached into every corner of life and society, ranging back and forth between work, social life and education, they were united in their enthusiasm about progress but agreed unanimously that the common people had to be educated in simple hygienic practices.

Sarah's pet subject was children. She pointed out that infant mortality was as low as it had ever been.

Now that children had to go to school and be educated, the outcome could be nothing but good for everyone.

Although retired; the two men retained a strong interest in the world of the workers. They pointed out that workers were uniting and had formed strong Unions to represent their basic human rights and to work toward better pay and conditions. Things were definitely improving all over the country, not just in Glasgow. However; they all agreed it would take a few generations till things got really good for the ordinary folk.

"Goodness!" exclaimed Sarah - pointing to an ornate clock resting on the sideboard - "will you just look at the time."

John reached into the side pocket of his waistcoat and produced a giant gold turnip of a watch and flipped open it is gold lid.

"Goodness!" he echoed. "Where has the evening gone?"

Murdoch - sitting back in his chair with a little half smile on his face - just sighed and observed:

"Ah well now; you cannot set the world to right in an hour, now can you?" Inwardly he wished the other two would stay on longer but he knew that Sarah's remark about time was a precursor to their departure.

Ah well! He thought... *all good things must eventually end.*

Shortly after, Sarah and John donned their outdoor clothing and took their leave promising to *do this again!*

Chapter 33

*J*ohn was seventy-four years old now and Sarah almost four years his junior at seventy. Both of them kept reasonably well, apart from all the usual aches and pains which accompanied advancing years.

Although only a year younger than his brother; Murdoch at the age of seventy three looked years older. Time and bad luck had rendered their accounts and the price paid was there for all to see.

However: the three of them continued to visit each other and kept in touch on a fairly regular basis

Sarah liked to walk and often did so. She would ask John to accompany her, but often he was doing something else or just plain couldn't be bothered! So she would go on her own. Sometimes she would meet people she knew, but there weren't so many friends around her age left now so, as time passed, this would happen less and less.

The younger members of John and Sarah's ever widening immediate family often came to see them. Some of the grandchildren would call for a quick visit to say hello or to see if there was any help they might need. There were a lot of them!

Murdoch and Mary alone had eleven children and she was pregnant yet again. The poor woman never had breathing space. She was either nursing a new infant or carrying one inside her. There was so little time between them. Yet Mary managed very capably.

It had crossed Sara's mind that since four out of the first five of Mary' s children were girls...when they grew up, they would at least be of invaluable help to their mother. *How on earth did so many of them manage in that small railway cottage?* Having had the luxury of bringing her own children up in a large house, this was a big mystery to Sarah. It caused her to reflect on her good luck.

If Uncle Edward had not left them that beautiful property, without doubt she would have continued working in the Lennox house and John on the farm. *At the ages they were now, they would both have been long retired, and have had to leave their tied cottage without savings to buy somewhere to live. Where would they have gone? Thank you yet again Uncle Edward!*

Almost three years passed quietly. Two of the summers were sunny and warm, the other not so good with a lot of rain.

Winters were different each of these years. One had been very cold with snow and frost and the other two quite mild and wet. Despite this, the Munro brothers and Sarah kept fairly well considering their advanced years. In the eyes of younger people around them; in particularly their grandchildren, they were considered to be ancient!

At the beginning of that third summer, Murdoch was not feeling very well... hadn't been for most of the late spring. He complained of chest pains and breathlessness. The local doctor told him it was his heart and that he had better take it easy. His legs started to swell and he found it difficult to walk. The years were catching up with him fast! However, he kept cheery and was not short of company. Sarah, John and some of his nieces often visited him and all were more than kind.

One lovely warm sunny day in August, Sara had been doing a little gardening at the front of the house, but her back ached from bending. She decided she had had enough for that day so put her gardening tools away.

John was tending the vegetable patch at the back. He, too, felt he had done enough and as usual, decided to put his feet up and read a book.

With the passing of the years, the two of them did less and less in the garden. Old age prevented them from working there for much more than about an hour at any one given time.

Sarah decided to go for a walk along the side of the Forth and Clyde Canal, but John, as usual, declined an invitation to join her - making the usual excuses she had become accustomed to. Consequently, Sarah did as she always did - set off on her own.

She strolled along slowly, taking in the scenery and have a rest from time to time. Seats had been placed at intervals along the canal bank for that very purpose. Often during one of these rests, she would sit for a while just thinking and letting her mind wander.

Eventually, she decided to have her first rest and sat down on one of the benches between the lock gates.

When she was settled, she began thinking about the first time she had set eyes on John Munro all those years ago.

The minute he had walked into the kitchen at the Lennox's farm, she had thought he was wonderful...tall, good looking and spoke with the nicest soft lilting accent she had ever heard. She just fell in love with him on sight. She remembered how she had vamped him, but that he was stubborn and would not commit himself to marrying her until he was ready.

They had had a good marriage with lots of love, but also, due to her Irish temper and his stubbornness, lots of quarrels and arguments.

Their good fortune had also added something special to their relationship. For most of their married life they had not had any serious financial worries. John had always been a good, thoughtful husband and an excellent father to their children... taking great interest in whatever they were doing. She thought of how lucky she had been in her choice of husband.

Her thoughts then turned to her children.

The two boys, John and Edward had done well in the shipbuilding industry. Both had good jobs and liked living in Glasgow. John had remained a bachelor, but his brother Edward, although nearly thirty four, had met a more mature lady and was considering marriage.

As for the girls: Joan also loved living in Glasgow. She had secured a very good position in one of the bigger city banks. She too had opted to stay single. Her three sisters had all married well.

Sarah was now rested. Rising, she continued on her way along the gravel path by the side of the canal; still consumed by thoughts of her family. All in all, she thought, everyone seemed to be happy with their lot! Again she reminded herself of the good fortune in having been left all that property. Had it not been for that twist of fate, doubtless she would have continued to work on the Lennox farm or some other farm. Equally doubtless, her girls would not have had the opportunities they had grasped so eagerly and would have ended up being in service as she herself had done at the beginning of her working life. Once more, she silently gave thanks to old Uncle Edward and his legacy.

She continued to worry about her first son Murdoch. He had so far stuck the job at the Lenzie railway station. But Sarah knew him only too well and guessed he only did so for the sake of his children. Her mother's instinct told her he was bored with the job and eager to spread his wings. She could understand this; the pay was not very good at all, barely sufficient for an average family. But Murdoch and Mary did not have an average family. There were so many of them in that household now that sometimes they were struggling to feed all the brood they had. If only they would call a halt to the baby production line!

Quite often she went over to visit and take some little extras and food for them. Fortunately, some of the older ones were now of working age, so that helped to bring in a little extra money.

Thus, steeped in a mixture of happiness and worry, Sarah continued on her walk. Suddenly she became aware that she had walked further than she had intended and decided she had better head for home. John would be getting worried about her; he always did if she was a bit later than normal. Dusk was falling

Chapter 34

John was indeed getting a little concerned at his wife's prolonged absence. It seemed to him that Sarah had been away an awfully long time, much longer than normal. That was strange!

Normally Sarah would have been back by this time and making the evening meal, but there was no sign of her. He thought he would wait a little longer to see if she turned up. If not, then he would go along to the canal in the direction she had taken and most probably meet her coming back.

Likely she had met an acquaintance - a friend even, and they would be sitting talking, not realising the time. *That was probably it,* he thought, trying to convince himself. He waited for another fifteen minutes... still no sign of her. Now he was becoming worried, this was very out of character. *Where the heck could she have got herself to?*

John waited no longer and set off in the direction of the canal.

There was no sign of Sarah on the road to the canal. He could see along its banks for a very long way but she was nowhere to be seen. Walking farther along the bank, he met with a lady he and Sarah knew; she was coming from the other direction. She declared that she had not seen Sarah since the previous week.

Now John *was* worried.

His next thought was that she may have gone to see Murdoch, but then again, she didn't usually go there on her own. *Perhaps she had gone over to Janet's, house... or one of the family members who lived nearest to them?* He made his way to Janet's.

When he arrived, Janet told him she had not seen her mother that day. John was beginning to experience the first stages of desperation.

"What are we going to do, Janet? She has to be somewhere! I am really getting very worried about her; this is not like her; she doesn't normally do this."

Janet tried to reassure him.

"Do not worry father, I will go to Susanna's place and enlist her help to look for mother. They have the pony and trap, so we will be able to get around faster to different places to try and find her. I think it would be best if you go home in case she turns up and you are not there, then *she'll* be the one doing the worrying!"

"So silly of me!" exclaimed John. "That's a good idea! But will you go now to Susanna's?" he queried.

"Of course, father, I will go right this moment." She said, reaching for her coat and bonnet. "It will take me a little time to get over there."

"Right!" said John... "I will get back home then."

Thereafter; Janet closed and locked the front door behind her and set off for her sister's house as fast as she could to tell her what was happening and recruit her help in looking for their mother.

As soon as Susanna heard the news, she reacted positively... taking charge

"We will get the pony and trap out and William will take us round the area to see if we can find mother. We'll try Uncle Murdoch's first, she may have gone to see him. If she is not there, we ' ll drive out to young Sarah's although I cannot think mother would have walked as far as that."

As planned, they called on their Uncle Murdoch first. He declared he had not seen their mother at all in the previous few days. They wasted little time there; leaving him standing in the doorway, they started off in the direction of their sister Sarah's house. As they left, Murdoch called after them:

"I hope you find your mother soon. Keep me informed. I will be worried about her too until I hear from you again."

As soon as they arrived at Sarah's and told her that their mother was missing, she donned her coat and bonnet and joined them in the search. Before doing so, the sisters had a brief conference... each of them listing places where they thought their mother might be or have visited. This done, they set off in the trap, following her likely route.

Fortunately it was summertime. At that time of year in these high Scottish latitudes, the sun was late going to bed. Thus, they had the help of daylight until well after half past ten in the evening. At least – if necessary - they would be able to keep searching until then.

Eventually they arrived at their brother Murdoch's house. He was on duty at the station but Mary, his wife, confirmed that her mother-in-law had not visited there that day. Having exhausted all likely possibilities, they decided to return to their parent's house... just in case Sarah had returned home in the meantime.

On arrival, their father met them at the door. As soon as they saw his drawn, anxious face, they knew their mother had not returned – she had simply vanished from the face of the earth!

In former days, in such situations, John would have taken charge, taken stock of the situation and acted decisively... not this time. Age and anxiety had robbed him of his strength. He could only stand there and listen as his daughters took over and planned the next move... they would go to the Police Station and report the fact that their mother was missing. The officers there would be better trained and equipped to organise an official search.

The bar Sergeant at the Police Station had known the girls since they were babies.

"Do not you be worrying your heads off now ladies" he advised them, adding, "if I know your mother, she'll have found some new friend or other and forgotten she has a home to go to. She'll turn up... be sure of it! Just in case though, I will get things set up for a proper search. I think you should get away home now and look to your own families. Good night to you all!"

And so the sisters took his advice but agreed that before doing so, they would stop off at their father's house on the way home. Janet decided to go back to their father's house and keep vigil with him, but before doing so would go home to tell her husband what was happening.

When she arrived back at her father's house, Susanna and her other sister Sarah were still there. Their father sat in silence at the window, gazing intently toward the front gate, no doubt hoping to see the figure of his wife making her way toward the door in the gathering gloom.

"I suppose I would better go home too' announced Susanna "and tell my family what is happening. On the way I will go to Lenzie station and tell Murdoch. I will take you with me, Sarah. We can stop off at your house so that you can tell *your* family. After that, if you agree, we will go on to my house.

When I have told my lot what is happening, William will bring us back here, then I will send him home.

"Sarah agreed and the two sisters left Janet to keep their father company.

When the girls returned to their father's house, they all sat for hours in silence; each wrapped in a cold cloak of anxiety... none wanting to broach the subject or speculate as to the fate of their mother. None of them felt like eating.

Murdoch eventually turned up after he had finished at the railway station and joined his father and sisters in their vigil. Eventually John fell asleep in his chair. The man was worn out, exhausted.

As time passed, the girls began to feel the pangs of hunger. Murdoch had managed to eat before coming over to this father's house but the girls had not eaten or even had anything to drink for over eight hours. Sarah went through to the kitchen and got together some bread, butter and cheese. This, they washed down with warm, sweet tea. As they sat there eating and drinking, they spoke in whispers so as not to disturb their father.

They speculated for a long time as to what could possibly have happened to their mother. The girls were in tears, thinking the worst, but Murdoch tried to keep them optimistic...failing miserably.

The sun rose early in these northern latitudes and by 5am it was well on its journey across the sky. It was a bright, clear morning – one designed to promote hope in the most despondent of heart but the spark of hope in the Munro household was all but extinguished. Still no sign of Sarah!

The consensus was that they would all go to the police station and request that a formal search started. It was barely 5-30am when they arrived there.

Although the station door was closed, they caught the smell of bacon cooking... it was coming from the little house beside the station. Their frantic knocking on the door was answered by the same big station sergeant. He lived there alone and was getting his breakfast before going to work. Susanna gave him the news that their mother had still not turned up.

"Come away into the house he invited, I will get paper and pencil and take some notes. My constables will be arriving for work any time now. As soon as they do, we will go round the area and recruit men and, as I promised last night, organise a proper search. Most of the field hands will already be at work so there will be plenty of men to help us." He looked at the drawn anxious faces round him before adding - "looks to me like you all need a bit of rest. These are trying times I know, but you have done all you can. Away home and see your families – get a little rest and something to eat. As soon as I have any news, I will bring it to your father's house."

They thanked him profusely; followed his advice and returned to their respective homes... all except Susanna, who went home with her father to keep vigil with him.

As soon as the Munros had left, the Sergeant donned his tunic and helmet and opened the Police Station for business. Shortly after, his four young constables arrived. He informed them of the situation and sent them off in all directions to organise search parties. He, on the other hand, made his way to the nearest canal lock office and organised a search of the canal property and the canal itself. The latter involving the use of boatmen with grappling hooks. Secretly, he hoped these would not be needed!

And so, while the family sat around feeling totally useless, the local community and officials carried out a thorough search of the whole area...not leaving a single stone unturned.

They had not long to search. Shortly after 6-30am, the sergeant was on the north bank of the canal - on the towpath and a few hundred yards from the Townhead Bridge. There was still no report of the sighting of Mrs Munro and he was heading for the Police Station. Up ahead of him, he could see what seemed to be a bit of a commotion just beyond it. As he got closer, he saw a small boat containing two men. It was lying just off the north bank and there was a large group of men on the bank itself.

When he arrived on the scene, he found the group standing round a water-soaked body lying on the bank. One look told him they had found Mrs. Munro. Making sure of the identity, he went to fetch the doctor. After seeing to this, he mounted his bicycle and reluctantly headed for the house of John Munro. The sergeant liked his job ...most of the time. This time was a certain exception!

Arriving at the house, he was met at the door by John himself. The look on the policeman's s face confirmed John's greatest fear. The other man began by saying what John had hoped never to hear in his lifetime;

"I am so sorry Mr. Munro, but your wife is dead. We found her body in the canal. It seems she drowned."

At these words, Susanna, who was standing by her father's side, turned away, letting out a great cry of grief. John uttered not a sound, but his eyes grew round and unblinking... two huge tears welled from them and rolled down his cheeks

The sergeant continued:

"She was found at about 5 o'clock by one of the canal boatmen. Her body has been taken to the hospital. There, it will be examined to see if drowning was in fact the cause of her death. As soon as this is done, I will call back. I am afraid I will need one of the family to make formal identification.

When the policeman left, John went to the parlour and sat by himself. Poor man! He didn't know what he was going to do with himself. His thoughts were in turmoil. His mind felt numb; he just couldn't believe his precious Sarah was gone out of his life forever. How would he survive without her? This was not happening to him. Perhaps he was dreaming and would wake up with Sarah calling to him as she had always done; telling him to wash his hands and come sit at the meal table?

As John sat there deep in his grief, Susanna, in her ever practical way, thought of the rest of the family. Ensuring that her father would be all right, she composed herself and left to go to the houses of her sisters and brother and give them the news.

The family received the news of Sarah ' s death in exactly the same way their father received it - with complete devastation! How could this have happened? All of them had but one thought.... *poor father! How would he recover from this?*

They all stopped doing what they were doing and gathered at his house to share in his grief. The cruel hand of fate had eradicated their mainstay – the point of focus for them all. Sarah had been the most wonderful wife and mother. All that was left of her now were lovely memories... her brightness of spirit and especially her love for them all. They bravely tried not to weep for their father's sake, but as soon as one started, they all wept and wept. John stayed dry eyed for a while, but eventually he too could not hold back the tears and he wept with his daughters.

Murdoch was first to return to reality. He knew there was much to do and that his father was not fit to attend to all the formalities demanded by the state following a death. He therefore declared he would go to the police and see what had to be done. At his announcement, his father protested that he was quite capable of carrying out his duties as head of the family.

"I am fine now son! I will be needed to formally identify mother's remains, I"

"Absolutely not father" protested Murdoch. "You have more than enough here to contend with. Allow me to attend to all these things. Do not you think it would be better if you remember mother as you last saw her... before she went for her walk.

At his last question, the agony in John's eyes told Murdoch all he needed to know. His father's shoulders drooped visibly and with head down he mumbled;

"Aye, You are right my boy. There will be time soon enough when we will all have to say our final farewells" Secretly; John was grateful to Murdoch for offering, he didn't think he could have done it himself.

And so, Murdoch set off to fulfil the harrowing duty of identifying his mother's body. As he headed in that direction, his thoughts turned to all the happy times he had had with her at *Westcroft*. Silly little things came to mind: the time she had been so sympathetic towards Ben, the dog, and allowed him back into the kitchen at night when he had been put outside before their arrival - When Ben had died, she had shared his grief. All those memories of his mother's patience and love for all her children and her bright happy attitude to life flooded his mind. He could not control the tears streaming down his cheeks as he walked onwards. *What a loss she will be,* he thought. She had been so kind to Mary and all his children, bringing them gifts and just loving them all.

When Murdoch was ushered into the room where his mother's body lay, it immediately struck him in a silly detached sort of way that she did not look like herself. *How stupid of me* he thought. *How did I expect her to look after having been in the canal all night?*

However, there was no doubt whatsoever... the body lying there so cold and white was his dear mother - it was most definitely her. He gave a great sob of sorrow and despair and turned his back on her for the very last time.

Outside the room, he pulled himself together. Now he had the horrendous job of going back to the family and confirming the fact that their mother was dead. This would be the worst thing he had ever had to do in his entire life.

What a sad household! The grieving took a great deal of time and attention. However, they could not grieve forever. Next came the quest for answers as to how such a tragedy came about.

The family knew Sarah could not swim. Because of this, she had a fear of deep water. Therefore, under normal circumstances, she would never willingly enter the canal... not even to save some poor drowning soul so how did she end up in the water? *Did she feel dizzy or have a heart attack? Did she walk too close to the bank and trip or slip and fall in? Was she the victim of a crime - pushed in by someone? Or last but not least - the unthinkable - did she in fact simply take her own life by jumping in?* The entire family vehemently dismissed this last thought. No way would their mother commit or even contemplate committing suicide; her love of life even at her age - but principally the effect it would have had on her husband and family - would have ensured that such a thought would never have entered her mind. No! It must have been an accident. However, the exact circumstances of the accident would never be known...the mystery of Sarah's death would go with her to the grave; there, to forever remain a mystery.

Once the formalities were completed, a funeral was arranged. The turnout of mourners was overwhelming. As well as the immediate family living in and around the Kirkintilloch area, those members who had moved away to Glasgow had been notified and given time to attend. Although letters had been sent to John's brother Angus and sister Catherine who lived in the far north, they were unable to attend but had sent letters of condolence.

Sarah had been well known and liked by many people in the local community. She had had many friends and every last one of them turned out to bid her mortal remains farewell.

It was the custom in Scotland to invite funeral mourners back to the house of the deceased following the internment. However John's modest house would never have accommodated so many people. So when Susanna offered to have the people back to her house, the rest of the family were quite happy for her to do so. She had by far the biggest house and more than enough room. Besides, they felt they didn't want to do anything but grieve... not that Susanna did not grieve; but she was made of sterner stuff and as usual, rose gallantly to the occasion.

After Sarah's funeral, everyone went back to normal life - all except for John; he just could not gather himself together at all. Sarah was no longer there. He wasn't sleeping very well nor was he eating properly. He just felt utterly miserable all the time. The family often came to see him and on every occasion urged him to eat better and look after himself.

They also invited him to their homes for meals, but always he refused. He was behaving just as his father had done all those years ago when Janet, his mother died. Then; Grandpa Murdoch had had his daughter- in-law Sarah to shake him out of it. Now, since none of girls had their mother's Irish temper! There was no one to bully him!

Regularly, Susanna would come with the trap and take her father to visit his brother Murdoch. During these visits, the brothers would mentally cast off the years and travel back to the time of their youth.

The old days would regularly be brought out and dusted off. Now, here they were ... a couple of old widower men, having both lost their wives. But their individual circumstances were different; John had his children to watch over him whereas Murdoch had been left entirely on his own.

Janet and Sarah would do what was necessary for their father. They had been able to employ a man to do the garden for him and John was very grateful for that.

Often, after their visit, he would think how proud of them. Sarah would have been - she had taught them well. This thoughtful upbringing extended to their Uncle Murdoch. They were all fond of Murdoch and often visited him to see if he was needing anything.

Susanna was particularly good to him - sending one of her staff to clean his house and to occasionally do his laundry.

Time never stops for a rest...the year following Sarah's death saw a vast decline in Murdoch's health. His heart was bad and his dropsy much worse. The doctor attended him regularly and had a nurse call on him every day.

That August – a year to the day after Sarah's death - John was informed that his brother was failing rapidly - literally on his deathbed. Susanna came and collected her father and sisters and they all went over to Murdoch's house.

When they arrived, they found that the end was indeed near - the poor man was almost in a coma, but not quite. A faint spark was just discernible. As soon as John entered the room, the old man's eyes glowed with the warmth of recognition.

When the two brothers were alone, John held Murdoch's hand and spoke quietly to him in The Gaelic. He could see that his brother had not long for the world. Smiling gently he said...

"We have come a long way together, little brother, and share many memories. Rest peacefully now." As he said these words, tears dimmed his eyes. He and Murdoch had been very close all their lives - now his best friend and brother would soon be gone.

Everyone of his generation was leaving him. Soon it would be his turn to go. At times like this, he wished it would be soon. He felt he had nothing to live for. This world was for the young. He was an old man of seventy nine years.

Lost in these thoughts, John suddenly realised that he was alone in the room. His brother's mortal remains lay before him on the bed but their former owner had gone: departed forever. He gently laid his brother's cold hand on the bed and lowered his head beside it and wept.

And so, yet another Munro family funeral was arranged. This time, it was a more modest affair attended by close family members only.

However, because Murdoch was well known throughout the quarry and grindstone trade; many former associates turned out to pay their respects, joining the family mourners at the grave side. In fact the "quiet modest affair" with a few family members back to the house after the funeral was taking the shape of something beyond the facilities of Murdoch's modest home.

Again, Susanna rose to the occasion and her home became the venue for the mourner's reception.

When the last mourner had departed, another chapter in the Munro family story was closed.

In September of that same year and exactly one month after his brother Murdoch ' s death, John developed a discomfort in his throat. He gargled with warm water and salt thinking it would soon disappear. It did not, but grew steadily worse. He mentioned it to Susanna on one of her regular visits. Her answer was swift and sure:

"Right father! Get your coat and hat; we are off to see the doctor."

John protested to no avail... his daughter bundled him into the trap and there and then, took him to the local surgery.

After examining his throat, the doctor told him it was some kind of infection and gave him medicine to treat it.

The medicine did not do much for him and his throat became more and more inflamed and he could barely swallow- even liquids.

Susanna was very worried. She made her father stay in bed and called the doctor.

After examining him once more, the doctor stated that John had developed pharyngitis, but with care and attention; it should clear up in due course. Secretly, the doctor was worried about John's state of mind. He knew that old men of John's age often didn't care if they got better or not. Because of this they neglected to look after themselves or follow medical instruction. Often, infections took their toll of someone his age.

The doctor's assessment of John was correct. The old man became fevered and grew steadily worse. His daughters constantly worried about him. Susanna in particular, bullied him mercilessly – all to no avail. However, they realised that their father was a very old man.

Often John would remark; "It is time I was away." They knew for absolute certain that with every passing year, he missed their mother more and more. If age didn't get him, a broken heart would!

One night in late October, it became evident to Susanna that her father's demise was imminent and that he would probably not last the night. She sent for the rest of the family members who joined her in a vigil round the old man's bedside.

Towards dawn, John raised his head slightly off the pillow and looked towards the window. A half smile showed on his old, worn features - causing the wrinkles to smooth momentarily... making him look younger. He felt very cold... very, very cold... a reminder of the cold North Sea of his youth, perhaps?w

Looking far into the distance... further than anyone else in the room could see ... he perceived a young lad attempting to haul a small fishing boat up the pebble shore. The lad's features became clear to him. His smile broadened and he half raised his hand and murmured "Wait, Murdoch, I am coming – I am coming to help you. I will be with you soon."

The family turned their heads to see what their father was looking at but could not see anything. When they looked back at him they found he had left them. John had departed this world and gone to join his beloved Sarah and brother Murdoch.

With his passing an era came to a gentle end.

Acknowledgement

Thanks go to my dear husband Jim...for his advice, help and above all...his endless patience.

Anne Seth Currie Mitchell Munro.

Lightning Source UK Ltd.
Milton Keynes UK
UKHW011821200223
417338UK00001B/19